THE MASTER MUSICIANS

CARTER

SERIES EDITED BY R. LARRY TODD
FORMER SERIES EDITOR, THE LATE STANLEY SADIE

THE MASTER MUSICIANS

Titles Available

THE MASTER MUSICIANS

CARTER

DAVID SCHIFF

OXFORD
UNIVERSITY PRESS

OXFORD
UNIVERSITY PRESS

Oxford University Press is a department of the University of Oxford. It furthers
the University's objective of excellence in research, scholarship, and education
by publishing worldwide. Oxford is a registered trade mark of Oxford University
Press in the UK and certain other countries.

Published in the United States of America by Oxford University Press
198 Madison Avenue, New York, NY 10016, United States of America.

Library of Congress Cataloging-in-Publication Data
Title: Carter / David Schiff.
Description: New York, NY : Oxford University Press, [2018] |
Series: Master musicians series |
Includes bibliographical references and index.
Identifiers: LCCN 2017026769|
ISBN 9780190259150 (hardcover : alk. paper) | ISBN 9780190259174 (epub)
Subjects: LCSH: Carter, Elliott, 1908-2012. |
Composers—United States—Biography. | Carter, Elliott, 1908-2012—
Criticism and interpretation.
Classification: LCC ML410.C3293 S32 2018 | DDC 780.92 [B]—dc23
LC record available at https://lccn.loc.gov/2017026769

1 3 5 7 9 8 6 4 2

Printed by Sheridan Books, Inc., United States of America

To Judy

Contents

Figures

Author's Note

THIS IS MY THIRD BOOK ABOUT ELLIOTT CARTER'S MUSIC. THE changing perspective in these three volumes reflects the expansion of Carter's oeuvre over the last third of his life, my own development as a composer and writer, and many changes in the musical landscape worldwide.

I began work on *The Music of Elliott Carter*, published in 1983 by Eulenberg Books and Da Capo Press (MEC83 from now on), in 1978 when I was studying with Carter at the Juilliard School. At that time he had deposited most of his sketches at the Library for the Performing Arts at Lincoln Center, a branch of the New York Public Library, just a short walk from Juilliard and from my apartment. Although I hoped to keep the book accessible to the general reader, I included detailed technical information on every work Carter had composed, based on the material at the library and on our many conversations at lessons, rehearsals, and performances. While I gave a thorough account of the early, "pre-Carter" works in MEC83, my emphasis was on the mature oeuvre, which began, as it seemed at the time, with the Cello Sonata, completed on Carter's fortieth birthday. Intending to convey in detail Carter's own understanding of his development as a composer, I analyzed the music in accordance with his suggestions, and I used his idiosyncratic technical vocabulary (i.e., "chords" rather than "pitch class sets"). Carter read and corrected several drafts of the book (as did Charles Rosen and William Glock). Recently, in reading through his correspondence at the Paul Sacher Stiftung, I discovered that Carter habitually recommended my book to friends and institutions as a source of information about his music. When certain music theorists, led by Andrew Mead, criticized the technical discussion in the book, and my competence as a theorist, Carter defended my work vigorously, saying that I had accurately presented his own view of his music.[1]

I began work on a second edition of MEC in 1996, while on a full-year sabbatical leave from my teaching position at Reed College. Faber Books and Cornell University Press published this second edition in 1998. Because Carter had turned out so much music after the time I completed the first edition, I extensively rewrote and rearranged the existing material to make room for the new works. Because of these substantial changes, I consider MEC98 a distinct work, not just an updated revision. As I noted in the preface to MEC98, its more restrained tone sprang from my dissatisfaction with the style of MEC83, not from any change in my feelings about the music, but in writing the second edition I was also dealing with some important changes in Carter's oeuvre. Beginning in 1983, he supplemented his pursuit of long form composition with a series of shorter works. Many features of the miniatures would become the basis for his "late period" works, both short and long, from the mid-1990s onward. In refashioning MEC I strove to understand the relation between these two modalities, again through a close study of Carter's extensive sketches. Access to all the new sketch material was now more of a logistical challenge because in 1980 I moved to Portland, Oregon, and in 1988 the Paul Sacher Stiftung in Basel, Switzerland (hereafter PSS) acquired most of Carter's scores, sketches, and letters. (There is also a large collection of Carteriana at the Library of Congress.) Thanks to my time at the PSS in the spring of 1997, and considerable assistance from the staff there, I was able to extend my detailed technical discussion to his latest music based on the evidence of his sketches.

To prepare for writing this third study I returned to Basel twice, thanks to support from the Amphion Foundation, Reed College, and the PSS. In addition to studying sketches and manuscript scores for the many works Carter wrote after 1998, I spent much time reading through the large collection (10,000 letters) of Carter's correspondence in the PSS. Given the size of this collection, there is much more work for scholars to do in using it to get a better understanding of all aspects of Carter's life from 1935 onward. Even with the short time I had with the collection, I found many documents that revealed opinions and connections that do not appear in the published literature.

In returning to Carter's music one more time, now within the well-established framework of the *Master Musician* series, my approach differs from that of both MECs. While I devote much space to the music written after 1998, this book, intended for listeners rather than theorists, does not contain extended technical analyses of the music. (Interested readers may find analyses of the post-1997 works in John Link's forthcoming book on late Carter.) More important, though, I no longer feel constrained to elaborating Carter's own ideas about his music, particularly as expressed in the program notes that he wrote for his compositions, but also as found in his few autobiographical accounts. In this third study I discuss both the man and the music in ways that move beyond and sometimes against his own interpretations.

Note

1 See Andrew Mead, Review of *The Music of Elliott Carter* in *Notes* 40, no. 3 (March 1984). For a summary of criticism of my book by music theorists see Wierzbicki, 76–78.

Acknowledgments

M Y WORK ON THIS BOOK WAS MADE BOTH POSSIBLE AND ENJOYABLE THANKS TO the encouragement, support, and assistance I received. My first thanks must go to Professor R. Larry Todd who, as editor of the Master Musician Series of Oxford University Press, invited me to write a book on Elliott Carter, to Suzanne Ryan who has guided my interactions with OUP, and to Victoria Kouznetsov, my editorial assistant at OUP.

For the time and travel necessary for my research I am greatly appreciative of the financial support I received from Reed College, the Amphion Foundation and the Paul Sacher Stiftung. My connection with Amphion was largely through Virgil Blackwell who has been an essential source of information, scores, recordings, photographs, and extremely helpful suggestions throughout the process. I owe the entire staff of the PSS so many thanks for giving me access to the treasures of their collection in such an agreeable Rhine-side setting and making Basel feel like my second home; in particular I must thank Dr. Felix Meyer and Dr. Heidy Zimmermann for their immeasurable support, and for their friendship.

Many people shared memories and insights with me in ways that were decisive for the final shape of this book. David Carter graciously agreed to an extended phone interview that provided a unique father-and-son perspective. David reminded me several times of his father's "Thurberesque" sense of humor, a quality he helped me hear in the music for the first time. I was most fortunate to spend several hours with Heinz Holliger in Basel and to learn of his evolving appreciation of Carter's music, which he so clearly loved. My picture of Carter was fine-tuned through important conversations and communications with Richard and Dee Wilson, Ellen Taaffe Zwilich, Fred Sherry, Oliver Knussen, Gerard Schwarz, Janis Susskind, John Ashbery, Dominique Nabokov, Pierre-Laurent Aimard, Tamara Stefanovich, and Richard Derby. A second round of thanks must go to Ellen Taaffe Zwilich for providing me with wonderful photographic portraits of the Carters.

My work and equilibrium were much aided by a support community of fellow scholars, Anne C. Shreffler and Carol Oja, Max Noubel, and Jonathan Bernard. Professor Bernard's readers report was of tremendous help in the final editing process. My Reed College colleagues Virginia Hancock and Ellen Stauder were kind enough to read some early chapter drafts and offer helpful critiques. At Reed I was also most fortunate to receive essential ssupport from Trina Marmorelli, Director of Instructional Technology Service.

In retrospect my appreciation of Carter's music would not have been possible without the early guidance (beginning in the 1960s) of Allen Edwards, Marvin Wolfthal, Richard Hennessy, Paul Jacobs, and Charles Rosen, and without my longstanding friendship with timpanist Peter Kogan who, in 1971, arranged for me to attend the Cleveland Orchestra rehearsals of the Concerto for Orchestra, where I first met its composer.

Finally, not one word of this book would exist without the constant encouragement, assistance, prodding and infinite patience and forbearance of my wonderful wife Judy.

CARTER

CHAPTER ONE

Elliott Carter Now

E LLIOTT CARTER DIED ON NOVEMBER 5, 2012, FIVE WEEKS BEFORE HIS
104th birthday. He was composing music nearly to the end of his
life. His last notations, for *Epigrams*, betray little evidence of diminished
eyesight, small motor skills, or creative focus. His oeuvre, begun in 1928,
spanned eighty-four years, but of his approximately 150 published works,
half, including his only opera, were completed after he turned ninety. The
unprecedented arc of his career challenges the usual notions of periodization. If we still cling to the over-freighted notion of the "late style," when
would we say that Carter's began?

Carter's longevity similarly complicates attempts to fit his career into
some larger narrative of music history. While he was alive, critics often
attempted to place him in relation to some imagined *Zeitgeist*, but he
persistently thwarted such pigeonholing. For all its innovations, his music
did not fit the usual ideas of the avant-garde. For all his contrariness, he
was rarely pegged as a "maverick." At once conservative and radical, he
was an outsider who looked like an insider—or maybe the reverse.

Anyone writing about Carter today faces two large areas of uncertainty.
The critical evaluation of his work remains unsettled, and there are still
many gaps in our knowledge of his life. In the United States, performances
of Carter's orchestral works declined sharply after his death. As of this
writing only one major American orchestra, the Boston Symphony, has
performed his grandest orchestral composition, *Symphonia: sum fluxae
pretium spei*, and no American opera company has staged his only opera,

What Next? In Europe, Carter's reputation remains strong, yet even there critical acceptance remains far from unanimous. Carter often said that the fate of his oeuvre would depend on performers, but while his music has attracted musicians as distinguished, and different, as Daniel Barenboim, the Arditti Quartet, Pierre-Laurent Aimard, and Matt Haimowitz, other equally distinguished artists, such as the Emerson Quartet, Emmanuel Ax, Joshua Bell, and Michael Tilson Thomas, have not felt compelled to make it part of their repertoires.

To date no one has written a full-scale critical biography of Carter, and many questions about his life remain unanswered. The best source of information about Carter's life at present is *Elliott Carter: A Centennial Portrait in Letters and Documents* (CPLD from now on) by Felix Meyer and Anne C. Shreffler, published by the Paul Sacher Foundation in 2008. Carter's most extensive autobiographical statement appeared in *Flawed Words and Stubborn Sounds: A Conversation with Elliott Carter* by Allen Edwards (FW from now on), but it was published in 1971. The conversation with Enzo Restagno (published by I.S.A.M. in 1991) fills in some of the blanks from FW. Even with these resources, and in some cases because of them, there remain many lacunae in Carter's life story.

Carter often gave even friendly researchers the impression that he was "biography-phobic" (as Anne Shreffler described him after several extended interviews). On more than one occasion I saw him turn on a well-meaning interviewer in public with a combination of schoolboy hijinks and undisguised distrust. At such moments he could easily give the impression that he had something to hide, and in his writings there are indeed many surprising omissions. In FW, for instance, Carter made no mention of his paternal grandmother's Jewish ancestry, though that fact might have been salient to his avoidance of travel in Germany during the 1930s. Likewise, the name Nicolas Nabokov, a close associate for forty years and best man at Carter's wedding, never appeared. Nabokov's covert work as cultural commissar for the CIA-funded Congress for Cultural Freedom had recently surfaced, raising speculation about his impact on Cold War culture, queries that twenty years later would be turned in Carter's direction. Carter's suppression of his relations with Nabokov in FW only heightened suspicions about their mutual influences and shared motives.

If Carter could omit two non-trivial subjects from his own account of his life, we might assume that there were other omissions as well. In Frank

Sheffer's glacially paced film, *A Labyrinth in Time*, Carter, who was extremely camera-shy, wears a mask of thoughtful blandness, a pose very different from the punchy, contrarian manner he could strike in unguarded, off-camera moments. Even in friendly surroundings, though, Carter usually gave the impression of existing only from the neck up, at least during the forty years when I knew him. He was particularly circumspect about any romantic relations that pre-dated his marriage, and hardly ever discussed friendships that were not directly related to his musical career. Perhaps not surprisingly he was less than forthcoming in his writings, in public interviews, or even in private conversation, about the advantages his inherited fortune gave him in his career, and on some occasions he left the misleading impression that he had been disinherited.[1] In later years he occasionally misrepresented his past political allegiances (such as they were) to match the opinions of his audiences, particularly in Western Europe, where it was assumed that an artist like Carter would be a man of the Left.

Though he often attempted to cordon off discussion of his music from examination of his life, Carter's biographical evasiveness has inevitably played a role in the debate about the merits of his works. He did not make it easy for critics looking for a message in his music. He rarely described any of his works in personal or emotional terms, or through explicit political or religious ideas, offering, instead, technical descriptions or parallels with little-known works of literature. While his contemporary Olivier Messiaen linked his equally idiosyncratic musical innovations to familiar Catholic (or avian) images, Carter habitually explained his music by way of obscure literary references, from Theophrastus to Saint-John Perse. In this diffidently bookish stance, and perhaps other ways, Carter resembled Wallace Stevens, whose phrase "flawed words and stubborn sounds" served as the title for Carter's only book, and whose poetry he set in two cycles in his last years. Some readers view Stevens' idealist view that "reality is an activity of the most sublime imagination" as either an aesthetic limitation or a character flaw, or both, a judgment Stevens himself pondered in "As You Leave the Room":

> I wonder, have I lived a skeleton's life,
> As a disbeliever in reality . . .

Especially for his first thirty years, our knowledge of Carter's life might be termed skeletal, but that could be more a matter of incomplete information than flawed character. Until someone undertakes a full-scale critical biography, we can only speculate about whether Carter's habitual reticence was in some ways evasive, whether his music might have sprung from some suppressed backstory, or whether (and how) his apparent strategy of evasion somehow served a compelling aesthetic goal, as many readers have come to feel it does in Stevens' poetry. Perhaps Carter just felt that anything beyond his intellectual history was none of our damned business.

Given what we do know about Carter, however, it is possible, I hope, to view his life and work in new ways without indulging in speculation. Much writing about Carter during his lifetime, including my own, stressed his late-blooming development and the sharp change in his style and ambition around the time of his fortieth birthday. Today, however, his entire oeuvre appears more consistent than it had in the past. He titled his last composition *Epigrams*—a moniker equally befitting the *Three Poems of Robert Frost* composed seventy years earlier, however different their respective idioms. In his early years, and his late ones, he devoted much of his efforts to vocal settings of American poetry. His engagement with American modernist poetry, initiated in 1936 with a ballet score inspired by Hart Crane, would bear its full fruit only in his very last years with settings of Williams, Moore, Stevens, Cummings, Pound, and Eliot, poets Carter had first encountered when he was an undergraduate at Harvard in the 1920s. The understated, Thurberesque wit that characterizes many of his latest compositions is already audible in the Symphony no. 1 and *The Harmony of Morning*, from the 1940s. *Nine by Five*, a woodwind quintet composed in 2009, shares an ingenuity and humor with its predecessor, composed sixty-one years earlier. The no-possibilities-left-unexplored harp writing of *Mosaic* (2002) recalls the equally exhaustive harpsichord configurations in the Sonata for Flute, Oboe, Cello, and Harpsichord from 1952. Similarly, the brilliant toccata of *Caténaires* (2008) had a precursor in the eighth étude for woodwind quartet (1949), and, going back still farther, an ancestor in Fauré's Impromptu op. 102, a work Carter would have encountered chez Nadia Boulanger in the early 1930s.

These career-spanning resemblances suggest the need for an alternative to the older chronological division of pre-Carter and mature Carter. To this end, two persistent and highly idiosyncratic aspects of Carter's personality—psychological dualisms and pre-compositional calculation—now appear more pertinent to the entire oeuvre than the older periodization.

The first movement of Carter's Cello Sonata portrays the cello and piano as two contrasting characters. The piano marches along in strict time, while the cello emotes erratically. Only rarely do they share musical ideas or mime some gestures of shared purpose. This dramatic form of non-imitative counterpoint appears in all Carter's later works, even those for a single instrument, though the interaction of characters might range from friendly conversation to violent conflict or to the non-interactive parallel play of very young children. Carter frequently explained his idio-syncratic approach to polyphony in social terms, comparing his music to the relations between individuals in a democratic society, but his works, so many of which inhabit the intimate sphere of chamber music, often suggest interior dialogues between opposing selves.

Listening across Carter's entire oeuvre, and his life, we can detect re-current signs of psychological polarities, not unlike the split between Eusebius and Florestan in Schumann's music. I will term these poles Carter Light and Carter Dark. Musically, they appear in contrasted qual-ities of lightness or *leggerezza*, the word from Italo Calvino that Carter borrowed for the title of a late miniature, and weightiness or *gravitas*. These contrasts, though, parallel similar oppositions in Carter's person-ality (rebellious/respectful), and even his rarely stated politics (Trotskyite/anti-communist).

Carter sketched out a vivid description of the two sides of his creative personality in extensive preparatory memos (now in the PSS) for a so-nata for two pianos that he worked on, but never completed, in the 1950s. While no musical notations exist for this sonata, Carter wrote a detailed scheme for contrasting the characters to be portrayed by the two pianos. Piano I would be "showy, unstable, very emotional, pedantic, at times angry." Piano II would be "quiet, sober, serious, logical without being pedantic, self-effacing, but always with persuasive points that in the end are most telling, although not insisted on, touching, orderly, in which small details count for a great deal."[2] The asymmetry in these two apparently non-gendered characterizations may betray Carter's sympathy for the quiet voice of reason, the Apollonian comfort zone that often has the final say in his music, but the pairing with an unbridled daemonic partner shows that Carter, like Euripides and Nietzsche, recognized the Dionysian power of unreason in the psyche and in music. In both spheres a drive to create order would serve no purpose without a countervailing anarchic principle, which Carter, at least in this sketch, associated with rage and instability rather than eros. While Carter abandoned the sonata, he re-purposed its two characters in the works that follow. Their roles are enacted by the two violins in the Second Quartet, and by the harpsichord and piano in the *Double Concerto*.

These two contending impulses of Carter's music, his yin and yang, appear and reappear throughout his oeuvre, independent of his musical idiom or of genre, in major works and miniatures, within works but also between them. We can see Carter's practice of composing alternatively between these modes in the juxtaposition of the (dark) String Quartet no. 1 and the (light) Sonata for Flute, the Quartet no. 3 (dark) and the Brass Quintet (light), *Triple Duo* and the Quartet no. 4 (dark following light) and most monumentally with the two grand works of the 1990s, the *Symphonia* and *What Next?* But the dark and light strains were already present in the 1930s and 40s, culminating, respectively, in *The Minotaur* and Woodwind Quintet.

A second and perhaps even more idiosyncratic key to Carter's creative processes was his habit of pre-compositional calculation, often in numerical rather than musical notation. In a letter of recommendation written in 1942 to help Carter obtain work in military intelligence, Lincoln Kirstein described his Harvard classmate as a mathematician, a curious label since Carter took no math courses as an undergraduate, but perhaps an astute view of Carter's mental processes. Examining Carter's sketches, we encounter many hundreds, perhaps thousands, of pages that seem to bear no relation to music: numerical calculations, schematic curves plotted on graph paper, groupings and re-groupings of notes in "chords" of various sizes, usually with a numerical label. (Further adding to the evidentiary confusion, Carter occasionally wrote dates, addresses, and telephone numbers on his sketches that at first glance appear to be part of his composing.[3]) Carter's calculations were not restricted to musical sketches, however. In reading through his letters at the PSS, I found that he habitually scribbled them on the back of letters and envelopes with no apparent relation to a specific piece, as if they constantly issued forth from an underlying mental mechanism. Often I found the same calculations worked out in many different settings. Perhaps Carter needed to re-calculate tempo relations in particular because he never compiled a systematic rhythmic thesaurus comparable to his Harmony Book.[4]

The roots of this habitual calculus may go back to Carter's early years, when he systematically worked out the polyrhythms, such as 5:3 or 9:5, found in Scriabin's *Etudes* op. 42, even though he could not perform these virtuosic pieces, or to his intense study of counterpoint with Nadia Boulanger, but the rationale behind the process remains mysterious. Carter never explained how his endless calculations meshed with the expressive aspect of the music. To the contrary, he criticized the role that calculation played in the theories of Joseph Schillinger or in the extended serial procedures of the postwar European avant-garde. Carter's sketches do, however, provide overwhelming evidence that he composed music through this idiosyncratic and mysterious process right through his last work. While, in his very last years, he sometimes claimed that he was now simply putting notes on the page without pre-compositional calculations, the sketches suggest otherwise.

Ultimately listeners will decide on the value of Carter's music, but their judgment will depend on the efforts of future performers. Almost all of Carter's works have been recorded, but for many of them only a single recording is available. To date, moreover, many of the works, have been recorded only by a small circle of New York musicians. This state of affairs suggests that much of the music has not yet really been heard. A number of recent recordings have disclosed hitherto unsuspected qualities in the music. Compelling accounts of the *Holiday Overture* by Donald Palma and Kenneth Schermerhorn, and Harold Meltzer's refocused reading of the *Double Concerto*, have certainly changed the way I listen to both pieces. The character and impact of much of Carter's oeuvre may still await similar revelations.

Notes

1 I have found no evidence to support Wierzbicki's claims, stated at the very beginning of his monograph and repeated often later, that Carter lacked financial resources at any time in his life.
2 See CPLD, 123.
3 Clear reproductions of typical Carter sketches appear in CPLD p. 200 and p. 202. See also the article by Laura Emmery, "Rhythmic Process in Elliott Carter's Fourth String Quartet," in *Mitteilungen der Paul Sacher Stiftung*, no. 26 (April 2013).
4 Carter appears to brandish a small rhythmic notebook, though, at one point in Frank Sheffer's film.

CHAPTER TWO

Remembering Mr. Carter (A Double Portrait)

I FIRST MET ELLIOTT CARTER IN CLEVELAND IN JANUARY 1971. IN THE
leisurely fashion of that time, I was pursuing a doctorate at Columbia
in English literature with a focus on the nineteenth-century English
novel in general and Thackeray in particular. I was also preoccupied with
music of all kinds, but I assumed that my musical interests would remain a
sideline. With a little time on my hands during the winter break between
semesters, I asked my friend Peter Kogan, longtime timpanist of the
Minnesota Orchestra, then a percussionist with the Cleveland Orchestra,
if I might attend rehearsals and performances of Carter's *Concerto for
Orchestra*, which Pierre Boulez was conducting for the first time. Not
only was it Boulez's first performance of Carter, it was his first performance of *any* American music.

At the first rehearsal, Carter spotted me sitting alone in Severance Hall
and, after I explained why I was there, kindly loaned me an extra copy of
the huge score. Carter came to Cleveland on his own, without his wife
or any entourage and, even though we had just met, he invited me to
join him for dinner several times during that week, once with Maestro
Boulez. Aware of the importance of these rehearsals and performances,
and also new to the strange rituals of a professional orchestra, I took

Much of the content of this chapter appeared in slightly different form in my article "Magna
Carter," which appeared in *The Nation*, February 11, 2013.

detailed notes on the whole process. A few weeks later, on the advice of Lionel Trilling, whose seminar on "Sincerity and Authenticity" was the high point of my literary studies, I pitched an article about my Cleveland encounters, unsuccessfully as it turned out, to *Harper's Monthly*. After that I often saw Carter at concerts in New York, but I got to know him well only after I summoned up the courage to drop out of my literary studies at Columbia and crossed Broadway to enroll at the Manhattan School of Music. After receiving a master's degree in composition there, I entered the doctoral program at the Juilliard School as Carter's student in the fall of 1976.

Our connection became closer after I began work on a book about his music in 1978. An article I had written about *A Mirror on Which To Dwell* appeared in the short-lived *New York Arts Journal* in April 1977. Without telling me, Carter sent it to Sir William Glock, an old friend who had served as the editor of *The Score*, as music critic for the *New Statesman*, and most important, as Controller of Music for the BBC. Sir William was also expected to edit a book on Carter's music written by Michael Steinberg, music critic of *The Boston Globe*, but in 1976 Steinberg unexpectedly abandoned his book-in-progress (and the *Globe* as well). On the basis of my article, Sir William agreed to let me take on the project. Michael Steinberg later granted me a brief conversation about his research. He told me explicitly that he had decided to drop the project because he felt that Carter had not been forthcoming about many of the details of his private life.

My change of status from pupil to quasi-Boswell meant that, unlike Carter's other Juilliard students, I was invited to attend a New Year's Eve party on December 31, 1977, at the Carters' apartment at 31 W. 12th Street just west of Fifth Avenue and a few blocks north of Washington Square. Although located in Greenwich Village, the Carters' street had a feeling of solid bourgeois respectability. Each floor of the building, erected in 1900, had just two apartments, running from the 12th Street side to the north end of the building—somewhat like the awkward configuration known in New York as a "railroad flat." The Carters lived in 8W, the west half of the eighth floor. The set designer Beni Montresor lived across the hall, and Claus Adam, cellist of the Juilliard Quartet, lived on the floor below. You entered the apartment from the small landing to a narrow, dark hallway, then turned left to reach a large room facing south, the only room with a view, which was divided between a living room and Carter's studio, with piano. (On September 11, 2001, Carter had a clear view of the attack on the World Trade Center from his studio.) A right turn at the entrance would take you to the dining room and kitchen. There were two connected bedrooms at the center of the apartment. Helen Carter used one as her office. There was also a small third bedroom, probably originally for a maid. The apartment, in no way grand, was nevertheless comfortable and roomy, at least by tight New York standards. The unremarkable furnishings gave it a feeling of run-down, professorial gentility.

My wife and I had barely set foot in the Carters' living room to join the New Year's Eve festivities when a petite older woman approached us. She introduced herself as Minna Lederman and, without pausing for small talk, told me that she knew I would be writing a book about Carter, that she would instruct me how to write it, and that she had already made arrangements for us to meet at the Lincoln Center Library just a few days later. Not wasting a moment's time, Minna then gave me the short version of her advice: I had to explain how the young Carter, or "pre-Carter," turned into the much-honored, formidable mature artist. I should not have been surprised by her taking charge of my project. Minna had been the editor of *Modern Music* from 1924 to 1946, and her close friends included Aaron Copland, Virgil Thomson, and John Cage, all of whom, like Carter, had written for her magazine under her tight editorial supervision. This was the first time, however, that I had a sense of the incredulousness with which many of Carter's older acquaintances viewed his later exalted status. They simply did not see it coming. (We might recall that Zola based his novel *The Masterpiece*—*L'Oeuvre*—on the conviction that his childhood friend, Paul Cézanne, lacked the right stuff of genius.) When I said something to Minna about Carter's being disinherited when he went to study with Nadia Boulanger, common scuttlebutt at the time, she quickly set me straight: "That was just his allowance. There were trust funds, there was real estate, there was a lot of money." In retrospect I wonder how she knew all this, but Minna, whom I got to know much better later on, certainly never minced words. She shared a long history with Helen and Elliott, going back over forty years.

Once I got past the redoubtable Ms. Lederman I soon met Paul Jacobs, who would go to the piano to lead us in *Auld Lang Syne* at midnight, Charles Rosen, Ursula Oppens, and her parents, and other friends of the

Carters' including Leon and Nadia Temerson, their daughter Catherine and her husband, Israel Rosenfeld, William and Barbara Krakauer (parents of clarinetist David Krakauer), the classical scholar Seth Benardete and his wife Jane, the painter Richard Hennessy, and my old college friends Allen Edwards (who later became Carter's copyist) and pianist Marvin Wolfthal. This would be the core of the group that my wife and I would see at the Carters' on New Year's Eve for many years to come. (Helen Carter liked to say that nearly all their friends were Austrian Jews.) Occasionally there would be a guest composer such as Vittorio Rieti, Hugo Weisgal, or, most memorably, Nicolas Nabokov, who would delight everyone with his outrageous anecdotes and mimicry. Only later did I come to notice the absence of famous figures from the great Carnegie Hall world of music. The Carters did not socialize with celebrities like Leonard Bernstein or Isaac Stern or Beverly Sills. (When the Carters entertained A-list guests, like the Stravinskys, they took them to La Côte Basque, then the temple of New York's haute cuisine.) On New Year's Eve their most prestigious guests tended to be literary, including Robert Silvers, Barbara Epstein, and Elizabeth Hardwick from *The New York Review of Books*. If not star-studded, the gatherings were always full of brilliant minds, but, inevitably, Charles Rosen would dominate the conversation—and the next day either Helen or Elliott would call to apologize for Charles' grandstanding. I recall that at most of these occasions Carter was more a listener than a talker. Afterwards I would often remember one of Helen's notoriously barbed remarks rather than anything Elliott had said.

In my perception, the Carter household at the time felt very much like a mom-and-pop business, HelenandElliott, Inc., in which Elliott composed and Helen did everything else. She functioned as social secretary, travel agent, manager, and gatekeeper. She ran the household and took pride in her sophisticated American cooking. In this setting it was easy to get the impression that Elliott could barely fix himself a cup of tea. Up in the country house in Waccabuc, where their lakefront property covered fourteen wooded acres, Carter often worked and slept in a studio above the garage, about one hundred yards from the house. If not quite as isolated as Mahler's composing hut, it was nearly as sacrosanct. Helen had her hands full managing the house and property (and dog) and entertaining guests. A country weekend was just one of the many ways she rewarded performers of Elliott's music.

My relation to Carter evolved in stages from enthusiast to student to virtual member of the family. (Since the Carters' son was also named David, there was occasional confusion about which one of us was the topic of conversation.) Although Carter was ten years older than my father, and despite great differences in our family circumstances, we shared certain experiences that probably eased our connection (though we never talked about them). My family, like his, knew little about classical music and discouraged me from pursuing a career in it. Like Carter, I took a precocious interest in twentieth-century music, in my case sparked by a recording of *La Mer* that my family somehow acquired when I was six. As a teenager I preferred, as Carter had, to listen to new music rather than practice old music. Fortunately, two of my piano teachers (Kenneth Wentworth and James Wimer) recognized my skewed priorities as those of a budding composer rather than an unpromising pianist. Unlike Carter, though, I took up other instruments (tuba and bass) while still in elementary school, played in school bands and community orchestras and, with friends, in a couple of jazz combos. I spent two summers at music camp where, when I was about to turn fifteen, I heard the first performances of my compositions. As an Ivy League undergraduate I majored in English, as Carter had done, and did not begin serious musical study until my twenties. Perhaps we shared some of the self-doubts that can plague late bloomers in a prodigy-obsessed field. We certainly shared a love of Proust. Here is one of his favorite passages, in the Scott Moncrieff translation (Carter would quote it in French):

> . . . the field open to the musician is not a miserable stave of seven notes, but an immeasurable keyboard (still, almost all of it, unknown), on which, here and there only, separated by the gross darkness of its unexplained tracts, some few among the millions of keys, keys of tenderness, of passion, of courage, of serenity, which compose it, each one differing from all the rest as one universe differs from another, have been discovered by certain great artists who do us the service, when they awaken in us the emotion corresponding to the theme which they have found, of shewing us what richness, what variety lies hidden, unknown to us, in that great black inpenetrable night, discouraging exploration, of our soul, which we have been content to regard as valueless and waste and void.[1]

I had been listening to Carter's music for a decade before I met him. When I was fourteen I came across a recording of the Sonata for Flute, Oboe, Cello and Harpsichord. It reminded me of one of my favorite pieces of music, Debussy's Sonata for flute, viola, and harp. (Many years later I learned that Carter had indeed been studying the late Debussy sonatas closely just a few years before he composed his sonata.) From then on I purchased every recording and score that I could find.

When I was an undergraduate at Columbia from 1963 to 1967, I heard the Group for Contemporary Music perform Carter's Sonata for Flute, Oboe, Cello, and Harpsichord, and the Six Pieces for Timpani. Carter often attended these concerts, as did Edgard Varèse, Stefan Wolpe, and Milton Babbitt. Although Babbitt, Carter, and Wolpe are often lumped together as uptown academics, they seemed, at these concerts, to be less friends than rivals, each with his own group of devotees. Wolpe, who had taught at the counter-cultural Black Mountain College, appeared sympathetically as an embattled genius surrounded by disciples who carried him into concerts after he was crippled by Parkinson's disease. His music enacted the struggles of the twentieth century in a slashing, all-over manner that recalled Action Painting. Wolpe's followers seemed to find Carter's music suspiciously uncommitted and bland—maybe the right word is "*goyish.*" Perhaps aware that the Wolpe crowd did not take him seriously, Carter once responded with an apparently back-handed compliment to Wolpe's quirkiness: "He does everything wrong," he told me, "but it comes out right." Carter certainly admired Wolpe's boldness and integrity. Many years later I would discover that the Carters had aided Wolpe financially (through directed contributions to the Fromm Foundation) when he was no longer able to support himself by teaching.[2]

Milton Babbitt, by contrast, was an unapologetic academic. His off-the-cuff professorial remarks displayed the same convoluted sentence structures found in his printed scholarly prose and his theoretical ideas had a great appeal to Columbia and Princeton graduate students at the time. They thought he had all the answers. When I took a composition class with Harvey Sollberger at Columbia in 1971, for instance, it was assumed that everyone would write twelve-tone music using Babbitt's time-point method of rhythmic organization. (I rebelled.) For Babbitt's followers, Carter's "failure to serialize," to use their phrase, was an incomprehensible deviation from the true path. Carter and Babbitt maintained a professional friendship despite the fact that, as Carter told me, he disliked Babbitt's most often played piece, *Philomel*, for singer and electronics: "Here's this wonderful story and there is Milton going beep-beep in the background." I might note that Babbitt's music never appealed to me at all. After enduring an evening of Babbitt-inspired music, my friends and I began to refer to the performers as "The Group for Contemptible Music."

Even though Carter's music was a staple of the uptown scene, he did not appear to have a large group of followers, apart from my friends Allen Edwards and Marvin Wolfthal. I was too shy to introduce myself to Carter at the time. The strongest early impression I had of his personality came from watching the famous Lincoln Center performance of *Histoire du soldat* on July 15, 1966, when he acted (if that is the right word) the role of the Soldier, with Aaron Copland presiding as the narrator and John Cage stealing the show as the Devil. While Copland and Cage confidently projected their well-established personae, Carter spoke softly, mumbled actually, with a slight stammer, and gave very little sense that he was performing at all, which made his impersonation of the hapless soldier all the more touching.

Thanks to a Kellett Fellowship, I was a student at Cambridge University from 1967 to 1970. Early on, I gave a talk to the Contemporary Music Society on Carter's music, which was much less well known there than the works of Messiaen and Stockhausen, and I also attended the London premiere of his Piano Concerto by Jacob Lateiner and the Boston Symphony at the Royal Festival Hall. The British musicians I came to know in Cambridge, especially composers Roger Smalley and Tim Souster, both of whom had worked closely with Stockhausen, made me aware of how limited and provincial the aesthetic certainties of Morningside Heights really were (a lesson I could have had learned in New York had I ventured south of Houston Street). This change in perspective did not diminish my admiration for Carter's music, however. Back in New York, I even dragged my parents to the premiere of String Quartet no. 3.

When the published score of that quartet appeared in 1973 I noticed a serious error in the alignment of parts on one page and wrote to let Carter know. In return for this favor, I believe, he agreed to look at *Cross-Currents*, a large Carter-meets-Xenakis score for string orchestra and percussion (and two conductors) that I was working on at the time with John Corigliano at the Manhattan School of Music. One morning at 7 my phone rang and, in her distinctive "lock-jaw" accent, Helen Carter told me that Elliott would see me at their apartment that afternoon at 2. Carter spent several hours going over my piece—actually tearing it apart note by note. His suggestions were not at all theoretical, but of the nuts-and-bolts variety. He quickly grasped what I was trying to do, pointed out the numerous places which were still only a rough approximation of my intentions, and suggested specific fixes. I knew at once that he was the right teacher for me.

A few years later, when I finally became his student at Juilliard, I would meet with Carter for a lesson every Tuesday afternoon from 3 to 4, and then we would both go to the Composers' Forum, along with all the other Juilliard composition faculty and students. It was fascinating to observe the interactions between Carter and his faculty colleagues David Diamond, Roger Sessions, Milton Babbitt, and Vincent Persichetti—and between them and distinguished visitors like Peter Maxwell Davies or Witold Lutosławski.

At that time David Diamond was the only member of the Juilliard composition faculty who taught many classes in addition to private lessons. He was passionately opinionated and took a great interest in his students, and these qualities gave him a large following despite the fact that he often struck an ultra-reactionary pose, as if he were the second coming of Vincent D'Indy. Diamond demanded that all his composition students write sonatas in three movements, the last one being a fugue—this in the late 1970s! Unlike Carter, Diamond had been something of a *wunderkind* and received recognition with his earliest works. Now that the tables were turned, Carter, who had helped Diamond get the position at Juilliard so that he could obtain health insurance, seemed to take delight in bursting Diamond's bubbles in public. At one Composers Forum, Diamond, who had also studied with Boulanger, presented one of his own fugal works. Carter grilled him about fugal technique, and chided, "David, is there anything you wouldn't do?" This was Carter's rarely seen bad-boy side, which was also apparent when I compared some of his shot-from-the-hip opinions with Roger Sessions' habitual piety toward the classical masters. In his classes, Sessions celebrated the greatness of great music. He would spend an entire semester delineating the beauties of a single Beethoven Symphony, or Verdi's *Falstaff*. Carter, by contrast, had no qualms, for instance, about calling Schoenberg's rhythms "the squarest of the square," or in finding Berg's Violin Concerto "too sentimental," or in saying that much of Webern's music, like late Fauré, was too subtle to be performed—verdicts delivered with a twinkle in his eye as if he were getting away with murder. (In my experience, Debussy and Stravinsky were the only figures in twentieth-century music about whom Carter had nothing but good things to say.) Unfortunately, Carter rarely allowed his off-leash pit bull side to appear in his writings and printed interviews, which, I think, he tended to over-revise until they lost much of their edge. He had paid a heavy price, internally and externally, for the unguarded opinions he expressed writing for *Modern Music* in the 1930s and seemed determined never to repeat that mistake.

Given my long-standing enthusiasm for Carter's music, some people have expressed surprise upon finding that my own music is so very different from his. As far as I could tell, however, Carter did not impose his style on his students. At my lessons he would only mention his own music to point out mistakes he thought he had made (as Ravel is said to have done). Some of the music I composed when studying with Carter showed influences that ranged from Xenakis to Charles Mingus to Richard Rodgers. Like other composers of my generation, I had become disenchanted with atonality by the mid-1970s. The first piece I wrote for Carter was a Mingus-inspired duo for bass and piano. Carter expressed surprise that it used key signatures (unknown in atonal scores) but did not ask me to change the style. When, in my second year of study, I deliberately wrote a number of pieces along Carterian lines, even setting Hart Crane's "At Melville's Tomb," I found that he did not alter his teaching method at all.

Because Carter was so reluctant to discuss his own work with his students, I began to get a sense of how he composed only later as part of my research for MEC. When he saw me trying to decipher the voluminous mountains of preparatory sketches, graphs, and outlines he seemed almost embarrassed by the evidence of his protracted labors. Once, as I was looking at the sketches for the Brass Quintet at the New York Public Library, Carter mused, "you might get the impression from all those sketches that I didn't have any idea how to compose."

In my final year at Juilliard I completed my opera *Gimpel the Fool*, which premiered at the 92nd Street Y in May, 1979. The opera blended influences from klezmer music, Jewish liturgical music, Stravinsky, Mahler, Weill, Steve Reich—and, occasionally, Carter—and Carter's suggestions as I composed and orchestrated the music were both sympathetic and apt. (I was delighted to see both Carter and Reich in the audience on opening night.) Carter was so worried, however, that he might misadvise me in an idiom far from his own that he arranged for me to work with his old friend Trude Rittmann. For many years she had worked on Broadway, arranging overtures, dance music, and music behind the scene for Rodgers and Hammerstein and Lerner and Loewe. ("These tunesmiths," she explained, "didn't even know what an overture was.") It was delightful to meet Trude, and she taught me a lot of tricks of the musical theater trade, but Carter's advice remained extremely pertinent.

There was one compositional method Carter recommended to his students that clearly came from his own practice. He often advised me to compose backwards. Although he believed that the beginning of a piece should suggest everything that would follow, he also said that the opening was much too important an event to be just the first idea that came to the composer's mind. Instead of beginning at the beginning, he suggested composing the loudest moment of the piece first: "then you will know where you are going." Carter composed in this counterintuitive fashion throughout his life. He completed the first movement of *Epigrams*, his ultimate opus, last, just as he had done in the Cello Sonata sixty-four years earlier. Many years later, while looking at sketches for the *Rite of Spring* and *Symphony in Three Movements* at the Paul Sacher Foundation in Basel, I found that this was often Stravinsky's method as well. The first notes you hear in *Le sacre* were the last to be composed. In Carter's case, a hyper-sensitivity about the effectiveness of an opening may have stemmed from his experience with his early Symphony no. 1. The original version, written in 1942, launched right into an unprepared thematic statement that lacked atmosphere. In 1954, he rewrote the opening, front-loading a glowing chord that invited the audience in. People might assume that Carter was not audience-conscious, but he certainly knew the importance of grabbing the listeners' attention. When I showed him my first attempt to orchestrate the overture of my opera, for instance, he immediately saw that it would not be effective, and then suggested a simple fix—replacing the flute with a piccolo—that worked like a charm.

Although Carter certainly loomed large in my life as my teacher, he never acted as a mentor the way Roger Session, Milton Babbitt, and, in particular, Olivier Messiaen were said to have done, and he was even less a musical pedagogue like Nadia Boulanger. Relying on Helen to maintain social and personal connections, he rarely showed interest in his students' lives or careers. When in 1988 Oliver Knussen asked him to recommend pieces by his students for performances at Tanglewood, he categorically declined, citing ethical principles, even though the highly talented roster of his Juilliard students from the previous decade included Joel Hoffman, Tod Machover, Tobias Picker, and Ellen Taaffe Zwilich, because he did not think it proper for a teacher to recommend some of his students' works over others'. Paul Jacobs told me that even when Carter served as a juror in music competitions he would not utter a word in support of music by his students. A piece of mine was played at Tanglewood only at Olly's insistence—or so he told me. I doubt that Olivier Messiaen would have passed on such an opportunity to showcase the works of his protégés. Perhaps Carter's reluctance at any show of favoritism may have stemmed from his underappreciation by Nadia Boulanger, who had no hesitancy about advancing her star pupils.

At lessons, Carter focused solely on the notes placed in front of him. He would usually scan them silently, occasionally striking keys almost inaudibly on the piano, but when he saw something he did not like he did not hold back—a typical lesson would begin with the remark "you can't start a piece that way" and end with "you can't end a piece that way." He also did not seem to feel the need to give much encouragement, at least in my case. In three years of study with him the most enthusiastic words of praise that I heard were "that should work," but he did attend all of my New York premieres. Afterwards he might say that my music "worked" or perhaps even that it was "good." (I was surprised to discover, only after his death, that he had written positive and detailed letters of recommendation for me over the years, even before I started work on MEC.) I would emerge from lessons feeling pummeled, but I found that Carter's critique was almost always on target and not driven by abstract or ideological considerations. I was in my early thirties at the time. I think Carter's unrestrained criticism would have been very hard to take at a younger age. To some extent, though, his emotional distance helped to make the criticism tolerable. Unlike some teachers, including Boulanger, he did not make a student feel that musical weaknesses stemmed from personality flaws. Other than offering the general (and apt) advice that I needed to work harder, Carter focused his critique on my notes, not my character.

Once I took on the challenge of writing a book about his music, I accompanied Carter to rehearsals, recording sessions and performances, and traveled with him for performances in Los Angeles, San Francisco, Cincinnati, and Boston. My wife and I were frequent guests at the Carters' apartment and at their country home in Waccabuc, and at dinners at the Century Club in New York. Helen Carter never missed a birthday of our children and would call once a week to hear about their accomplishments. On July 4, 1978, we celebrated Independence Day (and Helen's birthday) at Waccabuc with Aaron Copland. At dinner I was given the place of honor next to the creator of *Billy the Kid*, the music that had made me want to become a composer when I was nine years old. Copland was already showing signs of Alzheimer's disease, but his charm, good spirits, and implacable self-confidence were not at all impaired. When Carter offered him a seat at the head of the table, Copland, without missing a beat, said "fitting and proper," using words from the Gettysburg Address that he had set in *A Lincoln Portrait*. Carter and Copland spent much of the afternoon settling old scores in a mostly jocular manner.

My close relation with the Carters continued at long distance after the summer of 1980, when we moved to Portland, Oregon, where I took a teaching position at Reed College and my wife became the cantor at Congregation Beth Israel. When MEC83 first appeared, Da Capo Press, its American publisher, threw a festive launch at the Lincoln Center Library. It seemed like every composer in New York living north of Tenth Street was present, and Peter Maxwell Davies offered a toast to Carter's music and my book. In August 1988 my *Scenes from Adolescence* was performed at Tanglewood as part of a program marking Carter's eight-ieth birthday. We celebrated his ninetieth birthday with him in London, where we heard the British premiere of his Quintet for Piano and Strings at the Barbican. Afterwards we both signed copies of the newly released MEC98. I was scholar in residence in Tanglewood in August 2008 for the week-long Carter centennial festival, where I heard many of his latest works, including *Sound Fields*, which reminded some listeners of Ives and others of Feldman; the delightful *Mad Regales*, which John Ashbery listened to with a broad grin on his face; and the brilliant piano toccata, *Caténaires*, Carter's shameless old-age crowd pleaser, which has since served as an encore all over the world. I missed the 100th birthday concert at Carnegie Hall only because Max Noubel had invited me to a simultaneous celebration at IRCAM, where I gave a talk entitled "Carter, Cage and all that Jazz." (I could play the bad boy, too.)

Despite my forty years of interactions with Carter, I am well aware of my limitations in giving a complete portrait of the composer. He had many close friends; they included performers who were intimately involved with his music, such as Charles Rosen, Paul Jacobs, Ursula Oppens, Oliver Knussen, Virgil Blackwell, and Fred Sherry, but also people he rarely saw but felt close to, particularly the Italian composer Goffredo Petrassi, whom he often termed his best friend. I was closest to Carter in his early late maturity, between the ages, roughly, of seventy and ninety. His personality may have been quite different in earlier years, and musicians who came to know Carter only in his last decade describe him in very different terms than I would use. I have the impression that Carter's relationships with students such as Frederic Rzewski, Alvin Curran and Joel Chadabe during the 1960s were closer and more collegial than the more distant stance he showed at Juilliard a decade later. Going back a bit farther, Peter Maxwell Davies, who met Carter in 1957 at Dartington, remembered him as a highly nervous chain-smoker with a debilitating stammer. A trace of the stammer was still detectable when I knew him, but the jitteriness, and the cigarettes, had vanished. Compared to the fast-talking Cage and Babbitt, however, Carter was a Moses, not an Aaron. The scars of his speech impediment may have remained deep in his consciousness, though. In one of his settings of poems by Louis Zukofsky, composed at age one hundred and one, Carter set his own stammer to music.

The Elliott Carter I remember was a New Yorker of a very particular sort—a cultivated New Yorker. He spent most of his time in a circumscribed, overwhelmingly white, stratum of the city—its universities, conservatories, museums, galleries, libraries, and concert halls, particularly the smaller ones like Alice Tully Hall, Grace Rainey Rogers Auditorium at the Metropolitan Museum, and the 92nd Street Y. He rarely needed to venture out of Manhattan except to get to the airport or to Waccabuc. Until SoHo was gentrified as an arts district he also had little reason to travel south of Houston Street. Wall Street, City Hall, Chinatown, Little Italy, and the Lower East Side were not on his map, and neither were Times Square, the Theater District, Coney Island, or Harlem. If the Carters traveled near Times Square it was to dine with other artists and intellectuals at the Century Club, located on W. 43rd Street right across from the offices of *The New Yorker*. Although he lived within walking distance of two legendary jazz clubs, the Village Vanguard and the Five Spot, Carter never visited them. He read *The New York Review of Books*, *The New Yorker*, and *The New York Times*, but not *The Wall Street Journal*, *Variety*, or any of the tabloids. He did not attend any houses of worship unless it was for a concert or a funeral, and he had no interest in the competitive sports to be seen at Yankee Stadium or Madison Square Garden. He never watched television but he did enjoy going to the movies, usually at an art cinema nearby rather than a first-run theater uptown. The Carters bought their food at Balducci's or the Jefferson Market, two fancy grocers a block from their apartment, and pastries from Dumas' French bakery. As might have been predicted by his Ivy League education, Elliott's clothes came off the rack at Brooks Brothers or J. Press. In short, except for composing, his was a stereotypical upper middle-class life, straight out of one of William Hamilton's *New Yorker* cartoons.

Notes

1 *Swann's Way*, 502–503.
2 Letters in the PSS show that the Carters regularly made tax-exempt gifts to the Fromm Foundation that were directed mainly to performers and supporters of Carter's music.

CHAPTER THREE

A Brief Life of a Very Long Life

I N HIS 1971 CONVERSATION BOOK WITH ALLEN EDWARDS, *Flawed Words and Stubborn Sounds*, Elliott Carter sketched out a short, highly selective picture of his first thirty years, tracing his intellectual development while omitting almost all other aspects of his life. Later interviews added some anecdotes to this official story but without changing its narrow focus.[1] In the future a proper biography may fill in the many omissions in this account, but the cropped view that Carter presented in FW served to spotlight his conscious artistic calling, which was quite determinedly that of a composer. Carter was neither a performer, nor a theorist, nor a pedagogue. For over eighty years, from his early twenties to his death, composing took precedence over all other concerns.

Carter seemed predestined, however, for a non-musical life. Soon after the American Civil War his grandfather, Eli C. Carter, founded a successful importing business, specializing in European "finery" (i.e., lace and linens). In time Carter's father, Elliott Sr., took over the firm, and from the moment of his birth in 1908 Elliott Jr. was groomed to continue the succession. The company, E.C. Carter and Son, was well respected in the realm of interior décor and, at least until the Depression, flourished profitably. Carter's parents, Elliott Sr. and Florence Chambers Carter, belonged to such privileged enclaves as the New York Athletic Club and Westport (Connecticut) Country Club. From the 1920s onward they lived in a fashionable duplex apartment at 136 East 64th Street (just west of Lexington Avenue) and had a summer home in Saugatuck, Connecticut. Every year, the family traveled to Europe to meet with lace producers in Belgium, France, and Switzerland. When Carter was seven his parents hired a governess to teach him the French that he would need for future work in finery. There were no musicians in the family circle and apparently little interest in classical music, even as a matter of parental pride. Carter claimed that his parents never attended any performances of his works. His mother enjoyed Broadway musicals, however, an interest she passed on to her grandson, David, but not to her son. Carter's parents must have had some sense of their son's musical inclinations because, as noted in FW, they decided that he should have piano lessons when he was in third or fourth grade (age 9). Carter, however, recalled that he hated practicing Chopin and scales and that "only when I went to high school did I really begin to take an interest in music."[2] It would be many years before he would give this interest precedence over the family's expectations that he would continue the business, or that he could overcome his fears of displeasing his parents. Carter later wrote that he discussed his desire to rebel against his family's designs for his future with Charles Ives in 1928 or 1929.[3] (He was uncertain about the exact date.) Even in the late 1930s, however, Carter continued to work for E. C. Carter and Son. He told me that he spent a dispiriting summer selling breath freshener (the company's attempt to develop a downmarket product in hard times) in upstate New York.

The three-generation family history somewhat resembles Thomas Mann's *Buddenbrooks* except that in Carter's case the artistic grandson displayed none of the stereotypical stigmata of degeneracy but lived a long and healthy life—even, thanks to his inheritance, a bourgeois one. While Carter often said that he rejected his parents' values,[4] his own life maintained many of the comforts of his New York childhood, though with little of his parents' Upper East Side extravagance. (David Carter described his grandmother to me as a pathological shopaholic who spent most mornings at Saks Fifth Avenue or Bergdorf Goodman, followed by lunch at the "21 Club.") Despite his parents' displeasure, Carter was not disinherited when he chose to pursue music, but was required to live within a budget. Letters show him consulting with his father on financial matters in a cordial way throughout the 1940s. From the time of their marriage in 1939, the Carters were able to travel across the country or around the world whenever they pleased, and they invested in real estate.

In 1945 they purchased the apartment at 31 W. 12th Street, and in 1950, a summer home in Dorset, Vermont. In 1952 they also acquired a house in Waccabuc, New York in northern Westchester County. Their wealth and holdings increased substantially after Carter's father died in 1955, though Carter often referred to these assets as a burden rather than an advantage.

Given what we now know, and what we don't, I will outline Carter's biography in three ways: first, stating the established facts of his family, education, and employment; second, tracing his professional recognition and critical reception; and, third, mapping the development of his oeuvre, an evolution which Carter situated within a broad framework of influences from European and American music and from literature, philosophy, film, theater, and dance. This third life story, the biography of the music, will make up most of this volume.

C.V.

BIRTH: December 11, 1908, in New York City to Elliott C. Carter Sr. and Florence Chambers Carter.

DEATH: November 5, 2012, in New York City.

MARRIAGE: July 6, 1939 in Chatham, Massachusetts, to Helen Frost-Jones (July 4, 1907–May 17, 2003).

SON: David Chambers Carter, born January 4, 1943.

EDUCATION: Horace Mann School, New York, graduated in 1926.

HARVARD UNIVERSITY: B.A. (English Literature), 1930; M.A. (Music), 1932.

PRIVATE STUDY AT LONGY SCHOOL BOSTON: (1926–32?) and with Nadia Boulanger at the *École normale de musique*, Paris (1932–35).

EMPLOYMENT HISTORY: Ballet Caravan (1937–39), St. John's College (1940–42), Office of War Information (1943–45), Peabody Conservatory (1946–48), Columbia University (1948–49?), Queens College, CUNY (1955–56), Yale (1960–62), Cornell (1967–?), Juilliard (1964–85). (Exact dates for the teaching positions are hard to nail down because most of them were short-lived and part-time. Carter walked away from some of them, sometimes in the middle of a term, when an opportunity for travel presented itself. Carter told me that Douglas Moore had fired him from his position at Columbia, but he did not explain the reasons for his termination.)

Elliott Cook Carter Jr. was born on December 11, 1908, in New York City, the only surviving child of Elliott Cook Carter Sr. (1886–1955) and Florence Chambers Carter (1887–1970). At the time of his birth the family lived on W. 95th Street. They later moved to 420 Riverside Drive, and, when Carter was at Harvard, to 136 E. 64th Street. According to Carter, his grandfather, Eli Cook Carter (1845–1923), ran away from the family farm near Binghamton in upstate New York to enlist in the Union Army.[5] After the Civil War he founded an importing business in New York City and married Marion Levy, the daughter of Jewish immigrants from Silesia. Late in his life Carter recalled that while his grandmother no longer practiced the religion of her parents, she made no secret of her origins. According to the Jewish tradition of matrilineal descent, Carter's father would have been born a Jew, but not Carter himself. There is no indication, however, that Elliott Sr. ever considered himself to be Jewish. His wife, Florence Chambers Carter, was of Northern Irish descent and belonged to the Presbyterian Church. Helen Carter briefly joined the Presbyterian church in the early 1940s, when she remained in Santa Fe while her husband was in New York. In letters between them at the time, Elliott addressed Helen's religious turn with a bemused sympathy and obvious surprise. In conversation about his childhood, Carter also recalled that his paternal grandfather had a mistress in New Jersey whom, with his wife's knowledge and despite her displeasure, he visited every Sunday.

Carter attended the Horace Mann School, an all-male private day school founded in 1887 by Nicholas Murray Butler, the longtime president of Columbia University, as part of Teachers College. (The school moved from Morningside Heights to its present campus in the Riverdale section of the Bronx in 1914.) Among Carter's contemporaries at Horace Mann, two (not mentioned in FW) would become successful song writers: Johnny Green, composer of "Body and Soul," and Paul Francis Webster, an African American who would write the lyrics to Duke Ellington's "I Got It Bad (and that ain't good)" and Sammy Fain's "Love is a Many-Splendored Thing." Horace Mann admitted non-WASP (but mostly well-to-do) students at a time when many of the prestigious boarding schools in the northeast would have excluded even someone like Carter with a single Jewish grandparent. In FW Carter noted his friendship with classmate Eugene O'Neill Jr., son of the playwright, who later became a Greek scholar before committing suicide at age 40.

In 1924, when Carter was fifteen, Clifton J. Furness, his music teacher at Horace Mann, kindled his interest in contemporary music and introduced him to Charles Ives.[6] Ives, Carter and Furness attended concerts together, and Carter later recalled returning to Ives' E. 74th Street home after a concert to hear "his 'take-off' at the piano of Ravel's signature 'Daphis and Chloe' chord and of the repetitiousness of Stravinsky." Ives felt that "most all contemporary composers had chosen the easy way out."[7]

With the help of a letter of recommendation from Ives, which praised his interest in literature and music and sense of humor, but did not refer to any musical abilities, Carter was admitted to Harvard in 1926.[8] Many years later Henry Cowell retrieved a composition that the young Carter had submitted to *New Music*, the ultra-modern periodical underwritten by Ives. Carter later wrote: "It wasn't much good, I must say. It's a wonder Ives or anyone else could have seen anything in it."[9]

At Harvard Carter majored in English literature while also singing in the Harvard Glee Club and studying the oboe at the Longy School. Carter's unimpressive Harvard transcript, full of "Gentleman's Cs," may indicate that he prioritized music over academics. Clifton Furness followed his protégé to Harvard to pursue a doctorate in literature, and on December 12, 1928 and May 15, 1929, Carter and Furness presented piano duet recitals in Hartford, Connecticut, of music by, among others, Stravinsky, Schoenberg, and Ives—but Carter's self-described "meager pianism" at the time limited his actual involvement.[10] Oddly there is no surviving correspondence between Carter and Furness after 1932, although Furness became a noted Whitman scholar before his death in 1946. In the summer of 1927 Carter traveled to Tunisia to transcribe Arabic music for the Baron Rudolphe d'Erlanger. His earliest surviving composition, a setting of "My Love is in a Light Attire" from James Joyce's *Chamber Music*, dates from 1928 and is dedicated to Laura Williams, a singer who specialized in Arab music. [11]

Carter's Harvard contemporaries included an impressive cohort who would go on to make a mark on American culture: Lincoln Kirstein, founder of the New York City Ballet, financier and philanthropist Edward Warburg, architect Philip Johnson, Leroy Anderson (future composer of "The Syncopated Clock," "Sleigh Ride," and many other light music classics), harpsichordist Ralph Kirkpatrick, literary scholars Harry Levin and M.H. Abrams, and James Agee, the future author of two classic works of American literature, *Let Us Now Praise Famous Men* and *A Death in the Family*. In FW Carter wrote that he also came to know a group of much older Boston composers, including Henry F. Gilbert (who died in 1928), Edward B. Hill, Arthur Foote, and Charles Martin Loeffler—though he took little interest in their music.[12]

After receiving his AB in 1930, Carter stayed on at Harvard for two more years to obtain a master's degree in music in 1932. His teachers included Walter Piston and, for one semester, Gustav Holst. One of his fellow students was the future musicologist Donald Grout. Before leaving Harvard for Paris, Carter composed music for the Harvard Classical Club's production, in classical Greek, of Sophocles' *Philoctetes* for male chorus, oboe and darabukka, the Arabic drum he had encountered in Tunisia. On March 15 and 17, 1933, this music became Carter's first performed work, but he was already in Paris and could not attend.[13]

At Piston's suggestion, and against his parents' (and Ives') wishes, Carter went to Paris in 1932 to study with Nadia Boulanger, as Piston, Aaron Copland, Virgil Thomson, and Roy Harris had done before him. In his later years Carter said that he had first hoped to study with Schoenberg, but that the Viennese master was in transit from Boston to Los Angeles at the time. Actually, Schoenberg arrived in the United States in October 1933, after Carter was already in Paris, and settled in Los Angeles in 1936, with a teaching position at UCLA, only after Carter had completed his studies with Boulanger. Both Carter and Schoenberg may have been in Paris for a brief time in 1933, but there are no records of any contact between them at the time, or any time later.

With Boulanger, Carter devoted himself in particular to the rigorous study of 16th and 18th century counterpoint. He also recalled studying Renaissance choral music with Boulanger and singing this repertory in a chorus conducted by Henri Expert. Equally important were the intensive study of Bach's cantatas, and exposure, at exclusive previews chez Boulanger, to Stravinsky's latest works, including the Duo Concertant, *Perséphone*, and the Concerto for Two Solo Pianos (all of which influenced his later compositions). Carter described the music he composed for Boulanger as being mainly influenced by Prokofiev, but he did not consider any of the compositions he completed under her tutelage worth saving. On his departure, the letter of recommendation she wrote praised him as a musician, but not as a composer.[14] Given that Carter had arrived in Paris with few musical accomplishments beyond singing in a college chorus, Boulanger's endorsement as an "excellent musician" was no small achievement.

Carter returned to the United States in 1935. After a few months in Boston, he returned to New York and in 1936 he became musical director for Ballet Caravan, a touring dance company created by Lincoln Kirstein, though it is not clear what that job entailed. Carter soon composed the score for *Pocahontas* for Ballet Caravan. Choreographed by Lew Christensen, a preliminary version of the ballet, with piano accompaniment, premiered on August 17, 1936, at the Colonial Theatre at Keene State College in New Hampshire. (The orchestral version premiered in New York on May 24, 1939.)

In New York Carter soon befriended Aaron Copland, William Schuman, David Diamond, Samuel Barber, and Marc Blitzstein, all associated with the League of Composers, and he began to write reviews for the League's journal, *Modern Music*, edited by Minna Lederman. The League was the rival to the "ultra-modernist" International Composers Guild/New Music Society, which was funded by Ives and whose programs featured many of the composers whom Carter had admired before he studied with Boulanger: Cowell, Varèse, Ruggles, Ornstein, Crawford, and Rudhyar.[15] The aesthetic divide between the two groups at times appeared to be an ethnic opposition as well since many of the League's members and patrons were Jewish and several, but not all, of the ICG ultra-modernists were virulently anti-Semitic. A decade after his return from Paris, Carter would play an active role in merging the two rival organizations to form the League-ISCM, but at first he chose to ally himself with the Copland-oriented camp that was very much in ascendance during the late 1930s.

Even in his earliest writings for *Modern Music* Carter demonstrated an independent mind and a broad knowledge of the contemporary scene. His earliest article (in MM 14, no. 2 [Jan.–Feb. 1937]) passed judgment confidently on works by such established figures as Webern, Pizzeti, Respighi, Milhaud, and Honegger, and alluded knowingly to the Hollywood composers Max Steiner and Alfred Newman. Carter's punchy pronouncements led Minna Lederman to dub him "Fighting Kid Carter," but in a few years it also propelled him to reject, in public, the musician who had almost been a father figure—an Oedipal moment that Carter

later termed "disastrously traumatic."[16] The occasion was the first complete public performance of Charles Ives' *Concord Sonata*, which Carter
reviewed in *Modern Music* 16, no. 3 (March 1939).[17] After an affectionate
portrait of boyhood afternoons spent with Ives and his "strong, wiry
Yankee vitality," Carter took a surprising negative turn, writing that he
was "sadly disappointed" by the music, which he found "basically conventional" and "full of the overdressy sonata school." He took Ives to task
for adding irrelevant dissonances to an old score and accused the music of
"a lack of logic which repeated hearing can never clarify." Within a few
years Carter began to make amends, as evidenced by the laudatory article
"Ives Today: His Vision and Challenge," which appeared in *Modern Music*
in 1944. By 1946, in a preface written with Paul Rosenfeld for a projected
book about Ives, Carter presented him as an American Mussorgsky
whose music "emotionally connects us with the facets of the American
temperament—its humorousness and its nervousness, and its mysticism."[18]
But the damage to the relationship with Ives remained: "I never had the
heart to see him again."[19] Actually, Carter had had no direct contact with
Ives after 1930, though he corresponded with Mrs. Ives in the later 1940s.

In the years immediately following his return from Paris in 1935, Carter
sketched but never completed many compositional projects, including a
collection of madrigals, a flute sonata, two string quartets, a symphony,
and an opera. As he had done with the music he composed for Boulanger,
he destroyed almost all of these works. Even as late as the 1950s he would
abandon major works in progress—a second symphony and a sonata for
two pianos.[20] Most of the works that do survive from the late 1930s
sprang from Carter's Harvard connections. He composed *Tarantella* for the
Harvard Glee Club, *To Music* for his graduate school roommate, Stephen
Tuttle, and the score for *Pocahontas* for his Harvard classmate Lincoln
Kirstein. Ten years later Kirstein would again commission Carter for the
score to the ballet *The Minotaur* for the Ballet Society, the company that
would become the New York City Ballet. Neither *Pocahontas* nor *The
Minotaur*, two substantial orchestral scores, found much success either as
dance works or in the concert hall. Even the choral works, whose literary
sophistication seemed tailored for elite academic vocal ensembles, were
rarely performed because of what were seen as their technical difficulties.
The Harvard Glee Club, for instance, could master only one of the three

movements of *Emblems*. Unlike the choral and ballet scores, all of Carter's instrumental works written before 1952, including the Symphony no. 1 and *Holiday Overture*, were composed on spec, without commissions.

Soon after resettling in New York, Carter met Helen Frost-Jones, a sculptor studying at the Arts Student League in New York. They were married on July 6, 1939. Their son, David Chambers Carter, was born on January 4, 1943. The best man at the wedding, which took place on Cape Cod, was the composer Nicolas Nabokov (cousin of the novelist) who had moved to New York from Paris in 1932 and whom Carter had met through Lincoln Kirstein. Nabokov, whose music had been performed by the Ballets Russes and the Boston Symphony, gave Carter advice on orchestrating the original version of *Tarantella*.[21] In 1936 and 1937 Carter traveled to Aurora, New York, where Nabokov was teaching at Wells College, for lessons.[22] In 1938 Nabokov conducted the premiere of *Let's Be Gay*, which Carter had composed for the Wells College chorus. A ballet set to Nabokov's orchestration of Bach's Goldberg Variations opened the program on May 24, 1939, that presented the world premieres of Carter's *Pocahontas* and Copland's *Billy the Kid*. Taking on the role of advocate that Copland, for whatever reason, avoided, Nabokov would help Carter in many capacities over the years to come and secured his first teaching position, at St. John's College in Annapolis, Maryland, in 1940 and 1941.

In 1942 Carter left St. John's (a pattern that would repeat many times later) and worked on compositions while living on Cape Cod and in Santa Fe, New Mexico. While Helen remained in Santa Fe, he returned to New York (moving back into his parents' apartment) while trying, unsuccessfully, to secure a job in Army or Navy intelligence. Surprisingly, given his bilingual childhood, he was told that his French was inadequate for intelligence purposes. In 1943 he went to work for the Office of War Information, a propaganda agency founded in 1942 to present the American "war message" both at home and abroad through the Voice of America. As part of his work, Carter produced a recording of Schoenberg's Piano Concerto with Eduard Steuermann. Copland, Barber and Blitzstein also did some work for the OWI.[23]

In 1946 Carter began to teach at the Peabody Conservatory of Music, and in the summer of 1948 he presented an analysis of his Piano Sonata at a class that Edgard Varèse was giving at Columbia University.

Teaching, however, would take a secondary role in Carter's life as recognition for his composing mounted. In 1950 he received a Guggenheim Fellowship that allowed him to spend a year working on his String Quartet no. 1 in the relative isolation of Tucson, Arizona. The recording of the quartet by the Walden String Quartet and its European premiere in Rome in April 1954 by the Parrenin Quartet, at a festival of contemporary music produced by Nabokov (and funded by the Congress for Cultural Freedom) established Carter's reputation among a small but influential circle of composers and new music advocates. In particular, the Rome performance marked the beginning of two of Carter's most important professional and personal friendships, with William Glock and Goffredo Petrassi.[24]

Although Carter taught at Yale, Cornell and Queens College (CUNY) before joining the faculty of the Juilliard School in 1964, his life from 1951 onward centered on composing, either at his New York homes, or during extended stays at the American Academy in Rome, the American Academy in Berlin, or the Rockefeller Institute at Bellagio—usually arranged with assistance from Nicolas Nabokov. Official recognition came with his first Pulitzer Prize, in 1960, for the String Quartet no. 2, followed by a second Pulitzer for the String Quartet no. 3 in 1973 and many other honors, worldwide.

From 1970 until the mid-1990s the Carters' life remained stable, but a significant professional change came in 1981, when Carter left his New York publisher, Associated Music Publishers (G. Schirmer), and signed with the British publisher Boosey and Hawkes. This realignment was soon reflected in the commissions Carter received. While all of his works from the Variations to *Night Fantasies* had been written for American performers, he composed *In Sleep, In Thunder* (1981) for the London Sinfonietta, *Triple Duo* (1983) for the Fires of London, *Penthode* (1985) for the Ensemble Intercontemporain, and the Oboe Concerto (1988) for Heinz Holliger and the Collegium Musicum Zurich. Both massive works of the 1990s, *Symphonia: sum fluxae pretium spei* and the opera *What Next?* received premieres by European ensembles (the BBC Symphony and the Deutsche Staatsoper, respectively). Perhaps not coincidentally with this new European presence, Carter was awarded the Ernst von Siemens Prize in 1981, after being nominated by Boulez. Sir

William Glock spoke at the presentation of the award. Carter was only the fourth composer to be so honored, after Britten, Messiaen and Boulez.

As both Helen and Elliott encountered health problems they reluctantly sold the Waccabuc house in 1990, moving to a retirement community in Southbury, Connecticut. Carter was treated (successfully) for heart disease, hearing loss and prostate cancer throughout the last twenty years of his life. Helen Carter died on May 17, 2003, after a long, painful struggle with Lyme disease.[25] After her death Carter continued to live in the 12th Street apartment, where he was looked after by a small group of devoted friends including Virgil Blackwell, Fred Sherry, Carol Archer, Lucy Shelton, and his housekeeper and caretaker Lorna St. Hill. Carter's 100th birthday in 2008 was celebrated with concerts at Carnegie Hall, Tanglewood, and IRCAM. He completed his last work, *Epigrams* for violin, cello and piano, just six weeks before his death on November 5, 2012.

Reception history

Carter was a late bloomer surrounded by a glittering cohort of prodigies like Dmitri Shostakovich, Olivier Messiaen, Benjamin Britten, Samuel Barber, William Schuman, David Diamond, and John Cage. Leonard Bernstein, ten years younger than Carter, leapt to fame with his ballet *Fancy Free* in 1944, while Carter's music had yet to attract much attention. In the 1940s American concert music found a new and assured national identity in Copland's ballet scores, the symphonies of Harris and Schuman, and many of Barber's compositions, including the Second Essay for Orchestra, the Piano Sonata, and *Knoxville: Summer of 1915*. Copland's *Appalachian Spring* and Barber's *Adagio for Strings* joined Gershwin's *Rhapsody in Blue* in the short list of works by American composers instantly recognized by the general public.

Although his own music from this time was stylistically similar, Carter had difficulty competing in this field. Serge Koussevitsky, who conducted the premieres of Sessions' Symphony no. 1, Gershwin's Second Rhapsody, Barber's *Knoxville* and Bernstein's *Age of Anxiety*, among many other new American works, declined to perform *Pocahontas*, Symphony no. 1, or *Holiday Overture*, despite recommendations from Copland. The note sent by Copland to Koussevitsky about *Pocahontas* on September 25, 1939,[26] is far from glowing: "[Carter] has never been played as yet by any major orchestra, and this is his first important orchestral work. I need not tell you about the quality of the piece as you can see that for yourself." Nevertheless Carter did not entirely lack for recognition, or positive reviews. The Suite from *Pocahontas* won the Juilliard School of Music publication prize and *Holiday Overture* won first prize in the Independent Music Publishers Association contest. Virgil Thompson, who returned to New York from Paris to become music critic for the *New York Herald Tribune*, praised the Piano Sonata as a "sustained piece full of power and brilliance" (March 13, 1948).

We can trace Carter's gradual emergence from obscurity during the 1950s through a number of articles. All appeared, we should note, in journals with a limited and professional readership, not *Time* or *Life*. In January 1951 an extensive review of the Cello Sonata by Richard Franko Goldman appeared in *The Musical Quarterly*. Goldman, who had also studied with Boulanger, called the sonata "one of those rare works that tempt one to extremes of praise."[27] In the cover story of the *American Composers Alliance Bulletin*, Summer 1953, Abraham Skulsky charted Carter's development through the First Quartet. A page from *The Minotaur* appeared on the cover, and the issue also contained a list of works with excerpts from many reviews, all but one highly positive. In the June 1954 issue of *Encounter*, William Glock, reviewing the Rome premiere, deemed the String Quartet no. 1 "a work of which American music may be proud." Glock, who later became Controller of Music at the BBC and a powerful advocate for Carter's music, had been invited to Rome by Nicolas Nabokov (who also had a hand in the funding of *Encounter* by the CCF). At Glock's request, Carter presented his own view of contemporary music, and his place in it, in "The Rhythmic Basis of American Music."[28] An updated, expanded survey of Carter's work by Richard Franko Goldman, appeared in *The Musical Quarterly* XLIII/2 (April 1957), where Goldman called Carter "the one composer of importance who has recently come to the fore" and said that his music "represents what is perhaps the most significant American development of the last ten years."

In the 1960s two influential books devoted entire chapters to Carter: Joseph Machlis, *Introduction to Contemporary Music* (1961), and Wilfrid Mellers, *Music in a New-found Land* (1965). Mellers, placing Carter on an equal footing with Ives and Copland, prefaced his discussion of

Carter with a quotation from Wallace Stevens (see Chapter 13). Forty-five years later, Carter would set these same lines at the conclusion of *The American Sublime*, his penultimate farewell to music.

Following the Pulitzer Prize that Carter received for the String Quartet no. 2 in 1960, his music received its most prestigious endorsement in 1963 with the publication of *Dialogues and a Diary* by Igor Stravinsky and Robert Craft. On February 19, 1962, Craft had conducted a performance of the *Double Concerto* at the Monday Evening Concerts in Los Angeles and Stravinsky attended all the rehearsals.[29] In their first book of conversations, published in 1958, Stravinsky, who, we should recall, had a close personal and professional relationship with Nabokov, had already advised composers to follow Carter's notation of melodies divided between instruments in the First Quartet.[30] Carter may have shown Stravinsky the score of the quartet in 1957 when he attended the first performance of *Agon* at a concert in Los Angeles that celebrated the Russian master's seventy-fifth birthday. A few years later Craft asked Carter to send Stravinsky the score of the Quartet no. 2. The detailed commentary on the *Double Concerto*, replete with a comparison to Berg's *Kammerkonzert* and a suggestion that the piece would be easier to play if the spatial arrangements were reversed (an option included in the revised edition of the score), is evidence that Stravinsky/Craft gave the work serious scrutiny. Stravinsky's verdict: "There, the word is out. A masterpiece, by an American composer."[31]

In writings throughout the 1950s, Carter bemoaned the lack of support for new music in the USA, especially in contrast with the generous funding for the performances and publications of the European avant-garde. While there were numerous examples of successful new American compositions during this time, the most visible of these—Menotti's *The Consul, The Saint of Bleecker Street* (both of which received Pulitzer prizes) and *Amahl and the Night Visitors,* Bernstein's *West Side Story*, and Barber's *Vanessa* (also a Pulitzer winner)—were all in styles far from the atonal, electronic, and aleatory explorations heard at Darmstadt. For younger European observers these populist works exemplified America's entrenched provincialism. In his briefly influential *Since Debussy: a view of contemporary music,* critic André Hodeir disposed of all American music on two pages, terming even Carter, Babbitt, and Wolpe neo-classicists, and likening the climate of American music to that found in the Soviet Union.

Inevitably American composers attempted to challenge such views, and responses began to increase around the time that John F. Kennedy was elected President in 1960 and the "middlebrow" culture of the Eisenhower era was questioned within the new President's Ivy League entourage. In the summer of 1959 Carter lectured at the Princeton Seminar in Advanced Musical Studies. Papers from the seminar appeared in *The Musical Quarterly* (46, no. 2 [April, 1960]) as "Problems in Modern Music." In the preface to that volume, Paul Fromm, the seminar's bene-factor, wrote that it sprang "out of the conviction that Americans need no longer depend upon Europe for their resources" and would study "on the highest level . . . the most significant trends in contemporary musical thought."

Fromm, a musically-trained Chicago wine importer, had taken an in-terest in Carter's work after hearing a performance of the First Quartet in 1953. In 1955 he commissioned the work that would eventually appear as the *Double Concerto*. Carter offered many apologies for not completing the commission on time but Fromm was a patient patron. (In letters to Fromm, Carter always referred to the work as "your *Double Concerto*.") The *Double Concerto* premiered at the Metropolitan Museum in September 1961 (with soloists Ralph Kirkpatrick and Charles Rosen) as part of the Eighth Congress of the International Society for Musicology, along with Milton Babbitt's *Vision and Prayer* and Leon Kirchner's Concerto for violin, cello, ten winds and percussion. Paul Fromm underwrote the performances. All three featured works were conspicuously distant from Menotti, Barber, or Bernstein in their musical idioms.

That concert became a model for new music performance in the USA during the 1960s, especially after the founding, in 1965, of the National Endowment for the Arts, which, for the first time since the New Deal, provided non-covert government funding for composers and performers. In New York, newly hatched ensembles dedicated to contemporary music included the Contemporary Chamber Ensemble, founded in 1960, The Group for Contemporary Music, founded in 1962, and Speculum Musicae, founded in 1971. These three groups performed Carter's music, along with works by Babbitt and Wolpe and younger serialists such as Charles Wuorinen and Donald Martino, and eventually became identified as "Uptown" music in contrast to the "Downtown" styles of Cage, Feldman, Brown, and the emerging minimalists.

In 1962 Carter contributed an article to the first issue of *Perspectives of New Music*, a Princeton-based, self-conscious (and Fromm-funded) American riposte to *Die Reihe*, similarly given to abstruse musical analysis; Carter, however, soon became disenchanted with the journal's insular preoccupations. Although many of the established music critics disparaged the academic tone of *Perspectives*, and the "uptown" scene in general, Carter found his work championed by two younger non-academic critics, Michael Steinberg at the *Boston Globe*, and Eric Salzman, who wrote for *The New York Times* for a while, but was mainly influential through his book *Twentieth-century Music: An Introduction* (1967). He situated Carter's work in a category of "the new performed music" that emphasized their virtuosity and dramatic character.

In the 1970s Speculum Musicae, originally founded by Luciano Berio as the new music ensemble at the Juilliard School, became in effect Carter's house band and premiered both *A Mirror on Which to Dwell* and *Syringa*. Its members included pianist Ursula Oppens, violinist Rolf Schulte, cellist Fred Sherry, and clarinetist Virgil Blackwell, all of whom would remain closely associated with Carter's music for the rest of his life.

With his second Pulitzer Prize in 1973, Carter's place in the musical hierarchy seemed secure. Throughout the 1970s his music was featured at the New York Philharmonic, where Pierre Boulez had replaced Leonard Bernstein as musical director. Andrew Porter, music critic for *The New Yorker* from 1972 onward, lavished praise on every new work. Only *The New York Times* remained doubtful, to say the least. Reviewing the New York Philharmonic's 1970 premiere of the Concerto for Orchestra, Harold C. Schonberg, the *Times*' chief critic, termed the music "essentially uncommunicative, dry and a triumph of technique over spirit." Schonberg's successor Donal Henehan found *A Mirror on Which to Dwell* "incomprehensibly brittle and dry" except for listeners who "value scrupulous, rather severe craftsmanship above all other musical values." (26 February 1976). With Henehan's successor, John Rockwell, the *Times*' longstanding conservatism flipped to a "post-modern" stance equally, if not more, dismissive of Carter's music. (Rockwell had made his mark at the *Times* by his advocacy of Philip Glass and Bruce Springsteen.) In *All American Music*, Rockwell began a chapter on Carter with the statement "if there is any kind of consensus as to America's 'best' living composer, it is Elliott Carter," and then devoted the next nine pages to amplifying the scare quotes placed around "best," so that by the end Rockwell dismissed Carter's oeuvre as "curiously constrained, flawed by a lack of inner clarity and expressive directness."[32] Along the way Rockwell recycled many of the familiar *New York Times* complaints: the music was "excessively knotty"; Carter made "a fetishism of complexity." Rockwell did, however, acknowledge that parts of *A Symphony of Three Orchestras* and the Third Quartet, two of Carter's knottiest and most complex works, "had an irresistible greatness."

An anti-Carter backlash soon surfaced in American academia as well, led by Richard Taruskin (U.C. Berkeley), a polymath Stravinsky scholar, who equated Carter with everything he deemed malignant in modern music (contempt for the audience, indifference to politics, complexity for its own sake), in the multi-volume *Oxford History of Music*. Taruskin consigned Carter's music to a "cul de sac full of absurdly overcomposed monstrosities" (5:305). As a further example of changing tastes Michael Broyles' *Mavericks and Other Traditions in American Music* devoted no space to any of Carter's compositions, just mentioning him in passing as a non-maverick academic composer. Similarly, Alex Ross' hugely influential *The Rest is Noise: listening to the twentieth century* devoted barely a page to Carter and, echoing Taruskin, attributed his success to "the tireless mechanism of Cold War cultural politics"—whatever that might mean.[33] The anti-Carter turn in American musicology coincided, however, with a far less visible pro-Carter movement among music theorists, spurred on by the publication, in 2002, of Carter's *Harmony Book*, edited by Nicholas Hopkins and John F. Link, which would be followed in 2012 by Guy Capuzzo's study of *What Next?* and a volume of *Carter Studies* edited by Marguerite Boland and John Link.

Carter waited a long time to find advocates for his music in the orchestral world, a wait that finally ended when he gained the support of two distinguished conductor/pianists. In the 1990s James Levine, musical director of the Metropolitan Opera and of the Boston Symphony, and Daniel Barenboim, music director of the Chicago Symphony, the Orchestre de Paris, and La Scala, joined the ranks of Pierre Boulez, Heinz Holliger, Michael Gielen, and Oliver Knussen as Carter devotees. Barenboim played a crucial role in commissioning Carter's opera, *What Next?*, and Levine commissioned and premiered a long list of works both large and small. Carter repaid their support with many appreciative dedications.

As Carter approached his hundredth birthday some previously hostile critics granted him grand-old-man status and praised the later works for a new-found clarity. As we shall see in the account of the music that follows, the very late period also produced some of Carter's darkest and most perplexing compositions.

Notes

1 As he approached his hundredth birthday, Carter allowed himself to present a less guarded account of his early life in an interview with Jörn Jacob Rohwer published, in German, in *Das Magazin* in 2008.

2 FW, 39.

3 CIR,139.

4 CPLD, 24.

5 Restagno, 6.

6 CIR, 107.

7 CIR, 135.

8 CPLD, 25.

9 CIR, 139.

10 CPLD, 25.

11 CPLD, 26–27.

12 FW, 47.

13 CPLD, 30.

14 CPLD, 33.

15 See Carol Oja's account of the evolving competition between the two factions in *Making Music Modern*, 177–200.

16 CEL, 111.

17 CEL, 87–90.

18 CPLD, 72.

19 CEL p. 111.

20 See articles by Felix Meyer and Stephen Soderberg in CS for more information on Carter's unfinished or unpublished works.

21 CPLD, 37.

22 Giroud, 135.

23 See Annegret Fauser, *Sounds of War* pp. 76–93 for a detailed account of the OWI's work.

24 In "Afterwards: Nicht Blutbefleckt?" published in *The Journal of Musicology* 26, no. 2 (2009), 274–284, Richard Taruskin would portray the entire Nabokov-Carter connection in a sinister light, attributing Carter's international success to his friend's CIA connections. Charles Rosen, whom Taruskin also accused of writing Cold War propaganda, defended himself and Carter in "Music and the Cold War," which appeared in the *New York Review of Books*, April 7, 2011. In a review of Vincent Giroud's biography of Nabokov that appeared in the August 5, 2016 TLS, Taruskin, citing his own adage that "in the long run we are all wrong," struck a much more measured and balanced tone, cleared Nabokov of charges of "clandestine sponsorship" since the CCF was always a visible agency, and even called Carter the "pre-eminent American standard-bearer of elite modernism in music."

25 See memorial tribute by Robert Craft, "Remembering Helen Frost Carter," in *Down a Path of Wonder*.
26 See Copland and Perlis 1, 283.
27 Goldman, 69.
28 CEL, 57–62.
29 The program also included Bach Cantata no. 210, Schoenberg's Chamber Symphony op. 9 and the premiere of Stravinsky's *Anthem: The Dove descending breaks the air*. The soloists in the Carter were Leonard Stein, harpsichord and Pearl Kaufman, piano.
30 Igor Stravinsky and Robert Craft in Conversation, 124.
31 *Dialogues and a Diary*, 47–49.
32 Rockwell, 45.
33 Ross, 405.

CHAPTER FOUR

A Modernistic Education (1924–1935)

Prologue

The overused term Modernism makes most sense when it denotes an evolving, many-sided disputation about the relation of art to the rapidly changing conditions of modern life, rather than a coherent movement or body of ideas. Within the framework of American culture, arguments about modernism have turned on questions of origins, national character, race, politics, audiences, and the idea of art itself. The hierarchy and analysis of these issues changed from decade to decade. For some American observers in the first third of the twentieth century, modernism appeared to be a European import that arrived in "scandalous" blockbuster events like the Armory Show of 1913, or the American premieres of *Le sacre* in 1922 and *Pierrot Lunaire* in 1923. Others (notably Gertrude Stein) claimed to the contrary that modernism was made in America, site of the first modern total war; home of Edison, Ford, the Wright Brothers, Scott Joplin, and Sidney Bechet; birthplace of the skyscraper, factory-sliced bread, and jazz. They could point out that during the 1920s almost every significant European modernist composer appropriated some aspect of jazz in order to give the music a contemporary flavor.

While some modernists, like the futurists, celebrated the noise and violence of the present day, others, like Eliot or Hemingway, saw only desolation and disillusion. Some critics, like Edmund Wilson, equated modernism with the French symbolist movement and its hermetic attempt to "purify the language of the tribe," an idea that Mallarmé, further complicating the question of origins, associated with his American predecessor, Poe. We might call Wilson's perspective the High Modernist view. Others, like Gilbert Seldes, a Low (or Broad) Modernist, celebrated the rapidly evolving lively arts of American popular music and movies. For Wilson the quintessential American modernist was T.S. Eliot; for Seldes, it was Irving Berlin.

In the bohemian Greenwich Village that took shape in the first two decades of the twentieth century, some modernists made common cause with socialists, feminists, and anarchists, at least until the first red scare of 1919. Others seemed indifferent to political ideas or were drawn to Mussolini's fascism. The relation of artistic and political radicalism was not self-evident. What was the political content of Duchamp's "Nude Descending a Staircase"?

Even before Elliott Carter began high school, much of the infrastructure and many of the literary landmarks of American modernism were already in place. In 1908 Alfred Stieglitz founded Gallery 291 to promote the new art of photography. Between 1915 and 1923, in the wake of the Armory Show, and with the help of a steel mill inheritance, Walter and Louise Arensberg created a Dadaist salon that brought together newly arrived European artists like Duchamp, Picabia, and Varèse with American modernists including Georgia O'Keefe, Isadora Duncan, Man Ray, William Carlos Williams, and Wallace Stevens. In 1918 Gertrude Vanderbilt Whitney founded the Whitney Studio Club, predecessor of the Whitney Museum. In 1920 the Provincetown Players achieved notoriety with their first professional production: Eugene O'Neill's *The Emperor Jones*. Modern American poetry seemed to emerge fully formed with the publications of Ezra Pound's *Hugh Selwyn Mauberley* in 1920, Wallace Stevens' *Harmonium* and Marianne Moore's *Poems* in 1921, T.S. Eliot's *The Waste Land* and William Carlos Williams' *Spring and All* in 1922, the miracle year that also saw the publication of Joyce's *Ulysses*, banned in the United States but, as Carter recalled, read by everyone he knew. Beginning in 1918 *The Dial* promoted new poetry, painting, and, in the "Music Chronicle" of critic Paul Rosenfeld, the latest music. Rosenfeld's *An Hour With American Music* (1929) provided a superb overview of the emerging scene. By 1920 Charles Ives had completed all the works that would eventually be seen as the foundation of American experimental music including *The Unanswered Question, Central Park in the Dark, Three Places in New England,* the *Concord Sonata,* and the Fourth Symphony.

The Awakening

> *Only when I went to high school did I really begin to take an interest in music. (FW, 39)*

In the first weeks of 1924, just after Carter turned fifteen, New York seemed to erupt with new music. On January 13 the International Composer's Guild presented Varèse's *Octandre. Le sacre du printemps* had its Carnegie Hall premiere, with the Boston Symphony conducted by Pierre Monteux, on January 31. Paul Whiteman's "Experiment in Modern Music" at Aeolian Hall on February 11 launched Gershwin's *Rhapsody in Blue.* And that was just the beginning of the year. As Carol Oja documented in *Making Music Modern,* new music groups in New York proliferated throughout the twenties, performing a large number of European and American works in all contemporary styles. While the Metropolitan Opera and New York Philharmonic took a conservative stance, new orchestral works and operas were also heard thanks to the productive rivalry of Serge Koussevitsky at the Boston Symphony and Leopold Stokowski at the Philadelphia Orchestra. Both ensembles performed regularly at Carnegie Hall.

World War I had interrupted the flow of new music from Europe, a break compounded by the wartime ban on German music and performers. Although works of the first generation of musical modernists—Strauss, Debussy, Mahler, and Busoni—had become well known before the war, the armistice opened the musical floodgates, making the American new music scene both vibrant and confusing. Two decades of music seemed to appear at once. Schoenberg's expressionism and Hindemith's *Neue Sachlichkeit,* Stravinsky's primitivism and his neo-classicism landed nearly simultaneously, rubbing shoulders with works by American composers as different as Gershwin, Antheil, Ruggles, Cowell, Carpenter (soon joined by Copland, Piston and Sessions), and a group of futuristic emigrés: Ornstein, Rudhyar, and Varèse. The path for a young composer was anything but obvious.

The path Carter would follow certainly did not fit the usual model of musical development. At fifteen, thanks to the influence of Clifton Furness, he suddenly became a new music enthusiast, but he was not yet a musician either by conscious calling or visible attainment. Although he soon began to compose, he did not devote himself to mastering the piano (though he did perform the piano part for his *Pastoral* in 1944) or any other instrument. He would take up the oboe only when he went to Harvard. While in high school he never performed in any instrumental ensemble, nor did he find himself a composition teacher, though there were qualified ones close by, such as Rubin Goldmark, who had taught Gershwin and Copland, or Percy Goetschius, who taught Richard Rodgers at the Institute for Musical Art (which, in 1924, became the Juilliard School). Resisting the usual forms of a musical apprenticeship either because of family opposition or his own ambivalence, Carter acted more like a student of literature who might be devoted to Shakespeare or Milton, or Eliot and Joyce without ever contemplating becoming a poet or novelist. He attended concerts and studied scores and books about new music, often acquiring them during his family's annual business trip to Europe. By the time he graduated from Harvard his library included these volumes (some rather arcane):

> BUSONI: *Sketch of A New Esthetic of Music* (1907)
> HENRY COWELL: *New Musical Resources* (1930)
> ALOIS HÁBA: *Neue Harmonielehre* (1927)
> JOSEF HAUER: *Lehrbuch der Zwölftöne-Musik; Vom Melos Zur Pauke* (1925); and *Zwölftontechnik*
> RENÉ LENORMAND: *Étude sur l'harmonie moderne* (1912)
> ARNOLD SCHÖNBERG: a Festschrift with tributes by Karl Linke, Anton von Webern, Heinrich Jalowitz, W. Kandinsky, Egon Wellesz, Robert Neumann, Erwin Stein, Karl Horwitz, Paul Königer, and Alban Berg (Munich, 1912)

This highly specialized collection[1] shows that even before he had studied much music theory the young Carter was drawn to the speculative, constructivist worlds of European expressionism and American ultra-modernist music, perhaps as much to the theoretical accounts of the music as to the music itself. He took little interest in jazz and after hearing *Rhapsody in Blue* did not pay much attention to Gershwin's music either in the theater or the concert hall, although he sat next to Gershwin at the American premiere of Berg's *Wozzeck* in 1930. He admired Varèse's futuristic compositions, but not Antheil's, and, though he had a sentimental attachment to John Alden Carpenter's *Skyscrapers*, he did not particularly favor music with American themes. Most of the young Carter's preferred composers—Scriabin, Schoenberg, Hauer, Hába, Cowell, and Cowell's mentor Charles Seeger—envisioned radically new musical idioms, often with a mathematical, or at least numeric, component, and a spiritual, theosophical aspect as well.[2] In short, the teenage Carter seemed positioned to pursue experimental music, but while he would employ many constructivist techniques in his later music, he often criticized them severely. He questioned "mechanistic" approaches to composition, whether in Joseph Schillinger's *System of Musical Composition*, which he reviewed in *Modern Music* [Summer, 1946], terming some of its ideas "like a Pythagorean refrain, with not too musical results,"[3] or, later on, in some works of European serialism, in which he found "a stultifying intellectual poverty that no amount of arithmetic patterning will overcome."[4] These negative assessments, though aimed at the music of others, expose one thread of Carter's own prolonged internal arguments, arguments that at times stymied his development, but eventually would fuel his creative career. Despite his strongly stated reservations, for instance, Carter employed mathematical methods for organizing pitch and rhythm, however "Pythagorean" and "not too musical" they might be, in all the music he composed from 1948 onward; and yet these methods would co-exist with an abiding wariness about their arbitrary character.

A parallel, equally persistent interior debate began to take shape as Carter encountered early examples of neo-classicism. One of the first to impress him was Walter Piston's Three Pieces for flute, clarinet, and piano, which he might have heard at a Copland-Sessions concert in April 1928 (or at Harvard in 1926). Many years later he would recall the fresh sound of its anti-romantic clarity, especially compared to the Scriabin-inspired murkiness of much of the other music he heard. The anti-romantic turn also appeared in Stravinsky's Piano Sonata and Hindemith's *Kleine Kammermusik* op. 24, both performed in New York in 1925. As new music seemed to veer wildly from expansive, visionary styles to contracting, well-ordered ones, and as the idea of tradition began to overtake the idea of the future in modernist aesthetics, the course of musical progress became less clear with every new season—though perhaps not for Charles Ives.

Carter met Ives through the music teacher at Horace Mann School, Clifton Joseph Furness (1898–1946), a pianist who had studied at Northwestern University, an admirer of Scriabin and a follower of Dr. Rudolph Steiner, founder of Anthroposophy. Sensing the spiritual side of Ives' music, Furness began writing to Ives in 1921, reporting that he was already giving lectures on the newly published *Concord Sonata*. Ives repaid Furness' interest by securing him a teaching post in English and music at Horace Mann. According to Ives' biographer Jan Swafford, "Furness would become one of the closest artistic friends Ives ever had."[5] In later life Furness became a Walt Whitman scholar, despite reservations about the poet from Ives, and especially from Mrs. Ives. Furness was typical of the small group of loyalists that Ives cultivated that would also include the organist, composer and Scriabin enthusiast T. Carl Whilmer, Henry Bellamann, who would later become Dean of the Curtis Institute of Music, and Henry Cowell, Ives' future biographer (among many other attainments). The fifteen-year-old Carter may have been an amusing addition to this circle but played a far less important role than the older devotees.

The impressionable young Carter quickly took up Furness's interests in Steiner, Scriabin, and Ives. Carter recalled first hearing Ives's music, parts of the *Concord Sonata*, at a séance-like performance by Furness's friend, the theosophical pianist Katherine Ruth Heyman, a Scriabin specialist and also a friend of Ezra Pound's. Sometime after that, Furness and Carter attended concerts with Ives, sharing his box at Carnegie Hall and then returning to the Ives home for a lively post-mortem, though it is hard to tell from Carter's accounts how many such concert outings there were. Carter recalled meetings with Ives at an apartment on Gramercy Park and later at the Ives homes on East 74th Street and in Redding, Connecticut, where, in 1928 or 1929, he spent a day, his last meeting with Ives, hoping to get advice on pursuing a life in music, which his parents opposed. On that occasion he also showed Ives some music he had composed in a neo-classic style, an indication that he was already departing from the experimentalist path. The music, he recalled, did not meet with Ives' approval.

The impact of Ives' personality, opinions and music on Carter's development is a complicated subject, to say the least. Carter's publicly aired ambivalence about Ives would spark controversy throughout his life, especially over the issue of musical quotations, an intertextual practice for which Carter often faulted Ives, but which musicologists would come to see as essential to Ives' music.[6] Further thickening the plot, Carter's critique of quotations in Ives comports oddly with own his quotations of Ives' music in the Cello Sonata and Quartet no.1 which allude (albeit in a private way) to the *Concord Sonata* and first Violin Sonata, respectively.

In 1946, Carter was involved in the first publication and performances of *Central Park in the Dark* and *The Unanswered Question*, and even proposed writing a book about Ives. The swing back to a pro-Ives position coincided with Carter's turn from the League's populist aesthetic and his reconnection with ideas and techniques from such ultra-modernists as Henry Cowell, Ruth Crawford, and Conlon Nancarrow. Carter joined the editorial board of the ultra-modernist *New Music* in 1945 and played some role in the merger of the League and ISCM (the continuation of the ICG) in the early 1950s.

In retrospect Carter's sense of kinship with Ives is more surprising than his frequently aired discomfort with many aspects of Ives' music. They came from different generations and different cultures. Ives grew up in the small town atmosphere of Danbury, Connecticut, and became a Yale athlete, captain of the football team. Carter, born and raised in New York City, became a Harvard aesthete. In the *Essays Before a Sonata*, Ives, the "nostalgic rebel" as Stephen Budiansky called him, wrapped his innovative music in the ideas of mid-nineteenth century thinkers like Emerson, Herbert Spencer, and Matthew Arnold, and he presented the ultimate goal of music in visionary, spiritual terms: "we would rather believe that music is beyond any analogy, and that the time is coming, but not in our lifetime, when it will develop possibilities inconceivable now—a language so transcendent that its heights and depths will be common to all mankind."[7] The literary modernists Carter would come to admire while at Harvard—Eliot, Pound, Moore, and Williams—dismissed Victorian sages like Arnold and Emerson as relics of the past. The *114 Songs*, which Ives self-published in 1922, show that his literary taste similarly remained Victorian except for Vachel Lindsay's "General William Booth enters Heaven" and some light verse by forgotten contemporary writers like Maurice Morris and Anne Collins.

Ives illustrated the utopian and spiritual impulses in his compositions by infusing them with the melodies of the common people and their faith: popular songs, especially those by Stephen Foster, patriotic anthems, and Protestant hymns. For most of his life Carter, by contrast, showed little interest in spiritual matters whether in organized religions or beyond them, or, for that matter, in the populist, progressive political ideas that Ives espoused. After his early settings of Emily Dickinson and Walt Whitman, Carter never returned to the history and culture of the American nineteenth century for inspiration, and (apart from some Italian folk tunes quoted in his early *Tarantella*) he never made use of popular song. There might be hints of jazz in his music from time to time, but no hymn tunes, no "Camptown Races," no "Columbia the Gem of the Ocean."

How might we explain the discrepancy and time-lapse between the brief social contact Carter had with Ives, which preceded his decision to pursue a musical career, and the prolonged and profound influence of Ives on Carter's music? Tokens of Ives' influence began to appear overtly only with the Cello Sonata of 1948, which recalled the *Concord Sonata*. Ivesian echoes figure in almost every subsequent work. The String Quartet no. 1 quotes a theme from Ives' First Violin Sonata; the ending of the Sonata for Flute, Oboe, Cello, and Harpsichord resembles the very last bars of *The Housatonic at Stockbridge*; the seventh variation of the Variations for Orchestra evokes *The Unanswered Question*; the four-way dramatic argument and contrasting personae of the Quartet no. 2 recall the "Discussions" and "Arguments" movements in Ives' second quartet, and, in the Piano Concerto, the dense swirls of harmonies in the strings derive from *The Fourth of July*. The spatial configurations of the Concerto for Orchestra and A Symphony of Three Orchestras, while reminiscent of the European avant-garde, recall *The Unanswered Question* and *Central Park in the Dark*.

We might say that there were two versions of Charles Ives in Carter's life: the actual man whom he got to know a little bit in his teens, and the precursor-figure that Carter constructed as he formulated his own musical identity around the time he turned forty. In his writings Carter invoked Ives to support approaches to rhythm and texture, especially complex polyrhythms and the superimposition of contrasting ideas, even though the expressive uses he made of these devices were distant from the thematics of Ives' music. Had Carter decided to reconcile his parents' plans with a musical calling, the real Charles Ives might have served as a useful mentor on how to live a double life. But that was not the choice that Carter made. By 1930 he had terminated direct contact with Ives. The "traumatic" 1939 review of the *Concord Sonata* placed the break with the real Ives before the public. As we shall see, Ives as precursor, disguised as Aaron Copland and camouflaged with academic respectability, would struggle to emerge in the Piano Sonata of 1946, and then appear with a four-note fanfare in the Cello Sonata, the first piece that sounds like Carter and no one else—not even Ives.[8]

Harvard (1926–1932)

> *In 1926, my freshman class was addressed by Harvard's president emeritus and editor of the famous five-foot bookcase of the World's Best Books [Charles William Eliot]. He was very old, very eminent, very tottering. His advice to the rich and clean young gentlemen already tenderized by St. Paul's, St. Mark's, St. George's, Phillips Exeter, and Phillips Andover (with a few from the Boston Latin School) was "Flee introspection."*
>
> —Lincoln Kirstein (Kirstein 21)

The vivid memoirs of Carter's Harvard classmate Lincoln Kirstein can help us fill out the abbreviated account Carter offered of his Harvard years in FW. They illustrate the distance between the cultural climate at Harvard and the milieu Carter had encountered earlier at Katherine Ruth Heyman's spiritualist recitals. At Harvard anti-romanticism ruled, both as an educational philosophy and as a social ethos. At the same time, though, Kirstein's memoir gives ample evidence that the official Harvard ideology coexisted with a shadowy world of chemical and sexual exploration, a bohemian underbelly that was also part of the entitlements of a privileged upbringing. For Kirstein, the emblem of this counterculture was the *poète maudit* of the era, Hart Crane, whose life and work would play an important role, years later, in Carter's music.[9] Carter's own interest in Crane's poetry dated back to high school, when Eugene O'Neill Jr. lent him a copy of *White Buildings*.

The "manly" ethos espoused as Carter entered Harvard, reminiscent of another Harvard alumnus, Theodore Roosevelt, might have served to prepare Harvard's elite students to become captains of industry, Wall Street brokers, members of Congress, or State Department officials, but it also had a more intellectual presence at Harvard in the culturally conservative, anti-romantic writings of Irving Babbitt, especially his *Rousseau and Romanticism* (1919). Babbitt was a daunting polymath, learned in French and Sanskrit literatures. His mandarin rejection of Rousseau-inspired introspection lent legitimacy to the blossoming anti-romantic strain within modernism. He rejected the most influential thinkers of the previous century: "Every age has had its false teachers, but possibly no age ever had so many dubious moralists as this, an incomparable series of false prophets, from Rousseau himself down to Nietzsche and Tolstoy."[10] In *The Sacred Wood* (1928) T.S. Eliot, Harvard's most illustrious modernist alumnus, praised Babbitt for his ability to "see Europe as a whole" and then reformulated Babbitt's anti-romanticism as the very core of modernist aesthetics: "poetry is not a turning loose of emotion, but an escape from emotion; it is not the expression of personality, but an escape from personality," though he quickly added his own escape clause: "but, of course, only those who have personality and emotions know what it means to want to escape from these things." An attitude, and prose style, farther from *Essays Before a Sonata*, would be hard to find.

In FW, Carter prefaced his far less colorful account of Harvard by recalling his disappointment in finding that the music department had no interest in contemporary music and "considered Koussevitsky's modernist activities at the Boston Symphony an outright scandal." Carter thereby blamed the Harvard music department for a further delay in his pursuit of a musical calling, but the mainly literary education he received at Harvard would continue to play an important part in music he would write many decades later. Carter's Harvard transcript indicates that he completed one course in music (and received a C) in his first year. After that he studied English literature, French, German, and classical Greek. Only one, introductory, philosophy course appears on his Harvard record, but Carter attended Alfred North Whitehead's lectures that were subsequently published as *Process and Reality*. The distinguished philosopher, co-author with Bertrand Russell of the *Principia Mathematica*, boldly set out to redefine every aspect of philosophy in terms of quantum mechanics. Densely argued, yet far-reaching, even redefining God, full of neologisms and familiar words used in completely unfamiliar ways, and traversing much of the history of philosophy and science, Whitehead's lectures, unlike some of his more popular writings, were addressed to a few fellow philosophers, not undergraduates. Today they are still considered some of the most difficult literature in the field. Even considering Carter's mathematical instincts, it is hard to imagine an untrained twenty-year old following

Whitehead's complex exposition, but Carter nevertheless often cited these lectures as helping to shape his concepts of time and of musical form and, in later life, he often reread Whitehead's more popular works for pleasure. In FW he wrote that Whitehead's "stress on organic patterns, [has] molded my thinking—not only about music" (47). In a 1960 essay on Petrassi he cited Whitehead's definition of an event: "a unit of action in a total sequence in which the event contains within itself not only its own history but as well its prefiguration of possible futures and its own individual character."[11] Both statements align with Carter's long-term aesthetic values and his approach to musical structure.[12]

As a member of the Harvard Glee Club, Carter experienced the antiromantic turn in modern music first-hand when he sang in the Boston Symphony premiere of Stravinsky's *Oedipus Rex* on April 24, 1928. Stravinsky's score disavowed dissonance, avoided the brilliant orchestral alchemy of his earlier scores, employed triadic harmony, and seemed, at times, brazenly and unironically derivative of mid-nineteenth-century grand opera, the much-maligned genre of Meyerbeer. The shock, call it the shock of the old, felt by listeners mainly familiar with Stravinsky's Russian ballets is well reflected in Aaron Copland's astute review of the Paris premiere a year before. Noting that "music, more than any other art, has been profoundly influenced by the ideals of nineteenth century romanticism," Copland linked Stravinsky's turn toward an "objective attitude" and his "wholehearted acceptance of tradition" to the writings of Clive Bell and T.S. Eliot.[13]

In extracurricular fashion, Carter studied music theory and the oboe (with Louis Speyer) at the Longy School, founded in 1915 by Georges Longy, oboist of the Boston Symphony.[14] The content of Carter's studies at the Longy School, which he did not even see fit to mention in FW, remains obscure, but so does much of Carter's life and character at the time. In FW, for instance, he recalled, *en passant*, that, while at Harvard, he spent several "charming" summers in Munich with friends and sailed "on the treacherous Starnbergersee"—without mentioning the friends' names.

Despite his education at all-male schools, not all of Carter's friends were men. From a letter written to Helen in 1942, we learn of the passing (on September 18, 1942) of Edith Forbes Kennedy. Carter wrote that she "was a kind of mother to me and was the only one I knew who had faith

in me." Mrs. Kennedy, a married woman with three children, was a socially prominent Bostonian, who had been divorced from her husband,
Albert Kennedy, in 1929. This circumstance may explain the fact that
Carter never mentioned their relationship in his writings. A full portrait of her with a reference to her close friendship with Carter during
his Harvard years appears in May Sarton's *A World of Light* pp. 87–101.
We might wonder if the warmly lyrical *Elegy*, composed in 1943, was
prompted by her death.

Carter's classicist-oriented study of English literature at Harvard may
have reflected the university ethos, but his particular interest in Greek
took a surprisingly ethnomusicological detour in the summer of 1927
when he transcribed Arabic music in Tunisia for the Baron Rudolphe
d'Erlanger. (Carter never explained how he landed this assignment, but
most of his college summers were spent traveling abroad, as was the
family custom.) The project ultimately inspired the two earliest Carter
compositions still extant: a setting, dated 1928, of Joyce's "My Love
is in a Light Attire," dedicated to the singer Laura Williams, at whose
house Carter stayed; and, in 1932, incidental music for a production of
Sophocles' *Philoctetes* by the Harvard Classical Club, scored for unison
chorus, off-stage oboe, and darrabukka, the drum that Carter had brought
back from Tunisia. (Despite the song's title and dedication, Carter never
mentioned Williams in any other context.) The extensive manuscript
score for *Philoctetes* in Carter's hand at the PSS shows that he wrote in
the lyrics in classical Greek, perhaps assisted by Robert Fitzgerald (later
the famed translator of Euripides, Sophocles, Homer, and Virgil) who in a
letter to Carter referred to "our *Philoctetes*." Carter retained his command
of ancient Greek for many years to come, as he would demonstrate in
assembling the Greek texts for *Syringa* in 1978.

At the opening of the Joyce setting, perhaps one of a group of Joyce
songs that Carter recalled showing to Ives, he used quintuple meter and
bitonality. In the accompaniment Carter quoted a three-note motive
from the "Seikilos Song," one of the oldest examples of Greek music,
often termed the first composed song.[15] Throughout his career Carter
would use this motive as a musical signature (see Appendix). It appears
prominently in the *Pastoral* (1940), *The Minotaur* (1947), "Anaphora" from
A Mirror on Which to Dwell (1975), and the *Tre Duetti* composed in 2008
and 2009 (see *Duettino*, bar 8). (We might also detect the signature in the

rising-fifth themes of *Holiday Overture, The Harmony of Morning*, and the fugue subject of the Piano Sonata.) Carter's linking of ancient Greek culture with contemporary Arabic music was an original and provocative idea, however simply he was able to realize it in his music at the time. The impact of Stravinsky's quite different rendition of Greek classicism would, however, not appear until Carter's next score for the Harvard Classical Club, the 1936 production of Plautus' *Mostellaria*, in Latin, from which Carter derived his earliest published work, *Tarantella*—after three years of study with Nadia Boulanger.

Carter received his undergraduate Harvard degree on May 23, 1930, seven months after the stock market crash that precipitated the Great Depression. Apparently not much affected by the economic collapse, and having taken just one undergraduate music course, he gained admittance to Harvard's small master's degree program in music. He took classes in composition and orchestration with Walter Piston, who had returned to Harvard after studying with Nadia Boulanger from 1924 to 1926, and also recalled working with Gustav Holst who was a visitor at Harvard in the spring of 1932. As Howard Pollack demonstrates in *Harvard Composers*, Piston's lucid, sober, and eminently un-romantic music would serve as a model for much of Carter's music as late as the *Eight Etudes and a Fantasy* of 1949. Despite the fame and ubiquity of Piston's textbooks on harmony, counterpoint, and orchestration, however, Carter told me on several occasions that he found Piston to be an uninspiring teacher, and that after these two additional years at Harvard, from which only the fragments of music for *Philoctetes* remain, he still lacked the skills required to become a composer. Piston's most valuable advice as a teacher, Carter said, was to recommend that Carter follow in his footsteps and study with Boulanger.

Paris (1932–1935)

> *These were, of course, those terrible years between 1932 and 1935 in Paris when the fascist Croix de Feu staged a frightening street fight on the Place de la Concorde during the Stavisky affair, part of which I witnessed.*
>
> (FW, 52–53)

By way of this footnote in FW, Carter situated far more than his own musical apprenticeship with Nadia Boulanger. Amid the economic and political upheavals of the 1930s, modernism itself was under attack, from the left and the right, from without and within. Nazi Germany banned any music with Jewish ties, including that of Mahler, Schoenberg (and his students), Zemlinsky, Schreker, and Weill. The USSR officially suppressed "Formalism," its code word for modernism. In the United States the members of the Composer's Collective, including Aaron Copland, Marc Blitzstein, and Henry Cowell, strove to create an idiom with greater social relevance, "to be sung at meetings, on parades, and on picket lines."[16] Charles Seeger and his wife Ruth Crawford abandoned ultra-modernism for the study of American folk music.

In the 1930s, modernism in music may have seemed dead, yet somehow, despite the hostile circumstances, the leading modernists composed some of their greatest works: Stravinsky's *Symphony of Psalms*, Violin Concerto, *Duo Concertant*, and Concerto for Two Solo Pianos; Bartók's *Cantata Profana*, Second Piano Concerto, Violin Concerto, and Music for Strings, Percussion and Celesta; Schoenberg's Violin Concerto, Fourth Quartet, and *Moses und Aron*; Berg's *Lulu* and Violin Concerto; Webern's Symphony, Concerto for Nine Instruments, and String Quartet—many of which Carter would praise in his earliest articles for *Modern Music*.

In such fractious times, Mlle. Boulanger's classes, tea parties, and soirées must have seemed like a bastion of tranquility and civilization. Here Carter studied counterpoint in a rigorous fashion, honed his abilities in sight-singing and continuo playing, sang through many of Bach's cantatas, analyzed contemporary scores, and, on special occasions, met Stravinsky, Paul Valéry, Igor Markévich, and George Enesco. In his detailed reminiscences about Boulanger in FW and CEL Carter, characteristically, did not mention the names of any other students working with her at the same time, nor did he reveal anything about other friendships he may have had. In 1989 he told Enzo Restagno that he was friends with the painter Chaim Soutine at the time, and in a late interview with Jörn Jacob Rohwer recalled visiting the Louvre with Soutine: "he was the only painter that I ever really knew well."

Carter's recollections of Boulanger's routine interventions in his personal life square with similar accounts, thirty years later, from Philip Glass.[17] For Boulanger, no wall separated music from the self. The slightest error in a counterpoint exercise exposed a lack of personal discipline, an unacceptable disorder or casual disregard, that inevitably related to every other aspect of a student's existence, including, as Carter recalled, knowing what to order in a particular restaurant.[18] I once asked Carter about a staged Boulanger class I had watched on television, in which she slowly intoned the lesson of the day: "You must take risks! If you don't take risks, you should stay in your room. You should stay in your bed. You should die!" He affirmed that this was exactly the way she taught—and that after a while he just learned to stop listening to such exhortations. Carter also told me that Boulanger was not a theorist in the sense that Schoenberg or Hindemith were, but that the only thing that mattered to her was *métier* (i.e., technique). This apparently narrow concern, however, would have a huge impact on Carter's understanding of music, as he made clear in a conversation with Heinz Holliger published in 1994:

> She concentrated very intensely on the construction of musical phrases. When I showed up with my first pieces, which all sounded a little like Bartók, she took a Mozart score and showed me how he (Mozart) constructed his climaxes, how he ended his phrases, how he began them, how they increased in intensity or the reverse, and that touched me very directly. (*Sonus*, Spring 1994, 10)

Aside from his counterpoint exercises (some of which he transformed in 1939 into the charming and ingenious *Canonic Suite* for four saxophones), Carter preserved little of the music he composed while he was in Paris. Even after Boulanger's training he still felt that he was unable to write the music he wanted to write, and Boulanger, who had worked hard to promote the careers of composers such as Copland and Markévich, seemed unimpressed by his student efforts. Nevertheless, it could be argued that her influences on Carter were decisive for his later development. Under her tutelage Carter became a contrapuntist. Polyphony would inform every aspect of his mature musical style.

As Boulanger taught it, counterpoint was far more than the simple superimposition of independent lines. It entailed a disciplined coordination of the horizontal and vertical aspects of music, melody, and harmony, a comprehensive understanding of the terms of a musical idiom, and the development of strategies, mixing inspiration with calculation, for creating within strict limits. To compose a canon or fugue you cannot just start with a nice idea and hope for the best. Transforming time into space, you have to imagine how that idea will generate the architecture of the entire piece.[19] This transcendent concept of music was far from the "sewing machine" or "wrong-note" counterpoint heard in much of the new music of the 1920s, or even from Charles Seeger's more systematic ideas about "dissonant counterpoint," but it seemed clearly realized, in a contemporary form, in the disciplined, austere works by Stravinsky, from the *Symphony of Psalms* to *Perséphone* that Carter heard at Boulanger's home on the Rue Ballu, in the composer's presence. Carter may have perceived in Boulanger's understanding of Monteverdi and Bach, and in Stravinsky's apparent turn to the past, a much more compelling version of the systematic approaches to composition that had attracted him earlier to the theoretical writings of Cowell, Hauer, and Hába. It would take Carter another fifteen years, however, to work out a synthesis of all of these methods—and Schoenberg's as well—and apply them in his own compositions.

The first models of counterpoint that Carter would emulate in his own work were more modest in ambition and scope. In Paris he sang in a chorus conducted by the musicologist Henri Expert, an authority on Renaissance choral music, and "got to know the French madrigal school inside out" (FW, 55). Upon returning home in 1935 he found that several of his friends conducted choral ensembles. With their encouragement he composed a body of sophisticated secular choral music, a genre not particularly well-suited to hard times, but which brought together his literary and musical interests.

Notes

1 Carter gave me all his personal copies of these books in the 1980s.
2 For a concise account of the ultramodernist influence see Shreffler, "Elliott Carter and his America."
3 WEC, 120.
4 *Perspectives of New Music*, Spring 1963.
5 Swafford, 32.
6 See David Thurmaier, "'A Disturbing Lack of Musical and Stylistic Continuity'? Elliott Carter, Charles Ives, and Musical Borrowing, *Current Musicology*, Fall 2013.
7 *Essays Before a Sonata*, 8.
8 Carter presented Ives as precursor in two important articles: "The Rhythmic Basis of American Music" (1955) and "Expressionism and American Music" (1965).
9 See "Carlsen, Crane" in Kirstein, 38–71.
10 Hazard Adams, ed., *Critical Theory Since Plato*, 808.
11 CEL, 167.

12 See Jonathan Bernard, "The evolution of Elliott Carter's rhythmic practice," PNM 26, no. 2 (1988).
13 Copland on Music, 190.
14 In 1925 his daughter Renée Longy-Miquelle (1897–1979) took over as the school's director. In later years she would be a close friend and teacher of Leonard Bernstein, and, from 1963 up to her death, she brought a rigorous and traditional form of solfège to the Juilliard School. During that time Carter sought her advice on questions of rhythmic notation. At Juilliard, Mme. Longy taught a method of rhythmic dictation based on subdivisions of the beat, noting the number of subdivision and whether they were articulated, tied, or silent. Her system is extremely pertinent for performers of Carter's music.
15 The Seikilos Song appears in *Historical Anthology of Music: Oriental, Medieval and Renaissance Music*, edited by Archibald Davison and Willi Apel, Harvard University Press, 1949: 11. See also Appendix: Carter's Musical Signatures.
16 Copland Perlis, I, 223.
17 *Words Without Music*, 136–149.
18 Carter's accounts of taking Mlle. Boulanger out to dinner at a famed Parisian restaurant and also traveling with her to Venice should cast doubt on the notion that he was strapped for funds at the time.
19 See Stephen Soderberg's article on Carter's sketches in the Library of Congress (CS, 239–241) for evidence that Carter began work on the fugue for his 1946 Piano Sonata while studying with Boulanger. It took over a decade for the initial exploration to turn into the final piece.

CHAPTER FIVE

Musician, Wrestling (1935–1946)

CARTER OFTEN SHAPED THE TALE OF HIS MUSICAL DEVELOPMENT around a single, life-changing crisis:

> I worked up to one crucial experience, my First String Quartet, written around 1950, in which I decided for once to write a work very interesting to myself, and to say to hell with the public and with the performers too. I wanted to write a work that carried out completely the various ideas I had at that time about the form of music, about texture and harmony—about everything.
>
> (FW, 35)

The way that Carter described this dramatic turn recalls Martin Luther's "Here I Stand," but it also resembles the way some American art critics, around 1950, portrayed the emergence of Abstract Expressionism:

> At a certain moment the canvas began to appear to one American painter after another as an arena in which to act—rather than as a space in which to reproduce, re-design, analyze or "express" an object, actual or imagined. What was to go on the canvas was not a picture but an event.
>
> (Harold Rosenberg, *The Tradition of the New*, 25)

Carter's story, like Rosenberg's, mixed fact and mythology in a seductive way that seems increasingly problematic, though not necessarily deceitful, with the passage of time. In citing the First Quartet as the true beginning of his oeuvre he placed the music he had composed in the fifteen years after his return from Paris in 1935 in a limbo that became known as "pre-Carter." The statement from FW implied that the music he wrote before the First Quartet was fatally compromised due to pressures from either audiences or performers.

Some Carter scholars have proposed alternative ways of considering the early works that find elements of continuity with the mature style rather than an absolute disjunction. Jonathan Bernard cites many examples in this period of Carter's abiding concerns with complexity, "collectional" harmony, and the "long line" that was central to Boulanger's aesthetics.[1] Orrin Moe described the early music in more dialectic terms, splitting the works between neo-classical and expressionist lines that converged in the Cello Sonata but only achieved maturity with the *Variations for Orchestra*, completed five years after the First Quartet.[2] I think that this multi-track model mirrors many of the problems that Carter wrestled with in his life as well as in his music, but I would prefer to identify the contending impulses of "pre-Carter" with Walter Piston and Hart Crane. Since Carter was a Proust-lover I'll call these two directions Piston's Way and Crane's Way.

The contrast of these two paths is clearest in Carter's choices of texts. In most of his early choral works, including *Tarantella, Let's Be Gay, Harvest Home, To Music, The Defense of Corinth*, and *The Harmony of* Morning, he set poetry devoid of emotional interest, let alone any sense of tragedy. The music, though increasingly compelling, occupies a narrow emotional terrain between whimsy and melancholy. Carter composed most of these pieces for college choirs and glee clubs whose repertory centered on such clever diversions. With *Heart Not So Heavy As Mine*, however, Carter began to set poetry with far more emotional and intellectual weight. He would continue this darker thread in settings of Emily Dickinson, Walt Whitman, and Hart Crane. As we will see, Crane identified Whitman and Dickinson (and Melville) as his poetic predecessors. They became Carter's as well.

The competing claims of these opposed influences align, though not perfectly, with the Light and Dark components of Carter's creative process, with Nietzsche's contrast of Apollonian and Dionysian art, and with current understandings of the contrasting functions of the left and right halves of the brain, but they also represent conflicts inherent in being a "Harvard composer" in Depression-era America, the guise in which Carter first appeared.[3] As he attempted to launch his career, Carter took advantage of his Harvard connections, especially with G. Wallace Woodworth, conductor of the Harvard Glee Club, who led the first performance of *Tarantella* on March 5, 1937, and to his classmate Lincoln Kirstein, who, in 1936, hired Carter as music director of Ballet Caravan and asked him to write the score for *Pocahontas*, a ballet project inspired by Hart Crane's *The Bridge*. Carter thus reconnected himself with both the establishment and subversive sides of Harvard culture. His engagement with such different aesthetic ideals baffled many of his contemporaries, especially as many of them turned from aesthetic considerations to political ones. Carter's alternation of conservative and rebellious stances remains puzzling even today.

As Carter moved beyond the Harvard sphere, many aspects of his identity remained unresolved. The articles he wrote for *Modern Music* and his letters reveal opposed impulses and personae. The brashly opinionated critic in *Modern Music*, with his advocacy for hardcore modernist works by Bartók, Berg, Webern, and Schoenberg, seems to be a different person from the mild-mannered *petit maître* of *To Music* and *Harvest Home*, the *Pastoral*, or the *Elegy*. Likewise, the author of the futuristic "Artistic Credo" that Carter presented to Varèse's class in the summer of 1948, who described his music as "the kinetic projection of ideas, using perspectives in time," seems unrelated to the composer of the weighty neo-classical score to *The Minotaur*, written the previous year, with its reliance on eighteenth-century forms such as fugue and chaconne. As a composer Carter seemed to lack a recognizable voice. At once celebratory and impersonal, *The Harmony of Morning* seemed vastly different from the darkly erotic, death-haunted world of *Voyage*, written at the same time. In terms of both style and form, the four large orchestral scores, *Pocahontas*, Symphony no. 1, *Holiday Overture*, and *The Minotaur*, could have been written by four different composers.

Carter's political profile at this time seems as elusive as his musical voice. During the prolonged crises of the Great Depression and Second World War, his closest friends included leftist composers like Aaron Copland and Marc Blitzstein, who were creating socially conscious, activist works like *The Cradle Will Rock* or *The Second Hurricane* (both from 1937). At this same time, though, Carter devoted his energies to apolitical choral works written for elite Ivy League choruses, many of them based on obscure Latin or English poetry—texts devoid of any obvious "social significance." As CPLD notes (47), the political content of *The Defense of Corinth*, the only work that seems in any way concerned with contemporary affairs, could be read to support either intervention or isolationism, an ambiguity stemming from the conflict between Carter's Francophilia and his father's pacifism, but also from political divisions at Harvard. Even as late as 1947, his decision to set a poem by the reactionary, anti-New Deal poet Allen Tate associated Carter, intentionally or not, with a political and aesthetic position far to the right. (Tate's amalgam of political reaction and elitist modernism also attracted Robert Lowell at the time.) In conversation with Enzo Restagno many years later, Carter claimed that he had been a Trotskyite for a short time and that he had never been an anti-communist (34), but elsewhere his criticisms of Soviet music give a very different impression.[4] The Trotskyite line espoused in the *Partisan Review* in the late 1930s was politically anti-Stalinist and aesthetically pro-modernist, a stance that Carter may well have found attractive, however briefly. The only consistent political theme found in his articles and letters is a recurring complaint about the lack of governmental support for American music.

Even Carter's sense of his calling in music remained unsettled during his post-Boulanger years. Letters reveal periods of effusive optimism about a career in music, amid ongoing concern about how to escape from the many strings attached to financial support from his parents. Writing to Eva Goldbeck on June 3, 1935, the twenty-seven-year-old Carter confessed: "I have a life to start . . . but I see no way out unless I can earn enough to break away coolly in a considered way." Goldbeck, whom Carter had met through Clifton Furness, was married to Marc Blitzstein. According to Blitzstein's biographer, Howard Pollack, Carter socialized with the couple often (before Goldbeck's death in 1936) and showed Blitzstein his music. Apparently this close contact left a confused impression. Writing to David Diamond in 1942, Blitzstein described Carter as "a curious, serious guy, inept, and not a little touching."[5] Carter's own uncertainty about the direction of his life continued through the early 1940s. He even considered purchasing a 250-acre farm, an option he discussed with Helen and his father over the course of several months. He stopped pursuing the gentleman farmer idea only when he learned that it would not defer him from military service.[6]

Even today it remains difficult to get a full view of Carter's development in the decade after his studies with Boulanger because the musical evidence is incomplete. An account of his work by Claire Reis from 1938, reproduced in MEC83, indicates that by that date he had destroyed or never completed, a symphony, concerto for English horn, a set of madrigals, a flute sonata, an opera, and two string quartets.[7] With few remaining traces of these works, it is hard to determine why Carter abandoned them, but the sheer number of titles shows that Carter's prolific output in his last decades, so different from the slow deliberation of his middle years, had a precedent much earlier. Some important works from the early phase are not currently available on recording. There is no recording of the complete 1939 *Pocahontas*, and few people have seen its score. There is a single recording of the complete *Minotaur*, and the only recording of the suite, conducted by Howard Hanson, is out of print and hard to find. Amazon lists no current recording for the *Canonic Suite*, an important score, first published in 1939, in which Carter for the first time deployed his contrapuntal ingenuity in a personal way. Because of his later revisions, even the published scores obscure as much as they reveal. *Pocahontas* evolved considerably from its first performance on piano in 1936, to its New York premiere with orchestra in 1939. Carter omitted about half of the ballet score when he made a concert suite in 1941, and he revised the suite in 1961. The two commercial recordings of the score present the 1961 version and so give little sense of the impression the music might have made in 1939, let alone in 1936. Carter's Symphony no. 1 has a similar history. Though completed in 1942, much of its third movement contains themes derived from the earliest versions of *Pocahontas*. Following the premiere by the Eastman-Rochester Symphony on April 27, 1944, Carter cut a large section from the finale that reprised material from the opening movement. For the first performance in New York City, on January 16, 1954, Carter again extensively revised the score, rewriting the opening bars, and introducing many new indications for tempo and accentuation. The recordings of these "early" works therefore reflect many alterations made in the wake of Carter's 1951 transformation.

Piston's Way

Walter Piston's music is often described as "Parisian" neo-classicism, but both parts of that phrase are misleading, and even more so when they are applied to Carter. A better term would be "conservative," a stance slightly to the left of Howard Hanson, but to the right of Copland and Schuman, that Piston defended as a valid contemporary style: "It is not one of my aims to write music that will be called modern, nor do I set out to compose according to any particular style or system. I believe my music is music of today in both manner and expression, since I am inevitably influenced by the art, thought, and daily life of the present."[8] Piston also rejected "the self-conscious striving for nationalism." The measured tone of all these statements is not at all far from the conservative voice that Carter would employ in many of his writings from the 1930s onward.

Piston's aesthetic position often earned him grudging respect from contemporaries. In 1939, for instance, Aaron Copland wrote that "Piston belongs with Sessions as one of the most expert craftsmen American music can boast."[9] In a similar vein, Virgil Thomson described Piston as "the author of neoclassical symphonies and chamber pieces that by their fine workmanship may well arrive at repertory status when revived in a later period; for now they seem a shade scholastic."[10] Despite such implied or stated reservations, Piston was awarded the New York Critics Circle Award for his Symphony no. 2 and, in 1948 and 1961, received Pulitzer Prizes for his third and seventh symphonies.

Carter, the future "avant-garde composer", embraced Piston's conservatism more whole-heartedly. In 1946 his extended account of Piston's music appeared in *The Musical Quarterly*. Giving a more positive spin to Copland's faint praise of craftsmanship, Carter concluded that "Piston's work helps us to keep our mind on the durable and the most satisfying aspects of the art of music and by making them live gives us hope that the qualities of integrity and reason are still with us."[11] The respectful tone of this article, however, needs to be considered in relation to two others that Carter wrote around the same time. In "Ives Today: His Vision and Challenge," published in 1944, Carter had written that "few composers in our time have come to grips with the basic problem of musical expression as does Charles Ives," an endorsement Carter strengthened two years later in "An American Destiny." Also in 1946, Carter published "Fallacy of the Mechanistic Approach," a review which took Joseph Schillinger's *System of Musical Composition* to task (from a Pistonian perspective) for its "pseudo-algebraic formulas" yet found "many interesting contributions," including "the novel idea of deriving temporal divisions and irregularities by combining two regular patterns, such as three notes against four, into one line."[12] From this "contribution" Carter would soon derive the technique of metrical modulation.

The conflicting perspectives of these articles suggest that we need to re-hear Carter's music from this period in terms of its inclusions and exclusions, its surface and its shadows. For over a decade Carter chose to compose in an idiom unrelated to the ultra-modern music he had studied so enthusiastically in high school, far from the "high modernist" works of Schoenberg, Berg, and Bartók that he lauded in his critical writing of the same time, and, for the most part, also far from the jazz-inflected populism of Copland, Blitzstein, and Bernstein. Perhaps Piston's Way, sober, somber, and devoid of thrills, cheap or otherwise, offered Carter a safe haven from his own warring sympathies, and also from the more influential styles of Stravinsky and Hindemith, which lured so many of his contemporaries. Piston's preference for order over chaos, for structure over effects, would remain essential components of Carter's aesthetic.

Carter's affinities, and differences, with Piston's music are apparent if we listen to his Symphony no. 1 alongside Piston's Symphony no. 2. The two works are nearly contemporary and sound like fraternal twins. (Piston's uses a slightly larger orchestra.) Piston completed his symphony in 1943, a year after Carter finished his, but Piston's premiered in March 1944, a month before Carter's, and far more successfully. Both works contain three movements and last about 26 minutes. The first movements of both symphonies explore the rhythmic contrast between pulses in a 3:2 ratio (half notes and dotted half notes). The similarity of their rhythms would be more apparent to the eye had Carter heeded Fritz Reiner's suggestion and re-notated the parts of the movement in 3/4 in larger units of 9/4 or 6/4.

In the wartime setting of their premieres, both works conveyed little of the sense of urgency found in Samuel Barber's *Second Essay*, William Schuman's Fifth Symphony, or Leonard Bernstein's "Jeremiah" Symphony, all written at the same time, though Piston's finale, unlike Carter's, sounds a more strident tone. While Piston's Second seems to move gradually into the darkness of its time, Carter's First (not to be followed by a Second) seems to move backward toward a less anxious era, perhaps because its three movements appear in the reverse order from their sequence of composition. The first movement sounds far more sophisticated in its form and textures than the third, a contrast that Carter heightened in his later revisions. (In later life Carter chuckled over "all those quarter notes" in the finale.) The original reprise of first movement material in the finale may have been an attempt to create an impression of overall unity, but Carter, perhaps realizing that such a Franckian gesture did not comport with the humorous character of much of the music, excised it soon after the premiere. As Stephen Soderberg has shown,[13] the opening theme of the third movement started out as a fiddle tune for violin and piano composed in 1935 (and perhaps inspired by Copland's "Ukulele Serenade"). Carter recycled the theme in early sketches for *Pocahontas*, but not in the final version, then took it up again it to establish the rough-hewn, rustic mood for his symphonic finale. Carter told me that Duke Ellington complimented him on the short, jazzy clarinet solo that provides the movement with its climax, but I have found no evidence to confirm this momentous encounter.

While the third movement displays a pops-concert style rarely heard in Carter's music, the first two movements explore flexible tempos and fluid formal structures that anticipate his later style. Both of these movements combine Boulanger's idea of the *"grande ligne"*[14] with an open-ended elaboration of material that recalls Schoenberg's idea of developing variation and parts company with Piston's reliance on standard classical forms. In his original program note Carter wrote that the first movement was a hybrid of sonata and variation forms. When its themes return they take on new expressive characters, rhythmic inflections, and instrumental colors.

The first movement, with melodic ideas that suggest North Atlantic sea chanteys, evokes a maritime ebb and flow through carefully plotted treatments of tempo and pulse. Though the symphony is still tagged as neo-classical, these frequent modulations in tempo give the music a completely different rhythmic feeling from the metronomic regularity found in neo-classical scores like Stravinsky's Symphony in C, composed just a few years earlier. More like Sibelius' Symphony in C (no. 7) than Stravinsky's, Carter's first movement outlines a tempo arc, accelerating from its opening "moderately, wistfully" tempo, to an *"animato"* that is twice as fast, finding its way back to the original tempo only at the end. (The relations between tempos are more explicit in the 1954 revision.) Carter created the illusion of a fluid continuity by juxtaposing and cross-cutting short, contrasting episodes in a cinematic fashion. The interplay of contrasting and changing tempos creates an eminently Carterian rhythmic cross-weave, but without metrical modulations or complex polyrhythms.

While the third movement gives us a rare glimpse of Carter's youthful musical personality, and the first forecasts the "kinetic projections" to come, the second movement, the emotional core of the symphony, exemplifies a rarely noted lyrical warmth that Carter reserved for slow movements throughout his life. This distinctive subgenre runs from an unpublished Andante espressivo, originally one of the four Musical Studies from 1939, three of which would turn into the *Canonic Suite*, to the Adagio for violin and cello, part of *Tre Duetti*, written seventy years later. Comparison again with Piston's Second shows how both composers took great care in building the emotional intensity of their slow movements to a high point, but I think that Carter marked out this large curve less laboriously than Piston did. The lyricism of Carter's slow movement feels intimate, affectionate, and spontaneous, qualities not usually associated with Carter but that also appear in the letters from this time that he wrote to Helen in Santa Fe while he returned to New York, and his parents' apartment, to determine what role he might play in the war effort. Carter dedicated the symphony "to my wife" perhaps as a reaffirmation of their marriage (which was only in its third year and still childless) after this prolonged separation.

Carter had little luck with his symphony, which he recalled was performed—badly—by doctors' orchestras, but not by any major American orchestras until long after it was composed. *Holiday Overture* had an even rockier beginning. He composed it for the Boston Symphony, but Koussevitsky would not perform it. Carter said that he smuggled the parts out of the BSO library for a possible performance in Frankfurt that (contrary to some of his statements) never took place.[15] Copland, perhaps channeling Koussevitsky's objections, told the composer that it was one of those "typical, complicated Carter scores." I think he was almost right. The generic sound of the overture's thematic material, a Pistonian flaw, is counteracted by the ingenuity of its construction, a Pistonian strength, but the resulting Carterian narrative, in which opposed ideas converge, was difficult to discern.

Holiday Overture's confusing identity began with its pops–concert–sounding mis–title. Carter composed the score right after D-Day to celebrate the liberation of Paris, an intention that would have been clearer if he had called it "*Jour de fête.*" After its opening chord, virtually a quote from Milhaud's *Suite Provençale*, there are no obvious French tokens in the score of the kind Gershwin exploited in *An American in Paris*. Critics grasped at straws to describe the overture's style and content. After the first American performance, in Baltimore on January 7, 1948, the critic for the *Baltimore Sun* detected "the spirit of old-time minstrels," while Richard Franko Goldman heard "razzle-dazzle" and hints of Chabrier and Copland.[16]

To American ears the brash opening seems to promise a snappy concert opener like Barber's overture to the *School for Scandal*, or Bernstein's *Candide Overture*. At the point, though, where these works state a memorable lyrical melody, Carter's overture veers toward a contrapuntal texture built of "simultaneous streams of different things going on together" (FW, 101). The overture actually has two lyrical themes, neither one hummable. As the music unfolds, it is challenging, but not impossible, for both performers and listeners to reconcile the perky side of the music with the shadows cast by its increasingly complex counterpoint. The payoff for Carter's apparent waywardness comes only in the recapitulation, where the fast opening theme and the slower of the two lyric themes are superimposed. Unlike the similarly polyphonic recapitulation in Wagner's Overture to *Die Meistersinger*, however, the themes don't blend harmoniously, but clash with an increasing sense of portent, as if the music were uttering the famous line from *Death of a Salesman*: "Attention must be paid." In a short amount of time, the overture travels from *leggerezza* to *gravitas*—but it remains a challenge for interpreters to take the audience along for the ride.

Crane's Way

During his short life, Hart Crane (1899–1932) achieved fame for *The Bridge* and notoriety for his unconventional ways, which Robert Lowell, assuming Crane's voice, would portray in *Life Studies*:

I,
Catullus *redivivus*, once the rage
of the Village and Paris, used to play my role

of homosexual, wolfing the stray lambs
who hungered by the Place de la Concorde.

Enacting the role of gay *poète maudit*, Crane leapt to his death in the Gulf of Mexico in April 1932, when Carter was completing his studies with Piston at Harvard.

Among the founders of modern American poetry, Crane was the farthest in his life and art from T.S. Eliot, the Harvard graduate whose classicist aesthetic would reign over literary studies and practice through the 1950s. While Eliot assumed the appearance of a disciplined British bank clerk, Crane was the restless bohemian. The poems from "Prufrock" to "The Hollow Men" that made Eliot famous are grimly pessimistic. Crane's poetry, by contrast, aspired to ecstasy. Each poet constructed a tradition to support his oeuvre. Eliot's tradition, adumbrated in *The Sacred Wood* (1920), was British and European: Dante, Donne, Marvell, Baudelaire, Laforgue. Crane's tradition, spelled out in *The Bridge*, was American: Whitman, Melville, Dickinson. He lauded Dickinson as a "sweet dead Silencer, most suddenly clear/ When singing that Eternity possessed/And plundered momently in every breast . . ." This is the Emily Dickinson we hear in Carter's madrigals, *Heart Not So Heavy as Mine*, and *Musicians Wrestle Everywhere*. Crane concluded the fourth section of *The Bridge*, "Cape Hatteras," his ode to Whitman, with an imagined union of the two poets:

Yes, Walt,
Afoot again, and onward without halt,—
Not soon, nor suddenly,—No, never to let go
My hand
in yours,
Walt Whitman—
so—

In setting poems by Dickinson, Whitman, and Crane himself, Carter enacted a similar artistic union that would grant him voyage to areas of expression not found in his other early works but whose anarchic impulses were difficult to reconcile with the classicist principles of Piston and Boulanger.

Carter had first encountered Crane's poetry in high school when his friend Eugene O'Neill, Jr. showed him a copy of "White Buildings." O'Neill's famous playwright father had written a foreword to this volume. Carter's first Crane project, however, was the brainchild of Lincoln Kirstein, who, unlike Carter, had actually met the poet. The concept for the ballet *Pocahontas* sprang from the second section of *The Bridge*, "Powhatan's Daughter," particularly the passage titled "The Dance" (also Martha Graham's source for the title to *Appalachian Spring*). The story as Crane presented it is far more complicated than the romantic tale of Pocahontas and John Smith played out, back then, in school pageants. In language that was not just complicated, but often impenetrable, Crane's verse conjured up Pocahontas as an historical character and, at the same time, as the "Physical body of America"[17]:

> Thewed of the levin, thunder-shod and lean,
> Lo, through what infinite seasons dost thou gaze—
> Across what bivouacs of thin angered slain,
> And see'st thy bride immortal in the maize!

This grand oracular style, however was just one of the many voices that Crane used in "The Bridge." At times he mimicked the lyrics of Tin Pan Alley:

> And Rip forgot the office hours,
> and he forgot the pay;
> Van Winkle sweeps a tenement
> way down on Avenue A.

At times the voice sounds like a "country" musician: "Oh rain at seven/ Pay-check at eleven." Elsewhere we overhear fragments of raw, demotic prose:

> But I want service in this office SERVICE
> I said—after
> the show she cried a little afterwards but— . . . .

How could music reflect Crane's stylistic acrobatics? The score for *Pocahontas* approximates Crane's diverse language through stylistic eclecticism. The hammered rhythms of the opening evoke the cultures of pre-Columbus America with echoes of Chavez or Revueltas. When

John Smith appears, the meso-American syncopations give way to the gentler bounce of Hindemith. The charming, divertimento-like music for "Pocahontas and her Ladies" has a singable theme that could come from a Rudolph Friml operetta. The music for the torture scene is highly reminiscent of the primitivist style of Prokofiev's *Scythian Suite*. Finally, as Pocahontas departs with John Rolfe for England, they dance a pavane modeled on those found in the Fitzwilliam Virginal Book. The problem with this wide-ranging display of musical knowledge, however, was that many listeners wondered "Where's Carter?"

After three years of musical and choreographic development on the road, Ballet Caravan gave *Pocahontas* its New York premiere on May 24, 1939—when it was fatally overshadowed by Copland's *Billy the Kid*. No one needed to ask "Where's Copland?". His voice was instantly recognizable from the first notes of the ballet. Carter salvaged his music by making an orchestral suite that won the Juilliard Publication Award, but it remains rarely performed.

Even as he worked on *Pocahontas*, Carter found a more satisfying way to present a Crane-inspired multiplicity of voices in his four-voice choral setting of Emily Dickinson, *Heart Not So Heavy As Mine*, written in 1938. In 1945 he returned to Dickinson for a second madrigal, *Musicians Wrestle Everywhere*. Both works exemplify approaches to setting poetry that Carter would continue to pursue many years later, so I think they reward even closer inspection than I gave them in MEC.

In setting poetic texts throughout his life, Carter built on his experiences with Renaissance madrigals and Bach cantatas rather than on the traditions of the art song or opera. Instead of emphasizing melody, he constructed musical emblems that suggest the ideas in the text through polyphonic textures and rhythmic contrasts. In this treatment, the poet's voice appears not just in the vocal line, but in many facets of the composer's invention, including, at times, repetitions or reprises of phrases that reconfigure the original text. When this approach succeeds the listener can feel that the poem and music are describing each other, but the balance between the prerogatives of poet and composer can be precarious. Both Dickinson madrigals succeed in this violent refashioning, even though one is an intimate psychological mini-drama, the other, a mystical vision. Mournful and haunting, *Heart Not So Heavy As Mine* evokes the interpersonal anxieties of Carter Dark in a compressed, claustrophobic form. *Musicians Wrestle Everywhere*, by contrast, is Carter Light magnified to a dazzle.

On the surface, the poem "Heart Not So Heavy as Mine" contrasts a sad, shut-in speaker with a carefree passer-by. Dickinson obscures the genders of the characters by using the neutral "itself" for the *flâneur*. The sounds of the poem, its repeated, tolling alliterations (heart/heavy, wending/whistled/way/why, bobolink/bubbled/brook/bleeding/bugle, perhaps/pray/pass*) and "irritated" slant rhymes (mine/tune, way/why) set the stage for the unexpected sexually-charged image of "bleeding feet" and the climactic outburst, "Ah Bugle!". (* "Pass" appears in the current edition of the poems in place of "stroll" found in the score.)

Rather than dividing the ensemble to indicate the two characters, Carter scattered the text among the four voices, deploying counterpoint, harmony, and rhythm to contrast the two characters and also to weave them together. Without much dissonance and with simple rhythms, the music portrays two different spirits at once. In the first section, a melodic motive that recalls the Dies Irae and the world-weariness of late Brahms (and perhaps, though if so, ironically, Josquin's mock lament "*Faute d'argent*") states and repeats the title words of the poem with its last syllable held out to form a drone, passed from voice to voice, in a minor mode. The lighter-hearted passer-by appears in staccato, fragmented phrases that seems to move twice as fast, and in the major. The first section of the piece uses the seven tones of the B flat Aeolian scale which can imply B flat minor and G flat major. In the middle section (beginning with "It was as if a bobolink") Carter intensified the mood by the simple devices of a quicker tempo and harmonic transposition up a step to C Aeolian. This shift introduces two new pitches, D and G, stated dramatically to exclaim the agony of the line "Set bleeding feet to minuets." In the third section Carter superimposed echoes of both characters from the opening against the speaker's imaginings of a future meeting. He ratcheted up the harmony once again, by setting the words "Ah, Bugle!" on two jarring, alien pitches (for a jarringly, alien male image), not yet heard in the music: A and E. Their disturbance of the harmonic field sets up a final cadence on B flat that hovers between major and minor until a final, hopeful, resolution. Since Carter made use of all the pitches of the chromatic scale except for B natural in a systematic way, we might call the madrigal eleven-tone music.

> Musicians wrestle everywhere—
> All day—among the crowded air
> I hear the silver strife—

(CPED, 74)

Musicians Wrestle Everywhere expands the dialogue of voices out into the universe. Emily Dickinson begins this compact immortality ode with a gnomic image, then explains it, or rather proves that it defies explanation, though a series of negatives ("not bird . . . not 'Band' . . . not Tamborin . . . not Man . . . not Hymn") and biblically allusive guesses in quotation marks: "New Life," "Morning Stars," "the Spheres." The poem, at once earthly and celestial, seems to defy time and space. Rearranging the original order of the words and repeating lines and phrases, Carter's setting evokes ideas that the poet claims, repeatedly, cannot be put into words. Taking the hint from the phrase "silver strife," Carter evoked the musical wrestling as subatomic vibrations, figured in a five-part rhythmic polyphony, rather than as painful struggle. As in *Heart Not So Heavy As Mine*, the music uses a modal scale (A Phrygian), combining pitches into chords in a way that anticipates modal jazz. When Dickinson sets out her list of negative definitions ('It is not bird"), Carter's harmony wheels chromatically around the circle of fifths, enharmonically finding its way back to its original mode on an aptly glowing four-note harmony (A,B,D,E) to the words "time's first afternoon." In the closing section of the madrigal, where Dickinson replaces negations with possibilities ("Some say . . ."), Carter superimposed fading echoes of the opening polyphony against an emerging hymn-like texture. The tempo gradually slows as the poet's vision of immortality becomes ever more certain. The contending rhythms align, and the harmony comes to rest on, of all things, a C major triad, divided between voices so that the three upper notes, in the sopranos and alto, sound like overtones of the open fifth sung by tenor and bass. This Pythagorean sonority refigures the wrestling vibrations of the opening as the harmony of the universe.

In 1943 Carter returned to Hart Crane with a setting, for voice and piano, of the third poem of the group titled "Voyages" from *White*

Buildings, and he also set "Warble for Lilac Time" by Crane's poetic precursor, Walt Whitman. "Voyage" can be heard as a bridge between the slow movement of the Symphony no. 1 and the lyrical sections of the Piano Sonata, and the racing eighth notes of the Whitman song predict the meter-defying sixteenths in the sonata's propulsive first movement. In its style "Voyage" resembles the *Elegy*, composed, originally for cello and piano, around the same time, and we might even hear Crane's poem, which begins with the words "Infinite consanguinity," as the *Elegy*'s subtext. Carter's setting also suggests the model of Fauré's more tragic songs such as *"Au Cimitiere"* or *"Prison,"* the second to a text by another accursed poet, Paul Verlaine. Attempting to elucidate Crane's opaque text, Carter wrote a *précis* stressing the themes of love and death and summing up the poem "as a prophecy of [Crane's] personal voyage through life, which met its end when he willfully extinguished himself in the hands of the sea."[18] Carter made no mention of the homoerotic aspect of the poem, but many of his readers would have known the outlines of Crane's biography. (In later years, after composing *A Symphony of Three Orchestras*, which he described as a portrait of Crane, Carter could be surprisingly dismissive of his *poète maudit*. On one occasion he told me that he had come to think that Crane "was just drunk on words.")

Before considering the Piano Sonata—the first large-scale fusion of Piston and Crane—we should note that Carter's music evolved in zigzags rather than in a straight line. Turning from the Crane-inspired songs of 1943, he completed the brightly-colored *The Harmony of Morning* in 1944. Its opening theme closely resembles that of *Holiday Overture* (both contain his Seikilos signature), but the music unfolds without any of the overture's ambiguities. Instead of blending the two streams, this setting of the poem "Another Music" by Mark van Doren for women's chorus and chamber orchestra is Carter's most successful and unambivalently Pistonian composition. Written in an updated A major only slightly tinged with dissonance, it mirrors the three stanzas of the poem, the first describing sounds of nature, the second, instrumental music, the third, "another music," poetry, with a clear tripartite design of exposition, development, recapitulation—almost a textbook sonata form. The development even includes an instrumental fugato that moves from F minor to Eflat minor, keys far from the tonic. The structural dissonance of this passage, to use Charles Rosen's term, is resolved in the coda with a second fugato, for the chorus, in A major. The sopranos' climactic octave leap from A to A for the words "with truth" sounds like a Pistonian credo, affirming the tradition-sanctioned verities of tonal and contrapuntal organization, just as van Doren's text suggests:

> In the chambers of a brain
> Are bells that clap an answer when the words
> Move orderly, with truth among the train.

Piano Sonata

Carter worked on his Piano Sonata in 1945 while still employed at the Office of Wartime Information, and completed it, in peacetime, with the help of a Guggenheim Fellowship, in January 1946. Some of its ideas, however, went back over a decade earlier to Boulanger's classes. He told me that he discussed the sonata over weekly lunches with Samuel Barber, who was also at the OWI, and also planning a sonata—for Vladimir Horowitz—at the same time. Both composers felt that it was time to return to the grand piano style of Liszt rather than pursuing the more constrained approach to the piano found in Stravinsky's Sonata and Serenade, Hindemith's Second Sonata, or the piano-as-percussion of Bartók. Barber's sonata premiered two years after the first performance of Carter's (by Webster Aiken on February 16, 1947), and, unlike Carter's, immediately entered the repertory. Recordings by Beveridge Webster and Charles Rosen would later establish the nearly-equal standing of these two sonatas within the short list of major American keyboard compositions, alongside the two sonatas of Ives, the three sonatas of Roger Sessions, Copland's Sonata, and Cage's *Sonatas and Interludes*.

Carter had wrestled with Ives' *Concord Sonata* for twenty years, and he studied the score of Copland's Piano Sonata right after it appeared in 1942. He wrote Helen that "it is full of beautiful things but does not seem well formed." Both Ives and Copland appear in Carter's sonata, Copland by way of near-quotations from his Piano Variations, Ives *sub rosa*. In some ways, though, Carter's sonata has the appearance of an academic exercise. The first movement fills out a large-scale sonata form. The second movement contains an extended fugue, with a wealth of sanctioned contrapuntal devices. In scale and seriousness, moreover, it evokes comparison with Beethoven's "Hammerklavier" sonata, op. 106, though its tonal design resembles that of Liszt's Sonata. In its reliance on established precedents, the sonata seems to be one more instance of Carter's conservative side, and, by implication, a continuation of his harsh critique of the *Concord Sonata*, in notes rather than words.

In the analysis of the sonata and "artistic credo" that he prepared for Edgard Varèse's classes during the summer of 1948, however, Carter described it in terms of his interest in "the plastic flow of music and in contrasting rates of change" (CPLD, 77), and described his music as "essentially a kinetic projection of ideas, using perspectives in time" (79). Richard Franko Goldman noted how far these concerns took the sonata from classical models: "it has been described as a sonata consisting of a fantasia followed by a fantasia, but this is merely a way of suggesting that it is too unorthodox for conventional analysis or type-casting."[19] Carter's own analysis demonstrated that while the music appeared to be in two movements, there were actually three. The slow music that precedes the fugue was not an extended introduction, like that found in the "Hammerklavier," but an independent movement, interrupted by the fugue, that returns afterwards. A similar interplay of slow and fast material occurs in the first movement, whose slow introduction presents "material heard throughout the work: the jump of an octave reappears in the bass alternating between B and A sharp, which sound the two conflicting tonalities of the work." This initial slow music returns at several points in the first movement, a gesture found in Mozart and Beethoven, but which here suggest a slow tempo underlying the faster tempos heard in the two main themes.

While Carter reaffirmed his Pistonian lack of interest in "novel momentary effects," his analysis and credo avoided classical comparisons, emphasizing instead an interest in a "sense of flow" and "new temporal sequences." These are qualities more characteristic of Crane's poetry than Piston's music, and they suggest a Crane-inspired source for the sonata's un-academic innovations. Continuing the line of the Whitman and Crane songs, the sonata mirrors the historical and geographical sweep of Crane's poetry, its blend of Milton, Shelley, Whitman, and Charlie Chaplin, its imaginary bridge "from Far Rockaway to the Golden Gate." As a collage of voices, very much on Crane's model, the Sonata channels Beethoven, Liszt, Copland, and Fats Waller and co-mingles structural rigor with rhapsodic improvisation. Just as Crane depicted the collision of old world and new, the Piano Sonata stages a transatlantic debate, a Boulangerian critique of Ives—or an Ivesian dismantling of French academicism. The sonata's virtuosic demands cast the pianist as Carter's surrogate, a musician wrestling, but now in Crane's erotic terms:

> Light wrestling there incessantly with light,
> star kissing star though wave on wave unto
> Your body rocking.

Much as Crane invoked Dickinson and Whitman as precursors, Carter, perhaps confronting his two 1939 traumas (the *Concord Sonata* review and the premiere of *Pocahontas*), summoned up two predecessors—one overtly, the other, I would say, more by suggestion. With near-quotations from Copland's Piano Variations and Piano Sonata, Carter presented himself, for the first time, as an adherent, rival, and successor, honoring Copland's idiom at its most advanced, while pushing it well beyond its limits. If we momentarily placed the sonata on a Freudian couch we might also interpret the overt presence of Copland in the Sonata as a placeholder for the more fraught figure of Charles Ives. The music invokes Ives not by any allusions (such as would appear in the Cello Sonata and Quartet no. 1) but by its Emersonian sweep and, at its conclusion, its evocation of a Thoreau-like solitude—while at the same time "correcting" all the faults Carter had cited in 1939.

Despite its innovations and technical challenges, the sonata was performed by three different pianists (Webster Aiken, James Sykes, and Beveridge Webster) within a few years of its completion and garnered a kind of praise Carter had rarely received before, both for its novel sonorities, "ripplings, bells, echoes and harp-like arpeggios,"[20] and its "granitic" structure.[21] But even a tall stack of rave reviews could not have softened the impact of the critical slam Carter now received from one of his closest musical friends.

Notes

1 CS, 3–32.

2 "The Music of Elliott Carter," *College Music Symposium* 22, no. 1 (1982): 7–13.

3 See Pollack, *Harvard Composers*, for fascinating comparisons of Piston and the novelist James Gould Cozzens, and of Carter and Bernstein.

4 See CEL, 28–31 and 331–335.
5 Pollock, MB, 141.
6 Letter to Helen, PSS # 2183.
7 One quartet, from 1937, survived. A page of the manuscript appears in CPLD, 36.
8 Butterworth, 69.
9 COM, 158.
10 VTR, 459.
11 CEL, 174.
12 CEL, 16.
13 CS, 237–238.
14 See Bernard in CS, 28–32.
15 CPLD, 63.
16 Quoted in Skulsky, 13–14.
17 Paul Mariani, *The Broken Tower: The Life of Hart Crane*, 208.
18 MEC83, 326–327.
19 MQ, January 1951.
20 Carter Harmon, NYT, March 13, 1948.
21 Arthur Berger, NYHT, May 3, 1948.

CHAPTER SIX

Turning Points (1945–1948)

O N MARCH 14, 1948, ONE DAY AFTER WEBSTER AITKEN PERFORMED Carter's Piano Sonata in Town Hall, an article appeared in *The New York Times Magazine* entitled "The New School of American Composers." The author was Aaron Copland. After asserting that the generation of the 30s, Marc Blitzstein, William Schuman, Samuel Barber, David Diamond, and Paul Bowles (all but Blitzstein younger than Carter) were now well established, Copland discussed seven composers who represented "the best we have to offer": Robert Palmer, Alexei Haieff, Harold Shapero, Lukas Foss, Leonard Bernstein, William Bergsma, and John Cage. Copland, it's worth noting, did not spare the rod with his seven young masters. He called Shapero "the most gifted and the most baffling composer of his generation." Cage's music, he judged, "has more originality of sound than substance." Even Bernstein's music "at its worst" could be "eclectic in style, facile in inspiration." Nevertheless, all seven formed an "impressive group—one that need not fear comparison with the younger generation of any other country."[1] Although Copland had known Carter and his music very well for over a decade, Carter's name appeared nowhere in the article. Even though Copland's piece ran the very same day as a positive review for the Piano Sonata by Virgil Thomson in the *New York Herald Tribune*, it deemed all of Carter's music up to that moment as unworthy of mention.

When Copland's article was reprinted in *Copland on Music* in 1959, Carter sent him a short note, stating "I rather appreciate never having been singled out in your articles as so many passed-up past masters and dead wood were, since by this it is made more clear than ever that music has taken an opposite direction—one that can be talked about now and not reminisced about."[2]

Copland knew Carter's music better than anyone else. Why would he choose to ignore it in this highly visible article? Copland may have simply been reflecting the perceptions of the musical establishment. As of the spring of 1948 no major American orchestra had performed Carter's music. In an era rich with newly composed American ballet scores, neither of his ballets received the praise garnered by Copland's *Billy the Kid, Rodeo,* and *Appalachian Spring,* Bernstein's *Fancy Free,* Barber's *Medea,* or Schuman's *Judith.* Carter's pursuit of the choral genre, moreover, marked him as a marginal figure, writing for a boutique clientele. Copland, however, knew Carter's Piano Sonata well, and it was clearly not a negligible work, even if he might have viewed as an inexplicable anomaly.

By relegating Carter's music to silence Copland exacerbated tensions in their personal relationship. Copland took pride in his role in promoting the music of younger composers, but his efforts, such as they were, to interest Koussevitsky in Carter's music did not lead to any performances of Carter's four orchestral works at the BSO or at Tanglewood. In 1946, at Helen's prodding, Carter accepted a teaching position at the Peabody Conservatory in Baltimore, because, as she told me, "Aaron was doing nothing for him." This move strengthened Carter's ties to Nicolas Nabokov, who was also teaching at Peabody (while at the same time working at the State Department), and also connected him with Richard Franko Goldman, who would become one of his strongest advocates. Both men stood politically and culturally to the right of Copland. Nabokov was an anti-communist personally and professionally. Goldman was an Arnoldian critic of mass culture who, in 1954, would claim that "never have the uses of art been so debased as they are now; never has its status as a legitimate pursuit of man been so threatened."[3]

Yet at the very same time that Carter seemed to affirm, once more, his conservative side, he was also actively involved in several projects to promote Ives's music, renewed his friendship with Varèse, joined the editorial board of the ultra-modernist journal *New Music,* and began to re-examine the seminal works of musical modernism beginning with Debussy's three late sonatas. Not surprisingly *Emblems* and *The Minotaur* combined conservative and innovative elements, but in ways that made a confused impression.

Emblems, for men's chorus and piano, marks, as CPLD states, "the seemingly unlikely conjunction of the cosmopolitan and left-leaning Carter with the conservative Southern Agrarian Allen Tate" (86). One might question Carter's left-leaning credentials at this time, however, and recall that Tate's "Agrarian" label could not conceal his racist and reactionary opinions, even though his poetry was much honored in this period. *Emblems* begins with the sonorous a capella intoning of the words "Maryland, Virginia, Caroline," as if breaking with Piston's disdain for Copland's populist Americana, but it sets an inscrutable Crane-haunted poem that ends, emphatically, with an image that is undecipherable on the page, even more so when sung: "They've slept full and long, till now the air/Waits twilit for their echo, the burning shiver/ Of August strikes like a hawk the crouching hare." Even the Harvard Glee Club, which often sang *Tarantella* and *The Defense of Corinth*, was baffled, and, four years after receiving the score, could only perform its second movement.[4] Nevertheless Richard Franko Goldman praised the score as "an original, striking and unsurpassed piece in its medium."

The Minotaur sent similarly mixed signals. It juggled the neo-Baroque structures of fugue and chaconne with outbursts of polyrhythmic violence. The "Bull's Dance," launched with Carter's Seikilos signature, is a frenzied whirl of two against three. In the complete score, but not the suite, its rhythms undergo a transformation, turning into the pounding four against five cross pattern for the building of the labyrinth, a mythical detention center that Carter, in his conversations with Restagno, said he associated with Nazi concentration camps (31). The brutality of this music, however, gives way to a charming Pas de deux, inspired, as Carter told me, by the "*Idylle*" from Emmanuel Chabrier's *Dix Pieces Pittoresques*, salon music of a very high order. This potentially provocative mix of ideas failed to register even with Carter's friends. Goldman heard it as generic: "It might have been written by someone else of the neo-Classic persuasion."[5]

Perhaps because of these two ill-fated compositions, Carter often placed the two years between the completions of the Piano Sonata and the Cello Sonata in an autobiographical black hole. FW made no mention of *The Minotaur, Emblems*, or the Woodwind Quintet, completed just before

Copland's article appeared, or of the Sonata for Oboe and Harpsichord that Carter sketched while spending the summer of 1947 in Èze, a village on the Côte d'Azur.[6] In later years Carter downplayed even the quintet, one of his most frequently performed works, as "written in the kind of style [Nadia Boulanger] encouraged students during the middle 1930s to use, which, at the time I was a student, I did not like." [7]

On his fortieth birthday, about eight months after Copland's article appeared, Carter completed his Sonata for Violoncello and Piano. Turning from the jolly Jean Françaix-like rondo finale of the Woodwind Quintet to the Cello Sonata's first movement, we seem to inhale the air from a distant planet. In the Sonata Carter presented for the first time many of the techniques of his later music, including the dramatic superimposition of contrasting musical characters, harmony derived from a small number of pitch class sets, and metrical modulation. The four-movement form of the sonata anticipates the design of the First Quartet and also of the Concerto for Orchestra, written twenty years later. As if announcing in public his break with Copland, Carter signaled his allegiance to Ives with an overt allusion, a four note motto played prominently by the piano in mm. 19–21, and repeated by the cello in mm. 53–55, the only thematic material shared by the two instruments in this movement. The piano brings the motto back at the end of the first movement and twice at the end of the fourth. This motto recalls an idea stated quietly at the beginning of "The Alcotts" from Ives' *Concord Sonata*, the one movement of that work that Carter could perform himself. Ives brings it back, fortissimo, slowly, and broadly as the climax of the movement.

While Carter later described in detail the ideas, influences and desert locale that yielded the First Quartet, explanations for the stylistic turn from the Woodwind Quintet to the Cello Sonata are less clear. Some of Carter's contemporaries would mutter that the Copland article motivated Carter to "play the complexity card," but there is evidence that he was already exploring new directions in the early and mid-1940s. Two theoretical texts sparked a reconsideration of tempo that surfaced with the extensive numerical calculations that Carter made, for the first time, for the Cello Sonata—a method that would support all the music that would follow. Carter said that he derived this practice from an article on Beethoven's tempos by Rudolph Kolisch that appeared in *The Musical Quarterly* in 1943, and also (as he told Restagno) from reading

Schillinger's *System of Musical Composition*, which he reviewed, in a deceptively dismissive fashion, in 1946 (CEL, 41).

Kolisch's 1943 article "Tempo and Character in Beethoven's Music" is a detailed discussion of a still-controversial topic: Beethoven's metronome marks. Kolisch, founder and first violinist of the Kolisch Quartet, and Schoenberg's brother-in-law, framed his article with the question: "To what extent does tempo form an integral part of the composer's invention—an objective quality of the music itself?" Countering the notion that consideration of metronome marks was "inartistic," Kolisch demonstrated in detail the ways in which Beethoven associated metronome marks with the novel dramatic character of his music. Rejecting the old *tempi ordinari*, indicated by terms like andante or allegro, Beethoven, Kolisch claimed, used the metronome to indicate the precise mood of each movement. Kolisch illustrated Beethoven's systematic coordination of tempo, meter, and character in a table (see Table 6.1).

	ADAGIO	ANDANTE	ALLᵗᵒ	ALLEGRO					PRESTO
				moderato	ma non troppo		con brio	molto	
12/8	♩.=30	♩.=50							
4/4	♩=40	♩=60	♩=100	♩=126	♩=126		♩=168-176	♩=184-200	♩=200
4/8	♪=40-44		♪=88					♪=200	
6/8	♩.=30 (♪=92)	♩.=50	♩.=56		♩.=84	♩.=104	♩.=132	♩.=176	♩.=192
2/2	𝅗𝅥=30	𝅗𝅥=50			𝅗𝅥=84-88	𝅗𝅥=120	𝅗𝅥=132	𝅗𝅥=152-176	𝅗𝅥=184
2/4	♩=40	♩=40-66	♩=66-80	♩=80-88	♩=96	♩=126-132	♩=144	♩=176-184	♩=184
3/4			♩.=69-84		♩.=96-100		♩.=108-126	♩.=132	
9/8	♩.=44-46	♩.=56							
3/4	♩=30-44	♩=60-66	♩=80-116				♩=144-152	♩=162-207	♩=300
3/8		♩.=56	♩.=88					♩.=108	
3/8	♪=38-56	♪=72-92	♪=120						

This chart is a forerunner of the tempo calculations that Carter would use in his music beginning with the Cello Sonata. He worked out all the tempos for the sonata on a sheet of stationary from the Stafford Hotel in Baltimore, where he stayed while he was teaching at Peabody. As Stephen Soderberg notes, this sheet (digitally accessible from the Library of Congress) is "arguably . . . the first 'time screen'" (CS, 242). In this crucial turn in his development, Carter for the first time organized an entire work on the basis of proportionally related tempos. Here are the metronome marks for the sonata:

First movement: quarter=112 (from mm. 35 to 40 this pulse is notated as quarter note quintuplets in the right hand of the piano. The cello and the left hand of the piano move at a tempo 4/5ths the speed of the piano right hand, or 89.6.)

Second movement: half note=84; dotted quarter=112

Third movement: quarter note=35; eighth note=60; eighth note=80; double-dotted eighth note=80; quarter note=70; eighth note=70; eighth note=40; dotted eighth note=40; quarter note=48.

Fourth movement: quarter note=120; double-dotted half note=60; quarter=140; quarter=80; dotted quarter=80; quarter=120; dotted eighth note=160; quarter note=120; double-dotted half note=60; quarter note=140; quarter note=112.

We can see the proportional relations between these tempos if we re-write them in factors:

$112=4(7\times4)$
$84=3(7\times4)$
$35=5\times7; 70=2(5\times7)$
$60=3(5\times4); 120=6(5\times4)$
$80=5(4\times4); 160=10(4\times4)$
$48=3(4\times4)$

All the tempi are thus related by factors of 4, 5 or 7.

In Schillinger's *System*, as we have seen, Carter found even more precedents for deriving themes and forms by superimposing rhythms moving regularly at different speeds. While this was the only aspect of the system that Carter did not dismiss as "mechanical," Schillinger's encyclopedic charting of musical possibilities would serve as the model for Carter's own pre-compositional procedures.

We can find further evidence of Carter's changing aesthetic position in the study of the three late sonatas of Debussy that appears in CEL, but with the caveat that this document may reflect lectures Carter gave in 1947 (as he states in FW) or in 1959, and was then revised in 1994. The earliest of these dates would comport with the influence of these sonatas on Carter's Cello Sonata and his Sonata for Flute, Oboe, Cello, and Harpsichord, written in 1952. The article shows Carter's intimate knowledge of Debussy's scores and his particular fascination with their non-classical formal procedures:

> Indeed throughout the three works, there is a kind of spasmodic quality which can be seem in the detailed working of his melodies, harmonies and rhythms. It consists of establishing a pattern, dwelling on it by repetition of melodic motives, rhythmic patterns, and harmonic progressions, and then suddenly breaking loose from them to take up another pattern, in turn reinforced by the same sorts of devices. (CEL, 131)

The cello pizzicati in the scherzo of Carter's sonata sound like an homage to the guitar-like strumming in the central movement of Debussy's Cello Sonata, but Carter's formal procedures, even when aspiring to Debussy's formal freedom, seem much more similar to those of Alban Berg (whose influence also appears in the First Quartet, Variations for Orchestra, and, at least according to Stravinsky, the *Double Concerto*.) In Carter's dualistic aesthetic, a Debussy-inspired ideal of improvisation, which Carter often spoke of, would serve as a foil to Berg-like constructivism, an affinity he tended to downplay. Like Berg's *Lyric Suite*, Carter's Cello Sonata tells a story that continues from one movement to the next. We can hear the sonata, like Berg's suite, as autobiographical, but instead of representing an amorous affair, Carter portrayed his own compositional turning point. On repeated listening, the apparently conventional sequence of movements can be heard as a conceptual spiral, beginning with the second movement, circling back at the end of the fourth to the beginning of the first, and ending at the close of the first movement. (Carter composed the second movement first, the first movement, last.) Although there are breaks between the movements, each one, except the second, takes up an idea from the preceding, often by way of a transformation in tempo. The rapid quintuplet quasi-tremolo of the fast second movement reappears in the third in the changed expressive environment of an impassioned Adagio. The cello's cadenza-like passage work at the close of this slow movement reemerges at the onset of the fourth movement within the propulsive yet constricted fast lane of an Allegro. Stylistically the second movement starts out in the consonant, breezy idiom of Carter's earlier music.

Through a series of transformations, some of them "spasmodic" like Debussy's, the sonata's expressive mood becomes darker, the relation of cello and piano more contentious so that the fourth movement seems on the verge of a new language, which arrives, in the sonata's evoked temporal spiral, at the beginning. The sonata's double time scheme is the formal correlative to the superimposition of clock time and psychological time enacted by the cello and piano in the first movement. Although omitted from Copland's list of important composers of his time, Carter redefined time itself.

Carter first branded his music by its focus on temporality in the "Artistic Credo" he prepared for Varèse while he was completing the Cello Sonata. He later fleshed out his thoughts about time in several important essays (all reprinted in CEL):

"The Rhythmic Basis of American Music" (1955)
"The Time Dimension in Music" (1965)
"Music and the Time Screen" (1976)
"Time Lecture" (1965/94)

None of these essays, however, is a systematic analysis of musical time of the sort that Stockhausen presented in ". . . how time passes . . ." in 1958. Instead, Carter's method was to cite views that had influenced him (from Stravinsky, Koechlin, Husserl, Langer, and others) and then move to a history of his own stylistic development. He often emphasized the multiplicity of temporal experience, a phenomenon he illustrated with a passage from the chapter titled "By the Ocean of Time" in *The Magic Mountain*:

> It would not be hard to imagine the existence of creatures, perhaps upon smaller planets than ours, practicing a miniature time economy, in whose brief span the brisk tripping gait of our second hand would possess the tenacious spatial economy of our hand that marks the hours. And contrariwise, one can conceive of a world so spacious that its time system too has a majestic stride, and the distinctions between "still," "in a little while," "yesterday," "tomorrow," are, in its economy, possessed of hugely extended significance. (546)

Rereading Thomas Mann's evocative chapter, however, it is surprising to find that Mann (or, rather, the less-than-omniscient narrator of the novel) differentiates narrative time from musical time. Both music and narrative "present themselves as a flowing, as a succession in time, as one thing after another," but "the time element in music is single. Into a section of mortal time music pours itself, thereby inexpressibly enhancing what it fills. . . . A piece of music called a 'Five-minute waltz' lasts five minutes and this is its sole relation to the time element."[8] "Filling time" with music in itself is no trivial achievement; it is, Mann writes, "enhancing and ennobling," but a narrative, our narrator explains, can simultaneously fill time and tell a story about time (like *The Magic Mountain*). Music, he claims, lacks this double ability. From the Cello Sonata onward, all of Carter's music would attempt to disprove this claim.

The Cello Sonata also marked a turn in Carter's harmonic practice, although this was less obvious to the eye than its rhythmic innovations. Unlike the idea of metrical modulation, moreover, Carter did not discuss his approach to pitch organization until many years later. He demonstrated his use of the all-interval tetrachord (C, C♯, E, F♯ or 0,1,4,6) for the first time at Princeton in 1959, and did not lay out the more comprehensive harmonic schemes of his music until the essay "The Orchestral Composer's Point of View" in 1970. The seeds of his later development are present in the Cello Sonata, however. Here Carter first employed "collectional harmony" (to use Jonathan Bernard's term), deriving pitch combinations from a limited number of possibilities. The first chord in the piece contains the pitches F♯, A, A♯, and E♯. In tonal terms, this dissonant pitch combination seems almost illegible unless interpreted as a much-altered F♯ dominant seventh chord, a reading that seems plausible at first since it immediately resolves to the pitch B, stated in four octaves. The music does not seem to pursue this neo-tonal logic, however. The role of those four opening pitches becomes clearer if we rearrange and re-spell them as F, F♯, A, A♯. In this compressed form we can describe it as two major thirds (F–A, F♯–A♯) a half-step apart. This description also fits two apparently different combinations of pitches that appear in mm. 3 and 4. In m. 3 the piano plays a four note chord containing the pitches (from bottom to top) B, A♭, G, E. If we compress and re-spell them we once again find two major thirds (E–G♯, G–B) separated by a half step, and the same description matches the apparently different four-note sequence, F♯, A♯, E♯, C♯, heard in m. 4.

In subsequent works Carter would greatly extend the idea of deriving a large variety of harmonic events from a strictly defined source. He was drawn to collections of pitches with distinctive properties but which also contained the broadest harmonic potential, such as the two all-interval tetrachords and the all-triad hexachord (see Appendix), and twelve-note chords that contained all eleven intervals. Unlike many of his contemporaries, though, he never presented his harmonic practice as a system either in public or private, indeed he often seemed averse to the entire idea of systems.

Notes

1 *Copland on Music*, 164–175.
2 CPLD, 162.
3 Goldman, 3.
4 CPLD, 86.
5 Goldman, 40.
6 See CPLD, 84–85.
7 CPLD, 91.
8 Mann, 541–542.

CHAPTER SEVEN

Back to Modernism. Back to Futurism. Back to New York (1948–1975)

ITH THE CELLO SONATA, HIS LAST WORK USING KEY SIGNATURES, the first to employ metrical modulation, Carter's music became distinctive in its harmonies, rhythms, textures, and expressive content. The thirteen large-scale instrumental works he completed between his fortieth and seventieth birthdays display his particular gifts for sustaining a dramatic argument through innovative formal plans and a command of rhythmic flow. We can divide these compositions into three phases. In the first, which I'll dub neo-modernism, Carter melded aspects of the music of European modernists, in particular, Bartók, Berg, Debussy, and Schoenberg, with the music and ideas of American ultra-modernists Charles Ives, Henry Cowell, Ruth Crawford, Conlon Nancarrow, and Edgard Varèse. Creating his own tradition, he assembled an imaginary circle of precursors defined as much by its omissions (Stravinsky, Hindemith, Satie, Milhaud, Prokofiev, Gershwin, Copland) as by its inclusions. In the second or "vanguard" phase, beginning with the Second Quartet, Carter incorporated ideas from younger postwar European composers into his own idiom, in particular the spatial composition found in Stockhausen's *Gruppen* and Boulez's *Doubles*, and the cloud-like textures heard in the music of Xenakis and Penderecki. While both of these ideas are also found in Ives' music, Carter's encounters with the Darmstadt School yielded an edgier style that many critics termed avant-garde. In the third, or "New York" phase, beginning with the Third Quartet, Carter's idiom no longer drew on external influences, but evolved on its own terms.

To a great extent these three phases synchronize with Carter's trans-Atlantic wanderings in the 1950s and 60s. After the 1954 Rome premiere of the First Quartet, he spent extended time in Europe, reported back on a wide range of new music events in Dartington, England, and in Darmstadt, Venice, Rome, Zagreb, Warsaw, Amsterdam, Paris, and London in articles for *The Musical Quarterly* and *Perspectives of New Music*, and established friendships with composers like Goffredo Petrassi, Alexander Goehr, Peter Maxwell Davies, and Giacinto Scelsi. He composed most of the works of this period while in extended European residencies: the Variations for Orchestra, Second Quartet and Double Concerto in Rome, the Piano Concerto in Berlin, and the Concerto for Orchestra in Bellagio, Italy. From 1970 onward, however, his career once again centered in New York where, after a number of short-lived teaching positions at universities that often terminated because of his desire to travel, Carter now gave composition lessons (but with few other teaching responsibilities) at the Juilliard School. He would continue to teach at Juilliard, usually on just one day a week, until 1984. As his life became more anchored in Manhattan and Waccabuc, several major New York institutions now paid him some long-awaited respect. In 1970 the New York Philharmonic under Leonard Bernstein premiered and recorded the Concerto for Orchestra. In 1971, Pierre Boulez, newly-appointed music director of the New York Philharmonic, programmed the Concerto for Orchestra for the Philharmonic's European tour and commissioned *A Symphony of Three Orchestras.* In 1973 Carter received his second Pulitzer Prize for the Third Quartet. Also in 1973, the New York Public Library marked his sixty-fifth birthday with an exhibit of his sketches and scores at the Library for the Performing Arts at Lincoln Center. Speculum Musicae, which rose to the top ranks of new music ensembles in the early 1970s, premiered *A Mirror on Which to Dwell* in 1976 and *Syringa* on December 10, 1978, on the eve of Carter's seventieth birthday. Also marking that birthday, the City of New York awarded Carter the Handel Medallion, its "highest award given to individuals for their contribution to the city's intellectual and cultural life."

A. Neo-modernism

> *Any composer who has not felt—I do not say understood, but felt—the ne-*
> *cessity for the twelve-tone language is SUPERFLUOUS. For everything*
> *he writes will fall short of the necessities of his time.*
>
> (Pierre Boulez, "Eventuellement . . ." [1952])

In the aftermath of the defeat of the Axis Powers, the mass genocide first associated with the word Auschwitz, later termed the Holocaust, the dropping of atomic bombs on Hiroshima and Nagasaki, the rise of the Iron Curtain and the Cold War, and the threat of nuclear annihilation, many composers in Europe and America felt the need to reject the aesthetic ideas of the interwar decades and to develop a musical language that reflected radically altered conditions. For many the divide between old and new was made clear by the nearly-simultaneous premieres of Stravinsky's *The Rake's Progress* (Venice, September 11, 1951) and the *Dance around the Golden Calf* from Schoenberg's *Moses und Aron* (Darmstadt, July 2, 1951). While Stravinsky's opera was more recently composed than Schoenberg's, it was seen as the end point for the neo-classic style, a verdict affirmed within a few years by Stravinsky himself. Schoenberg's music, banned from most of Europe since 1933, seemed to point the way forward, though many of the young European composers, collapsing the distance between Schoenberg and his portrait of Moses, argued that the creator of the twelve-tone method never reached the promised land implied by his discoveries.

A few years before these premieres, T. W. Adorno's *Philosophy of Modern Music*, first published in German in 1948, had already mapped out the either/or, Schoenberg/Stravinsky view of the post-war environment in polemical terms:

> Schoenberg draws the consequences from the dissolution of all binding forms
> in music, as this existed in the law of its own development: he affirms the lib-
> eration of ever broader levels of musical material and the musical domination
> of nature which progresses toward the absolute. (213)

By contrast, Adorno accused Stravinsky of hebephrenia, "the indifference of the sick individual towards the external." Stravinsky's neo-
classicism was "music about music" that "continually directs its gaze

toward other materials, which it then 'consumes' through the over-exposure of its rigid and mechanical characteristics" (183–184). Many composers in Europe and America soon felt compelled to abandon their erstwhile neo-classicism and/or populism and adopt Schoenberg's twelve-tone method. The worldwide mass conversion to serialism peaked when Stravinsky himself became a twelve-tone composer, most notably with the score for the ballet *Agon*, which premiered in Los Angeles in 1957, on the composer's seventy-fifth birthday, with Carter in attend-ance. That same year, Aaron Copland, whose folk-inflected populism had dominated American music since the 1939 premiere of *Billy the Kid*, produced his first major twelve-tone work, the *Piano Fantasy*.

For the composers associated with Darmstadt, however, the deci-sive issue in postwar music was not Schoenberg's method, but Webern's particular way of deploying it. While the music of the Second Viennese School rebounded from thirteen years of Nazi repression, both Berg and Schoenberg appeared conflicted in their manner of breaking with tradi-tion, while Webern's oeuvre seemed unambiguously progressive. (Carter, riffing on Schoenberg's line that his music was not modern, just badly played, told me that Webern's music only sounded avant-garde because players at the time ignored the frequent expressive *rubati* in his music that articulate its phrases in a Brahmsian way.) Shot by an American soldier under still-mysterious circumstances soon after the war ended, Webern became the patron saint of the new European music. The widespread feeling that Webern's disjunctive, pointillist idiom was uniquely suited to mirror the atrocities, upheavals, and dislocations of recent times received its most powerful realization in Luigi Nono's *Il Canto Sospeso*, a setting for tenor, chorus, and orchestra of letters from victims murdered by Nazi forces, which premiered in 1954. (Carter termed the work a "master-piece" [CEL, 17].) Although post-Webernism was largely a European phenomenon, a series of Webern performances in New York in the early 1950s, some of which Carter helped arrange through his role in the newly merged League-ISCM, made a life-changing impression on many American composers, including John Cage and Morton Feldman.

In his writings and music from the 1950s Carter stood apart from the new orthodoxies of serialism and post-Webernism. In "A Further Step," an overview of contemporary music written in 1958, Carter rejected the narrowness of "serial technique, pointillism or expressionism" and, as a much more inclusive alternative, introduced the phrase "emancipated musical discourse," which he derived from Schoenberg's "emancipation of the dissonance." Most writings on Carter, including his own, discuss this expanded emancipation in terms of the musical techniques he deployed in the First Quartet and Variations for Orchestra, but it signals a momentous change in Carter's artistic ambitions and the way he now situated himself in musical history. Placing his own mission in relation to Schoenberg's, Carter wrote that works such as the Five Pieces for Orchestra and *Pierrot Lunaire*, had given "a glimpse of a new universe of emancipated discourse, unfortunately quickly abandoned when Schoenberg returned to the classical musical shapes upon adopting the twelve-tone system" (CEL, 6). Discarding his habitual mask of good manners, fighting kid Carter was back, gloves off, and, by implication, declaring himself not just the equal of the Einstein of twentieth-century music, but his rightful successor.

In his new guise as the emancipator of musical discourse, Carter presented himself as inheritor not only to the entire tradition that culminated in Schoenberg's music, but to other traditions as well. Before spelling out this claim in prose, he already gave it musical form in the First Quartet and Variations for Orchestra each of which builds on, and conceptually supplants, major Schoenberg compositions, while also alluding to music by Berg, Bartók, and American ultra-modernists, particularly Ives. Ironically, in portraying himself as the emancipator of music from neo-classicism (including the neo-classical aspects of Schoenberg's twelve-tone music), Carter deployed intertextual devices, composing "music about music" in ways he had avoided during his own neo-classical phase. In this respect his music became more like neo-classical Stravinsky even while sounding even less Stravinskian than it had in the past. We can therefore term Carter's midcentury style "neo-modernism."

In this neo-modernist phase, beginning with the Debussy and Ives allusions in the Cello Sonata and culminating with the Schoenberg vs. Ives disputation of the Variations for Orchestra, Carter propounded a grand synthesis of twentieth-century European and American idioms. Apparently contradicting his frequently stated objections to musical quotations, he encoded the terms of his synthesis within the music itself. Just as he had "signed" some of his earlier work with the three-note motto of the Seikilos Song, he now embedded in his scores traces of the works he was assimilating into his own idiom. Some of these intertextual clues are subtle echoes, some are more obvious invocations, and a few are actual quotations. In the First Quartet we find submerged quotes from Ives (Violin Sonata no. 1) and Nancarrow (Rhythm Study no. 1), echoes of Bartók's Fourth Quartet, Berg's Lyric Suite, and Debussy's Violin Sonata, and, on a conceptual level, at least two implied precursors: Schoenberg's String Quartet no. 1, op. 7, and Ruth Crawford's String Quartet, composed in 1931, particularly its first movement. (Carter never spoke about a connection of either of these two works to his quartet, though many listeners, including Felix Meyer and Anne Shreffler, have noted their resemblances. The writings collected in CEL make no reference to the Schoenberg op. 7 and cite only the last movement of the Crawford, not the first.) Without recourse to quotation, the Sonata for Flute, Oboe, Cello, and Harpsichord nevertheless recalls Debussy's late sonatas, Ravel's *Tombeau de Couperin*, the *klangfarbenmelodie* technique of Schoenberg and Webern, and, if we hear the harpsichord as a surrogate player piano, Nancarrow. In the *Variations for Orchestra*, the capstone of his neo-modernist transatlantic synthesis, Carter overtly (for once) retraced the formal plan from an older work, Schoenberg's Orchestral Variations op. 31, but at the same time he divided the orchestra into woodwind, brass, and string components in a way that evoked Ives' *Unanswered Question*. In Carter's *Variations* we can also hear echoes of Schoenberg's Five Pieces for Orchestra op. 16 and Alban Berg's Altenberg Lieder op. 4—and even a moment that that suggests (in the brass and timpani) the "Great American Symphony" rhetoric of Roy Harris or William Schuman. It's not surprising that when, in 1959, Aaron Copland finally offered some written praise for Carter's music, he cited Carter's "wide knowledge of the music of our time,"[1] though for Copland the flip side of eclecticism was the absence of a personal voice, a "flaw" in Carter's music that Copland often lamented both in private and (occasionally) in public.[2]

By bringing together European and American elements, Carter broke with notions of American exceptionalism that had driven the national styles of Roy Harris and Aaron Copland. Implicitly in Harris' Third Symphony, explicitly in Copland's *Billy the Kid* and *Rodeo*, the national identity was associated with westward motion, away from the multi-ethnic, jazz-saturated New York of Gershwin, and even farther away from Europe. In Carter's works, by contrast, American music and

European music now conversed as equals, but with the ultra-modernists Ives, Cowell, Crawford, and Nancarrow representing the American side, rather than the composers of the establishment such as Copland, Harris, Schuman, or Piston.

Carter presented his revisionist view of American music, and his place in it, in the 1955 essay "The Rhythmic Basis of American Music." In a deceptively understated and scholarly manner, he repositioned himself well beyond Boston neo-classicism, as the heir to composers ranging from Harris to Ives, and from Copland to Cowell and Nancarrow. He illustrated his argument with examples from Ives and Nancarrow closely related to the rhythmic idiom of his First Quartet.[3] Most readers at the time would have expected such an article about American rhythm to focus on jazz, but Carter quickly rejected that direction by claiming that "heard constantly from every corner, this music has lost its original freshness; the techniques have become shopworn, the performances routine and dull." At first reading this statement seems both uninformed and offensive, but as Carter continues it becomes clear that he is dismissing not the music we think of as jazz today, but rather swing-based commercial music, the crossover idiom heard in movies, radio programs, and pops concerts: "Orchestra musicians often do not play jazz well, and cannot under the conditions of concert life be afforded the rehearsals needed for good jazz. Today in out-of-the-way places one can still find fresh, lively jazz performances, and the improvisatory character of what is played is impossible to imitate with concert musicians" (CEL, 57). (In some interviews later on Carter said that he used to hang out in the jazz clubs on 52nd Street, but when I knew him he owned no jazz recordings and rarely spoke about jazz artists other than occasional references to Fats Waller and Art Tatum.)

Carter's critique of "jazz" was very much in line with the way Clement Greenberg, Richard Franko Goldman, and others attacked "middlebrow" American mass culture in the 1950s, but also with the advanced jazz ideology of the time. During the Second World War black musicians began to create a new style of jazz that broke with the equation of jazz with popular music and identified it with African American political aspirations and an avant-garde posture. Dizzy Gillespie summed up this double mission in the title of his 1946 bebop composition "Things to Come." (Duke Ellington had already premiered his similarly visionary *New*

World A-Coming in 1944.) Bebop, which came to public attention right around the time that Carter composed his occasionally bop-ish (even, at times, Monk-ish) Cello Sonata, made clear that jazz could no longer be considered a raw material waiting to be cooked by more cultivated white musicians. Instead, bebop became a model for musical emancipation on the classical side. In his rhythm essay Carter acknowledged that turn by quickly moving beyond composers like Leonard Bernstein and Morton Gould, who continued to fuse popular jazz and classical styles, and finding a more authentic approximation of the freedom essential to jazz improvisation in the "alternative" music of Charles Ives, Henry Cowell, Conlon Nancarrow, and Henry Brant, as well as in his own works.

To understand Carter's neo-modern compositions, we need to decode his intertextual hints carefully. In juxtaposing European and American sources he shaped a critique of both sides that allowed him to create a style, an "emancipated musical discourse," distinct from any of its appropriated elements. Bartók's Fourth Quartet, Berg's Lyric Suite, and Schoenberg's First Quartet and Variations provided Carter with models of large-scale architecture and expressive intensity rarely found in American music, except perhaps in the works of Roger Sessions. The Bartók and Berg quartets deployed coherent, advanced harmonic idioms, more dissonant than those found in Copland, more disciplined than those of Ives. American ultra-modernism, in the music of Ives, Cowell, Crawford, and Nancarrow, suggested fresh approaches to rhythm and texture, without the traces of Brahms and Mahler still found in Schoenberg and Berg, or of the Eastern European folk music in Bartók, and also a sense of national identity more complex than that found in the populist music of Copland or Harris. In Debussy's late music, Carter found a precedent for formal and semantic freedom: "Out of this accumulation for short, repeated melodic fragments, often standing in marked contrast with one another, a remarkable sense of dialectic emerges, of one musical idea suggesting the meaning of another, and the whole adding up to a kind of aesthetic satisfaction that is akin to that of the works of the past" (CEL, 131). Carter brought all these influences together through formal designs that emphasized processes of musical transformation. These processes are most apparent in the constant changes of musical tempo, sometimes abrupt, but more often flowing, that came to be associated with the technique of "metrical modulation."

   Like Boulez, Babbit, and others at the time, Carter felt that Schoenberg's rhythmic idiom did not comport with his harmonic innovations. Unlike these contemporaries, however, Carter did not develop a method of serialized rhythm associating pitches with durations (as Messiaen had done, once, in *Modes de valeurs et d'intensités*). Instead, Carter came to conceive the rhythmic activity of an entire piece in terms of a polyphony of tempos related in ratios such as 5:4 or 7:8. As one aspect of this new rhythmic concept he notated tempo changes in terms of similar ratios, with, for instance, the quintuplet eighth notes in one measure moving at the same speed as triplet eighths in the previous one. This device became known as "metrical modulation." The term first appeared in print in Richard Franko Goldman's review of the Cello Sonata (MQ, January 1951); a few years later it was taken up by William Glock in "A Note on Elliott Carter" (*The Score*, June 1955). Carter had explained the origins of the term and practice to Glock in a letter of May 9, 1955 (CPLD, 118). The term, though habitually used to describe Carter's music, was a bit misleading (Carter preferred "tempo modulation") because in his new rhythmic idiom the meter, the rhythmic organizer that makes a waltz sound different from a march, was rarely audible. The bar lines in tonal music, usually coinciding with the pace of harmonic change, create a rigid temporal framework akin to the hierarchy of the tonal degrees of the scale. In Carter's music barlines—seen but not heard—no longer play this role. Just as totally chromatic music "emancipated" pitches from that hierarchy, Carter's rhythmic practice released tempo from the constraints of meter. Durations and tempos would now interact without the stiff skeleton of regularly synchronized accents.

   In the ideological battles of the time, Carter's midcentury compositions struck many observers as a conundrum. They were clearly progressive but they resisted any alignment with serialism, the era's *cause célèbre*. Although Carter had sketched (and discarded) twelve-tone themes in the mid-1940s,[4] and used an eight-tone series in the First Quartet and several twelve-tone themes in the Variations, he never embraced Schoenberg's methods, let alone the developments of those methods by Boulez or Babbitt. When pressed he could get quite agitated on the subject. His detailed analysis of Schoenberg's Variations op. 31, broadcast by the CBC in 1957,[5] contained a brief explanation of the twelve-tone method, but with the following proviso: "As for myself, this system does not help in the kind of problems which my style of composition involves, and so I do not use it, much as I find it interesting." In a letter to Paul Freeman (April 1961), Carter, perhaps overreacting to a friendly inquiry that assumed he was a serialist, distanced himself even farther: "I do not consider the twelve-tone technique as having a true existence. I think that Arnold Schoenberg was a great composer but not a strict or true twelve-tone composer—if such a thing exists or can exist."[6]

Aside from demonstrating Carter's contrarian instincts, his resistance to twelve-tone technique can be explained in both aesthetic and theoretical terms. Many of the modernist works that he admired, such as *Le sacre, Erwartung, Wozzeck*, and *Intégrales*, predated Schoenberg's discovery, while others written after the advent of the method, such as Bartók's Third and Fourth Quartets, or Ruth Crawford's String Quartet, achieved harmonic rigor through other means. Carter explained his theoretical objections to Schoenberg's method to me on several occasions. He felt that the twelve-tone technique as commonly understood failed to deal with the vertical dimension of music, an aspect he emphasized simply by referring to the collections of pitches in his music as "chords" even when they appeared linearly. He also felt that the system's often misunderstood demand that no pitch be repeated until all the other eleven had appeared (a demand contradicted by all of Schoenberg's serial works) imposed an overly uniform rate of harmonic motion. He also found that the principle of "inversional equivalency" whereby, for instance, a minor second and a major seventh were considered to be structurally interchangeable, unnecessarily limited harmonic resources to six intervals rather than eleven. Despite these objections, however, Carter had no doubts about the importance of Schoenberg's music for his own development, as both the First Quartet and *Variations for Orchestra* make clear.

Carter was certainly not alone in laying claim to Schoenberg's patrimony, or in revising it. Carter's First Quartet appeared at nearly the same time as Messiaen's *Modes de valeur et d'intensité*, Boulez's *Structures*, Book I, and Babbitt's *Composition for Four Instruments*, all prototypes for total serialism, and also at the same time as Cage's *Music of Changes*, which extended Schoenberg's emancipation of the dissonance to abolish any distinction between music, noise, and silence. All of these works appeared at the time to be more radical than Carter's and exerted far more influence than his music or ideas.

Despite the growing respect for his music during the 1950s, Carter found himself in the discomforting position of being considered too radical in America, too conservative in Europe. In particular he expressed frustration with the lack of American performances for the *Variations*, after the premiere and recording by the Louisville Orchestra, because of claims that it was too difficult to program. No major American orchestra would record this work until the 1990s (with the Chicago Symphony under James Levine). In 1961, exposing his still-thin skin, Carter overreacted to a well-intended suggestion for a new opera from Kurt Hermann Adler, General Director of the San Francisco Opera, by writing, "my experience with my *Variations* has made me come to think that orchestras as well as opera houses in this country are too distressing to deal with."

Even when they performed the *Variations*, American conductors often treated Carter with surprising condescension. Eugene Ormandy, who conducted the *Variations* with the Philadelphia Orchestra in February 1962, re-orchestrated parts of the work without Carter's permission, and as late as the 1980s Loren Maazel proposed, very much to Carter's dismay, to cut a large phrase from its finale (bars 524–554). Carter replied that the passage was "indispensible." When the work was performed in Europe, on the other hand, younger musicians, such as Heinz Holliger, found its idiom old-fashioned. Holliger told me that it was only after hearing the Piano Concerto that he came to appreciate the validity and importance of Carter's independent approach. Pierre Boulez, who was fascinated with the rhythmic idiom of the First Quartet, similarly discounted Carter after hearing a performance of the Cello Sonata in Baden-Baden in 1955, and, like Holliger, did not re-establish an interest in Carter's music until the early 1970s.[7]

In retrospect the initial views of both Boulez and Holliger seem understandable. Carter's works of this period showed no traces of the influence of Messiaen, the teacher of the postwar avant-garde, and almost none of Webern, its posthumous godfather. They have little of the pointillistic, alienated quality of the new European music. Unlike Nono, Boulez, or Stockhausen, moreover, Carter composed for standard ensembles and in traditional genres. Today we can hear that his midcentury neo-modern works, for all of their innovations, also have much in common with the ostensibly more conservative music of the period. In its scale and spirit Carter's First Quartet resembles two other monumental postwar compositions: Britten's Quartet no. 2 and Shostakovich's Quartet no. 5. The Variations similarly converse more easily with Lutosławski's Concerto for Orchestra than Stockhausen's *Gruppen*. Carter situated his music right in the middle of the polarized international scene. To some observers his *via media* was a sign of timidity or confusion, the one road that does not lead to Rome, as Schoenberg would say. The example of Bartók might have suggested, to the contrary, that the middle road could be the most encompassing of all.

In 1951, funded by a second Guggenheim Fellowship, unburdened of his teaching commitments and East Coast musical politics, Carter composed his landmark First Quartet in the unfamiliar environment of the Arizona desert. He took breaks to explore the landscape with the naturalist Joseph Wood Krutch and to visit Conlon Nancarrow in Mexico. In this expansive work Carter, extending the strategies of the Piano Sonata, staged an extended drama of transformation on a double formal plan, one old, one new. As in classical quartets, but on the grander scale of middle or late period Beethoven, there appear to be four linked movements: Maestoso, Allegro scorrevole, Adagio, and a rapid finale without a verbal title. Each of these evokes a classical prototype: the first movement suggests the outlines of sonata form, the second can be heard as a scherzo alternating with trios, the third contrasts two different slow ideas, as Beethoven had done in op. 132. The last movement has the recurring elements of the classical rondo. These movements segue from one to the next (as in Beethoven op. 131 and Schoenberg op. 7), but the musical flow breaks off with two unexpected pauses which divide the music into three designated sections (I: Fantasia; II [untitled], III: Variations) whose boundaries do not coincide with the four-movement plan. This double formal scheme enables the listener to conceptualize the music in two ways (perhaps traceable to Whitehead's lectures): as a traditional music of essences and a new music of processes.

We can see how Carter achieved this interplay of old and new by comparing his quartet with its two unacknowledged but clearly audible forerunners, Schoenberg's String Quartet no. 1, op. 7, and Ruth Crawford's String Quartet. Like Carter's First Quartet, Schoenberg's op. 7 is an epic work, lasting over forty minutes. Much of it is written, like Carter's First, in invertible counterpoint, sometimes (unlike the Carter) in a fugal style but also in a non-imitative layering of ideas. Like Carter's quartet it rapidly develops away from its opening, and keeps on evolving and generating new ideas. It also segues from one movement to the next, though its processes of development and transition intertwine to such an extent that it is hard for a listener to say exactly where the first movement, which feels like a long sonata exposition, ends, and the second, a scherzo with themes derived from the opening movement, begins.

Not surprisingly, Schoenberg's post-Wagnerian harmonies and Germanic rhythms are in no way present in Carter no. 1, but a more important difference is in their treatment of musical themes. Schoenberg's quartet emphasizes thematic development in the sophisticated Brahms-inspired manner that he termed "developing variation." A listener would have trouble following the devious paths of its chromatic harmony or untangling its contrapuntal web if it were not for the constant presence of strongly defined motives that retain their identity no matter how they are transformed. The opening movement of Carter's quartet has a similar proliferation of themes (see either edition of MEC), but most of them share a rhythmic trait: they are composed of notes of equal value. Many of them are also made up of small intervals, seconds and thirds. In contrast to Schoenberg's procedure, Carter's themes seem similar to each other and, with one important exception, are not given a rhetorical character. Each theme, however, has its own tempo. They move, respectively, at these metronome speeds: 96, 36, 180, 48, 300, 540, 120, 135. In the first movement the themes are constantly superimposed in changing combinations, each overlay producing a distinctive polyrhythmic grid. These re-combinations constitute the process of the music, and are much more apparent to the listener than the motivic identity and development. For all their notational complexity the rhythms have a visceral drive that even suggests, at times, *Le sacre du printemps* (without the folk tunes or the ostinati).

The first movement of Ruth Crawford's still-astonishing String Quartet provided a less traditional model for Carter's emancipated discourse. It contrasts contrapuntal lines that are markedly different in speed, interval size, and character (*cantabile* vs. *marcato bruscamente*) in a dissonant atonal idiom without the motivic emphasis found in Schoenberg. Crawford's first movement, while at times strikingly similar to Carter's, is relatively brief. Carter's challenge was to sustain a texture similar to Crawford's on a scale similar to Schoenberg's. He accomplished this by giving changes in tempo the role that harmonic motion still played in Schoenberg's last-gasp romantic style, and which Schoenberg mapped out in his textbook, *Structural Functions of Harmony*. In Carter's First Quartet tempo modulation took the place of harmonic modulation.

The first movement of Carter's First was also the last piece he ever wrote that suggests the textbook three-part sonata form. Following the expansive opening cello solo (itself an echo of the beginning of Beethoven's "Kreutzer" Sonata), we seem to hear an exposition that ends with the return of the opening solo at measure 138, this time in the viola. The middle of the movement is wayward enough to feel like a development section, and, beginning at measure 312, there is a sense of a recapitulation. On re-hearing, the listener will note that the recapitulation actually begins covertly as a counterpoint, in the viola, to the climax of the development section. The more apparent recapitulation superimposes four themes that had previously appeared in sequence.[8] The success of this scheme, however, depends on a well-executed stylistic anomaly, a thematic device more like Schoenberg (or Beethoven) than Crawford. One of the eight themes, first heard at measure 70, has a lyrical quality that differentiates it from the others even more than its tempo. Its expressive weight allows it to play the role of the "second theme" or "*gesangsperiod*" in the nineteenth-century idea of sonata form. Its return, transposed up an octave and a minor third and re-assigned from viola to second violin, focuses the four-part counterpoint of the recap/coda, and gives it its emotional punch.

In the *Allegro scorrevole* Carter linked his own music to two composers (Copland termed them the "Bartók–Berg axis") whose styles, aggressively dissonant though in different ways, had until very recently been considered beyond the pale of American musical culture. (The Metropolitan Opera did not perform *Wozzeck* until 1959.) The rapid pace and broken texture of this second movement recalls the *Prestissimo, con sordino* from Bartók's Quartet no. 4 and the *Allegro misterioso* from Berg's Lyric Suite. (The slow music that interrupts the *Allegro scorrevole*, forecasting the slow movement, is also reminiscent of the *Tenebroso* section from the *Presto delirando* in the Lyric Suite.) The allusions to Bartók remind us of the dramatic change in his reputation that followed his death in 1946, a sudden upward revaluation that surprised even Aaron Copland: "One would have thought his musical speech too dour, too insistent, too brittle and uncompromising to hold the attention of the widest audience."[9] That turn, soon followed by the performances of all six Bartók quartets by the Juilliard Quartet, signaled a paradigm shift in American music, with a resurgent modernism taking the place of wartime populism. By invoking two notoriously difficult predecessors, Carter in effect justified the even greater demands of his new idiom.

The third and fourth movements are even more original than the first two. From the Adagio onward, transformational processes, more than intertextual references, define the musical action. In the Adagio we seem to hear the slow-motion collision of two inimical primal forces, a fire and a glacier. (Carter, of course, would have known Frost's poem about fire and ice.) The fire (in the viola and cello) gradually moves upward in register, while the glacier (violins one and two) seeps slowly downward. They converge, briefly commune, then climactically revert to their starting points, but once again the climactic gesture immediately collapses, this time in a whirling musical cloudburst that sweeps in new ideas, with allusions to Debussy and Nancarrow. After a second, mid-movement break, the new themes reveal their full potentials in the final designated movement, Variations. Here, processes of rhythmic transformation take precedence over thematic identity, as ideas return in ever-faster form. The technique of writing variations that accelerate is not new. Renaissance composers called such variations "divisions" since they use ever-smaller divisions of the beat. One skein of Bach's Goldberg Variations charts out the rhythmic mathematics of this idea in a way that parallels its companion skein of canons. Carter's Variations, however, lack a clearly differentiated theme. Instead seven short ideas, some introduced later than others, recur, sometimes juxtaposed, sometimes superimposed, in ever-quickening form. This process is easiest to hear in relation to the heavily accented theme of minor thirds that first appears twelve measures before the pause between movements II and III, and then continues right after the break. By the end of the movement they have evolved into flickering tremolos. Throughout this last movement tempo again plays the central role, as it had in the first.

With the First Quartet, completed when he was forty-three, Carter finally took the all-or-nothing risks that Boulanger demanded from her students. What could be more foolhardy than writing a forty-minute-long work of unprecedented and unrelieved rhythmic complexity, modeled

on music that was considered, at the time, either hopelessly old-fashioned
(and unplayable) like Schoenberg's op. 7, unplayable (and nasty sounding)
like Bartók's Fourth, or a nearly-forgotten experiment like the Crawford,
and without a commission or any guarantee of performance or recording?
Nevertheless, the quartet's premieres in New York (on February 26, 1953,
Walden Quartet) and Rome (April 11, 1954, Parrenin Quartet) and the
recording by the Walden String Quartet (released in June 1956) garnered
a level of praise and respect from critics and colleagues that Carter had
never received before. To this day many people admire the work even
though they don't find much to praise in Carter's other music. Recently
Philip Glass told a Portland, Oregon, audience that he was so impressed
with the perfection of Carter's quartet when he first heard it that he decided that music could go no further in that direction.[10]

Carter completed his next work, the Sonata for Flute, Oboe, Cello,
and Harpsichord, in 1952, before the First Quartet had been performed.
It was his first instrumental piece to be commissioned by a performer,
in this case the harpsichordist Sylvia Marlowe.[11] (The Symphony no. 1,
Piano Sonata, and Cello Sonata were all written on spec.) Uncertain
about how players would negotiate the polyrhythms of the First Quartet,
but also interested in exploring other means for freeing up the musical
continuity and discourse, Carter used a much simpler rhythmic language
here, but the forms of the three-movement sonata extend the innovations
of the First Quartet. The opening movement is an extended fade-out,
an exposition in reverse, beginning explosively and then subsiding in a
kind of anti-exposition. The second movement cinematically cross-cuts a
harpsichord piece with a different one for the remaining trio. The third
movement, where metrical modulation finally appears, begins with the
rhythm of a Venetian *forlana*, but subjects it to constant variation and
acceleration. The Sonata is one of Carter's most immediately engaging
compositions and was once frequently performed. Sadly, the double-
manual Challis harpsichord for which it was written has become hard to
find and maintain.[12]

Variations for Orchestra, Carter's midcentury summa, somehow survived
a misalignment of its commission and the composer's ambitions. It was
commissioned by the Louisville Orchestra, funded by the Rockefeller
Foundation, under a program intended "as a cultural instrument in the
Cold War."[13] Whatever politics may have been in play, Carter was unsettled

by the need to write a major orchestral work for a provincial ensemble with a small wind section, all the more so because the new work gradually assumed the character of a historical encounter on a grand scale.

In composing his *Variations* Carter confronted Schoenberg's similarly titled op. 31. The path to this summit meeting remains unclear. Carter heard a performance of op. 31 conducted by Hans Rosbaud in Baden-Baden on June 19, 1955, but he had been sketching his *Variations* since 1953. He completed the work only after hearing the Schoenberg and making a thorough analysis of its score. In 1957 he gave talks on Schoenberg's piece at Dartington and on Canadian radio.[14] Rosbaud, as if confirming the links between the two works, conducted the European premiere of Carter's *Variations* in Donaueschingen on October 19, 1957.

However it may have happened, Carter's work simultaneously honors and deconstructs Schoenberg's op. 31, which has often been considered the twelve-tone equivalent of the *Art of the Fugue*. Making the comparison himself, Schoenberg quoted the BACH motive at measure 24 of the Introduction, and many times later. Schoenberg scored his variations for a large orchestra, with quadruple woodwinds, twelve brass, a wide assortment of unpitched percussion plus timpani, xylophone, glockenspiel and flexaton, and harp, celesta, and mandolin, and strings. Carter, limited by the dimensions of the Louisville Orchestra used double woodwinds, nine brass, timpani, unpitched percussion, harp, and strings. The harp part, which comes to the fore in the fifth variation is, even today, notoriously difficult and is usually divided between two players.

The two works are virtually identical in length—about twenty-three minutes—and have a similar layout:

Schoenberg	Carter
Introduction	Introduction
Theme	Theme
Variation I moderato	Variation 1 Vivace leggero
Variation II Langsam (chamber orchestra)	Variation 2 Pesante
Variation III Mässig	Variation 3 Moderato
Variation IV Walzertempo (chamber orchestra)	Variation 4 Ritardando molto (chamber)
Variation V Bewegt	Variation 5 allegro misterioso

Variation VI Andante	Variation 6 Accel. molto (chamber)
Variation VII Langsam	Variation 7 Andante
Variation VIII sehr rasch	Variation 8 Allegro giocoso
Variation IX L'istesso tempo	Variation 9 Andante
Finale	Finale

In both works the central fifth variation plays a special role, though in Schoenberg it is the loudest and in Carter's the quietest (except for a few explosions and the surprising sound of the slapstick). Calling attention to the center point, both composers gave their variations an arch form—in Carter's case, an inverted arch. In both works the second half of the arch is (even) more intense and dramatic than the first. Carter framed his central fifth variation, which recalls the *klangfarbenmelodie* technique of the central piece, *Farben*, from Schoenberg's op. 16, with two new rhythmic devices that present the transformational processes of the two ritornelli in a compressed form. Variation 4 continuously slows down. Variation 6 accelerates.

Both composers used the variation form to write what are in effect one-movement symphonies in which many contrasting episodes sustain an ongoing argument. Schoenberg set out to demonstrate how unity, as manifest in the twelve-tone row, could give rise to a diversity of music. Carter sought to show how a diversity of elements could co-exist within a new unity. Both works presented these ideas as a cultural argument as well, with Schoenberg proclaiming his relation to the tradition of German music, and Carter pitting that European tradition against the American idioms of Ives, Harris, and of jazz.

Unity in Schoenberg's Variations has an ambiguous double aspect: in the Theme, the row appears as a harmonized melody whose motives return recognizably throughout the piece, but the tone row is also generating all the other notes, harmonies, and counterpoints. The row functions at once as the overt focus of meaning and the ever-present but impalpable syntax, at once style and idea. To create as much variety as possible, Schoenberg scored several of the variations for chamber orchestras, using mainly solo strings in Variations II, IV, VI, and VII. He also included two delicious vignettes of 1920s *zeitmusik*: Variation IV, with the theme in waltz time strummed on the mandolin amplified by harp and celesta, takes us to a Viennese café. Variation VIII sounds like a Berlin traffic jam. These contemporary references play off against the BACH motive, an emblematic reminder that great music, whether by Bach or Schoenberg are not just ephemera that happen "*von heute auf morgen,*" but will withstand the passage of time.

Carter's *Variations*, by contrast, celebrates all things ephemeral. At first the music appears similar in its strategy to Schoenberg's, with its theme emerging from a mysterious introduction, an image of chaos. The theme itself, or what appears to be the theme, begins with a five-note phrase that sounds like an inversion of the opening of Schoenberg's. One of its phrases even states a twelve-tone row. From its inception, though, with three chords in winds, strings, and brass, Carter's *Variations* sets forth its own three-way dialogue. There are not one but three themes: the long melody spelled out where we expect to hear it in the "Theme" and two others that Carter termed ritornelli. Across the entire work the first ritornello recurs in ever-slower forms, while the second becomes faster in every reappearance. Their variants, however, do not coincide with the nine designated variations of the main theme, but even that theme's variations refuse to stay within the expected boundaries. The main theme initiates its first, gigue-like variation even before it has completed its own exposition. The individual variations themselves interact, breaking down the apparently segmented structure. Variation 3, for instance, brings together the sharply contrasting moods (light vs. heavy) of the two previous variations. Variations 7–9 form a single unit: in Variation 7 three ideas are presented in alternating cross-cut statements by strings, woodwinds, and brass in a way that clearly alludes to *The Unanswered Question*.

Charles Ives died on May 19, 1954 while Carter was composing the *Variations*, and we might hear Variation 7 as a "Nimrod" to his memory, but Ives' spirit has been present, as a counterbalance to Schoenberg's, from the opening chords. The superimposition of different kinds of music found in *The Unanswered Question* and *Central Park in the Dark* is the driving force throughout Carter's Variations. In Variation 8, for instance, the slow, sustained woodwind idea of Variation 7 continues over an unrelated jazzy *scherzando*. The string and brass ideas from Variation 7 return in Variation 9, but now all three elements unfold simultaneously with a slowly building intensity heightened midway by a inexorably metronomic staccato line introduced over the other three elements by the trumpets (beginning at measure 455). The grandeur of this passage also recalls the craggy Ives of the *Robert Browning Overture*.[15]

Schoenberg launched the Finale of his Variations with two weighty allusions: the BACH motive heard as a mysteriously hovering *tremolando* in the flutes and violin, and a recitative-like phrase for the double basses that instantly brings Beethoven's Ninth into the conversation. These emblems of a great tradition usher in a series of short contrasting episodes whose mounting, chaotic energy is summoned back to order by a climactic trumpet statement of BACH. Carter's Finale also builds to a cultural summation, but through a whirling recall of its three elements that unfolds in two phases—and an Ivesian coda. The first phase arrives at an Andante espressivo, played *"con grand'intensità."* Max Noubel has compared the emotional lyricism of this passage with the Invention on a Tonality that follows the drowning scene in *Wozzeck* (42). The second phase builds to a climactic recitative-like declamation by the trombones, with a bravura counterpoint in the timpani, a combination of sounds and gestures heard often in the symphonies of Roy Harris and William Schuman, but complicated here by a third element, a slow tranquil line in the strings that outlasts the bombast. As the brass and percussion disappear, this string line ascends quietly in a variant of the first ritornello at its slowest speed, played against the fastest version of the second ritornello, descending in the woodwinds with a trembling halo in the harp. This afterglow fade-out recalls the serene close of Ives' *Housatonic at Stockbridge*, but might Carter already have been thinking about Wallace Stevens?

> Then the sea
> And heaven rolled as one and from the two
> Came fresh transfigurings of freshest blue.

("Sea Surface Full of Clouds")

B. An Avant-garde Composer?

> *Elliott Carter's ideas about rhythmic modulation are not experimental.*
> *They just extend sophistication out from tonality ideas toward ideas about*
> *modulation from one tempo to another. They put a new wing on the*
> *academy and open no doors to the world outside the school.*
>
> (John Cage, Silence, 72)

The New York Times headlined its obituary for Carter "Composer of the Avant-Garde Dies at 103," repeating a rubric that the "newspaper of record" had assigned Carter in 1967: "Carter's Tomorrow Concerto; Work by Avant-Garde Leader Has Premiere." Like other attempts at categorizing Carter, this label was a bad fit, but perhaps not entirely wrongheaded.

For much of the twentieth century, extending to the publication of Renato Poggioli's *The Theory of the Avant-garde* (Italian version in 1962, English translation 1968) the terms modernist and avant-garde were used interchangeably. Over the last thirty years, however, they have come to seem not only different but inimical.[16] In music we can trace three parallel strains of vanguard ideas. The mystical vanguard, which Carter encountered in his teens, begins with Scriabin's theosophy-inspired music, like *Vers la flamme.* The anti-artwork vanguard begins with Satie's "*musique d'ameublement*" and "*Vexations.*" The technology-centered vanguard begins with the noise music of the Italian futurists. In the 1950s these themes, sometimes in tandem, sometimes in opposition, reappeared in new guises. Fusing Satie's questioning of expression with the futurist cult of the machine, many composers pursued an ideal of depersonalization. For Cage, with his interest in Zen Buddhism and Christian mystics, this was a question of thinking of sounds "as sounds," with no connotations of human expression. For Boulez, Nono, and Stockhausen depersonalization served to subvert any lingering notions of the bourgeois self and entailed the quasi-mathematical organization of all musical parameters, including the motion of sounds in space. In his *Structures I*, Boulez pushed depersonalization to the brink, composing by algorithm. For similar reasons, though with different results, the mathematically-trained Xenakis generated his stochastic music with the assistance of computers. It was a short further step to leaving compositional choices to chance, whether by employing the *I Ching*, as Cage did, or, like Xenakis, aleatory mathematics. The incorporation of chance elements into music inevitably brought the notion of the artwork under question. This was a line that Cage, with his affinity with Satie, was happy to cross, as he did in *Music of Changes* in 1951. Most of the European avant-garde, including Stockhausen, who by the late 1950s had assumed the role of prophetic leader, while willing to experiment with aleatory elements, ultimately balked at abandoning the "work-concept." Meanwhile the ideas of a depersonalized totally-organized music and the scientific allure of technology encouraged the pursuit of synthesized music involving tape-recorded or computer-generated sounds or both.

The early monuments of Stockhausen's music, the rhythmically organized *Zeitmasze*, the *musique concrète* masterpiece *Gesang der Jünglinge*, the spatially organized *Gruppen* and the "open form" *Klavierstück XI* lent a great deal of credibility to all of these vanguard ideas, just short of dispensing with the "work."

Four years separate the completion of the Variations (in 1955) and that of Carter's next opus, the String Quartet no. 2, finished in Waccabuc on March 19, 1959. During this period he spent much time on the burgeoning European new music circuit. He was particularly impressed by Nono's *Il canto sospeso*, Boulez's *Le marteau sans maître,* and Petrassi's *Serenata*, whose instrumentation resembles that of the *Double Concerto*. In reports back from the ISCM festival in Rome in 1959, he also found much to praise in Messiaen's *Oiseaux exotiques*, Nono's *Incontri*, Boulez's *Improvisation II sur Mallarmé,* and Bo Nilsson's *Ein irrender Sohn*. After attending festivals in Venice, Zagreb, London, and Warsaw, he concluded that, at least in Penderecki's *Threnody*, "the extremely violent, almost 'anti-artistic' expression of the music justifies the means" (CEL, 36). On the other hand, he compared what he described as the neo-dadaist antics of John Cage and Dieter Schnebel unfavorably with the comic artistry of Harpo Marx, Grock, Buster Keaton, Charlie Chaplin, and Laurel and Hardy (34). This slam may have been payback for Cage's dismissal of Carter in *Silence*, which also included, for no apparent reason, a vignette about Helen Carter and TV dinners.[17]

Though Carter often sounded a we-are-not-amused tone in these critical surveys, his view of the scene was not far from that eventually taken by Boulez, who had been the leader of the avant-garde pack until he came to ideological loggerheads with Cage in a dispute about the relative importance of process and product. Like Boulez, Carter was skeptical about chance procedures, and, in particular, about the radical questioning of the artwork that he had encountered many years earlier in the ideas of Satie and Duchamp. While Boulez attempted to incorporate aleatory and electronic procedures in ways that preserved the notion of an autonomous composition, Carter never pursued these directions. His bumpy encounters with new music in Europe nevertheless had a decisive impact on the music he would write from the Second Quartet through *A Symphony of Three Orchestras*. These works no longer converse with the past. Like characters in Beckett's plays, as Carter noted, their performers have enough of a challenge trying to converse with each other.

Carter's "avant-garde" works sound different from similar works by Boulez, Stockhausen, Nono, and Xenakis because they simultaneously reflected Carter's admiration for much of the new European music while giving musical expression to his critique of the avant-garde:

> In considering this kind of music, one cannot help thinking that for some composers it might very well have become a matter of indifference just what shape the small details of a work would take, so long as a certain general effect is produced, and they came to think that it might be reasonable to let the performer choose how he wanted to make this effect—especially since so many listeners could not tell the difference anyway. (CEL, 35)

Carter built his response to such indifference into the structure and small details of his "vanguard" works. The four instrumental characters in the Second Quartet, for instance, appear in alternating frameworks of movements and cadenzas. In the work's movements, three players, in turn, attempt to play a role of leadership, with varying success, while in the cadenzas they act out their sense of isolation. The small concertino ensemble of the Piano Concerto, similarly, does not simply succumb to the large orchestral mass, which gradually takes the form of a dense, asphyxiating cloud, but responds in a series of woodwind solos, further elaborated by the piano. These lyrical utterances resist the looming catastrophe and somehow survive it.

The compositional techniques Carter developed for these works, by contrast, seem to resemble precisely those mechanistic, algorithmic aspects of serialism that he rejected so vehemently. Carter made no secret of these techniques. He published charts for the harmonic and rhythmic systems of the Second Quartet, *Double Concerto* and Piano Concerto in 1970.[18] In all these works he organized harmonies and rhythms on a global scale and with strict rules. In the *Double Concerto*, for instance, he paired harmonic intervals with specific metronomic speeds (CEL, 243). The Concerto for Orchestra took global organization even farther, as Carter revealed in "Music and the Time Screen" in 1976. Here he divided all the possible harmonic combinations of two, three, four and five pitches (11, 12, 28, and 38, respectively) systematically among the four orchestral groups and also associated each group with a distinct type of rhythmic motion: retarding, accelerating, slowing down from an ever-faster tempo, speeding up from an ever-slower tempo. He constructed the entire work on a four-part polyrhythm, 10:9:8:7, which he sketched out in detail on graph paper. (See MEC98, 299.) This multi-page, multi-colored graph was displayed in public at the exhibit of Carter's manuscript sketches and scores held at the Lincoln Center Library for the Performing Arts between December 1973 and February 1974.

Carter's voluminous sketches for the *Double Concerto*, a work in progress for six years, provide ample evidence that, in the wake of his encounters with the Darmstadt composers, he self-consciously reprogrammed his musical idiom rather than continuing in the neo-modern style of the *Variations for Orchestra*. The sketches take many forms, from the usual jottings of notes to extended verbal outlines to renderings of curves and slopes that could come from a calculus textbook. The numerous graphic speculations for this work, elegantly plotted geometric calculations of movement in time and space, could stand alone as visual art, or as conceptual art. When the concerto finally appeared, Carter, leaning on his literary studies, associated its astronomical perspective with the consolingly rationalistic cosmology of Lucretius from the first century B.C.E. and an eighteenth-century parody of such consolation and rationality, the *Dunciad* of Alexander Pope. The sketches, however, suggest more cogent connections to Einstein and Heisenberg—or Lewis Carroll.

The one technical aspect of advanced European music that Carter embraced with enthusiasm was spatial composition, a technique anticipated by Ives and Henry Brant and, going back much further, by Gabrieli, but revived in the mid-1950s around the time that stereophonic recording appeared. The most celebrated avant-garde example of spatial composition was Stockhausen's *Gruppen*, for three orchestras, which premiered in 1958. (Other examples from the same time Boulez's *Doubles* and Berio's *Allelujah II*.) The score for *Gruppen* included a detailed map for its seating arrangement, several pages of instructions about percussion instruments and beaters, and a scale of thirteen tempos from 60 beats per minute to 120. The scores for Carter's *Double Concerto*, Piano Concerto, Concerto for Orchestra, and A Symphony of Three Orchestras contain similar instructions. In the Second Quartet, Carter asks the performers to be placed "more widely spaced than usual on the stage so that each is definitely separated from the others in space as well as in character, although that is not necessary." In the Third Quartet he stipulated that the two duos be "as separated from each other as is conveniently possible, so that the listener can not only perceive them as two separate sources but also be aware of the combinations they form with each other."

In retrospect, spatial or stereophonic composition might appear to have been a passing fad, like Cinerama, but in Carter's music it took on an essential poetic role that may explain why critics now heard his music as avant-garde. Here Carter's music reflected the influence of the literary vanguard even more than the musical one—in particular the works of Beckett, Ionesco, and Genet, and their forerunner, Pirandello—which came to be called "theater of the absurd." In placing the players of the Second Quartet unusually far apart, Carter was composing the expanded gaps that separated the players on stage into the music, creating, in effect, spatial silences that questioned the possibilities of human interaction, understanding, and sympathy—the very foundations of musical expression. The self as represented in this music remained intact but as a fragile Giacometti-like reduction.

We can sense the more destabilized quality in Carter's "vanguard" music in comparing the openings of the First and Second quartets. Both begin with cello solos, but the expansive, sonorous exposition of the First gives way in the Second to a nervous five-note spasm, followed by silence. Later in the quartet the climax of the first violin part is an unaccompanied four-measure rest—musical antimatter.

Endowing spatial composition with a theatrical element, Carter expanded his repertory of musical metaphors to form what he termed "scenarios." In the Second Quartet, the four players may represent four distinct dramatic characters in a comedy of escalating miscommunication ending in a brawl. By rigorously delineating the four instrumental characters, Carter achieved systematic "polyvocality" where no single instrument or voice represented a controlling totality. (Literary precedents for this technique would include Joyce's *Ulysses* and Faulkner's *As I Lay Dying*.) While many of the individual lines are highly expressive, the work itself remains rigorously objective.

In some ways, though, the dramatic splintering of the compositional voice was a traditional idea. Carter often pointed to its source in the ensembles in Mozart's operas, or Verdi's, and in the case of the Second Quartet he also drew on the precedent of Ives' Quartet no. 2, whose first two movements are titled "Discussions" and "Arguments," although he often cited the more contemporary model of Beckett's *Waiting for Godot* and *Endgame*. In response to the pervading senses of alienation and absurdity in Beckett's plays, Carter employed abstract compositional techniques comparable in some ways to total serialism in order to demarcate the unbridgeable boundaries between players/characters. By assigning each instrument a unique vocabulary of harmonic intervals and a unique rhythmic style, he made it virtually impossible for them to play in unison, or even with the same rhythm. This fundamental alienation was so radical in its implications that Carter attempted to move toward a kind of reconciliation through a "fusion motive" that surfaces (not very audibly) in the last movement, a strategy that he would cite as a weakness in later years, but which strikes me as an effective dramatic ploy that sets up an even more intense statement of disunity. The attempts at connection (by the four characters, but also by the composer) explode in a climactic frenzy that hurtles the players away from any reconciliation and outward in musical space. In the coda the four players seem even farther apart than they were at the beginning. Perhaps not surprisingly, in his next work Carter turned outward from the social interplay of the Second Quartet to music that depicted the entire history of the universe, from big bang to big whimper.

Each of the three great concertos that Carter composed during the 1960s deserves a book of its own. They display an extraordinary command of all aspects of composition, but at the same time they differ greatly in their timbres, forms and expressive contents. Their range of mood, from darkly comic to darkly tragic to prophetically ecstatic, is all the more surprising because their organization of harmonic and rhythmic materials is similar. For a detailed account of their mechanisms the reader can consult either edition of MEC. Here I will first express the hope, perhaps a bit utopian given their difficulties, that all three works may be performed more frequently, both to solve many remaining performance problems and to reveal more of their distinctive poetry. Second, and following on the idea of poetry, I think it is time to cut the ties to the programmatic associations that Carter and others, including myself, attached to them. Little is gained, I now believe, in basing interpretations of the *Double Concerto* on Lucretius or Pope. Similarly, I would now question attaching too much significance to *Vents*, the poem that Carter placed in relation to the Concerto for Orchestra, even describing the connection in detail in a letter to Leonard Bernstein. In both pieces Carter's literary sophistication simultaneously clarified and obscured the music. The unusual, semicircular arrangement of instruments and the dazzling range of timbres and rhythms that Carter summoned up in the Concerto for Orchestra evoke a windswept continent without any need for a detailed extra-musical subtext. In recent years critics have linked the fact that Carter composed much of the Piano Concerto in West Berlin, a "free" city encircled by an oppressive Soviet-sponsored regime, to the spatial plan of the music, in which the solo piano and a septet of solo instruments are surrounded and even smothered by a large orchestra, and then concluded that the work itself was implicated in the Cold War. Felix Meyer, the Carter expert *sine qua non*, hypothesized that the repeated F sounded by the piano before it is nearly drowned in an orchestral deluge, was "a symbol for 'freedom', one of the keywords in the Iron-Curtain era" (CPLD, 191). But the German locale could easily have suggested other instances of oppression in the not-too-distant past. Why limit the concerto's powerful portrayal of victimization and survival to the particular politics of 1965? It tells the story of every outsider, outcast, or victim.[19]

Carter may have linked the *Double Concerto* to Lucretius and Pope simply to distinguish it from the avant-garde European works, such as *Gruppen* and *Doubles*, which it resembled, but I don't think we need consult those literary sources to hear it as a Chaplin-esque parody of the scientific pretensions of the Darmstadt scene. We might even hear it in more contemporary, Strangelove-esque terms, as a darkly comic response to the "science" of the nuclear arms race. Instead of sounding like a sleekly modern laboratory, like *Gruppen*, or gleaming like a well-polished gem, like much of Boulez's music, the *Double Concerto* creaks and groans and sputters like a dystopian planetarium, teetering on collapse. Its brittle sonorities, which must have appealed to Stravinsky, convey little of the expressive lyricism of the *Variations for Orchestra* or the string quartets. The entire work is defined by instruments of short duration, with the winds and strings of the two chamber orchestras serving as a backdrop. The contrast of staccato foreground and sustained background is particularly dramatic in the central movement of the piece, where the winds and bowed strings sustain a kind of chorale while the piano, harpsichord, percussion, and pizzicato strings play staccato figures that alternately slow down and speed up, and circle spatially clockwise and counterclockwise. Throughout the work, the two solo instrumental characters, each one combining the attributes of a mechanism and a performer, attempt to assert their individuality within an indifferent, impersonal environment, often with the comic resilience that Buster Keaton mustered in his 1922 short, *The Electric House*. In the Coda, though, the violent potential of depersonalization finally erupts in cataclysmic waves that ride on the unleashed resonances of metal percussion, cymbals, tamtams, and rolled drums. The dense clouds of sound in this section seem to prophesy the sound world of the Piano Concerto.

When Stravinsky praised the *Double Concerto* as a "masterpiece," after attending its premiere at the Monday Evening Concerts in Los Angeles as well as all the rehearsals, he also stated that Carter must have been influenced by the example of Berg's *Kammerkonzert*. It was a surprising comparison since the *Double Concerto* sounds more Stravinskian than Bergian and since Carter and Stravinsky shared a resistance to the *weltschmerzlich* side of Berg's personality. Carter, however, returned the favor by dedicating the Piano Concerto to Stravinsky and composing a markedly un-Stravinskian score with much more obvious affinities with Berg's music. The Piano Concerto is as emotionally hot as the *Double Concerto* was cool. Its non-classical two-movement structure resembles the configuration of Berg's Violin Concerto (four movements, in two linked pairs separated by a break) but, even more, its dramatic design. In both concertos an unspeakable horror seems to occur during the silence between the two halves. The playful, child-like quality in the first halves of both concertos gives way to tragic struggle. While Berg used musical allusions to identify his music with the tragic early death from polio of Manon Gropius, Carter's concerto seems more abstract. Carter wrote that it pitted the "crowd" of the orchestra, which eventually becomes a "suffocating blanket," against the piano's "individual." The "orchestral music . . . becomes more and more insistent and brutal as the work continues, while the piano makes more and more of a case for variety, sensitivity and imagination" (CEL, 273).

Other than the dedication, the one Stravinskian feature of the concerto is the seven-instrument concertino associated with the solo piano. Stravinsky had used a similar arrangement in his Capriccio. In Carter's concerto, however, the function of the concertino evolves as the relation between the piano and the orchestra grow increasingly hostile. In the first movement the concertino helps define a harmonic profile different from that of the orchestra. In the second it takes on a more dramatic function as the piano strives to counter the assaults from the orchestra.

A few years earlier Carter had praised the textural music of Xenakis' *Pithoprakta* and Penderecki's *Threnody to the Victims of Hiroshima.* Penderecki had found ways of producing the dense string textures of Xenakis without the computer-generated complexity of his scores. Carter, however, composed the swirling, smothering sound clouds that rise in the second movement of the Piano Concerto, without notational shortcuts or computer assistance, sometimes dividing the strings into as many as forty parts. He was proud of the scary appearance of the scores densest passages and posed in front of them with apparent glee. Beyond the mere fact of musical complexity, however, we should note that both the Xenakis and Penderecki works were related to events in the Second World War. Carter hinted at a similar subtext for the Piano Concerto in comparing the extended lyrical solos for bass clarinet, English horn, and flute that attempt to hold back the mounting tide of destruction to the false comfort offered Job by friends who cannot understand the depths of his despair. The second movement of the Piano Concerto rises to an emotional intensity unequalled in any of his other compositions, except perhaps for the Adagio Tenebroso of *Symphonia: sum fluxae pretium spei.*

Carter's Concerto for Orchestra premiered in 1970, at the height of the Vietnam War, and soon after the assassinations of Martin Luther King and Robert Kennedy. Carter divided the instruments into four groups, by register, rather than family; the score maps the setup in a huge semi-circle surrounded by the percussion. In a letter to Leonard Bernstein and in the published score, Carter explained this configuration by citing the epic, Whitmanesque prose poem *Vents,* written in 1946 by Saint-John Perse, *nom de plume* of the Nobel laureate French poet and diplomat Alexis Leger, an old friend of Nicolas Nabokov. The poem's title alone might encourage listeners to compare the Concerto's multidirectional discourse to winds blowing over the American continent at a time when social transformation was "blowin' in the wind." A nod to Dylan's era-defining ballad may be a little too irresistible, but it matches up with the work's impact on many listeners more forcefully than Perse's poetry. (Phil Lesh, bass guitarist of the Grateful Dead, thought so highly of the piece that he helped underwrite the cost of the recording conducted by Oliver Knussen.) In its rhythmic drive, molten textures, and glittering timbres the Concerto recovered much of the heroic feeling of the First Quartet. Like that quartet, the Concerto's evocative power transcends its technical complexities.

The Concerto, though, still presents performers with fierce challenges. While it is the most aurally sumptuous and viscerally appealing of Carter's orchestral works, it remains virtually unperformable within the tight rehearsal schedules that are the norm in the orchestral world. This problem, though, mirrors the expressive intent of the work. As part of its encompassing vision of American society, it simultaneously celebrates and subverts the orchestra, demanding that each musician, including each individual member of the large string section alternate, sometimes rapidly, between being a team player and a soloist. This task is made still more difficult through Carter's re-arrangement of the usual orchestral map and his inversion of the usual orchestral hierarchy, for here the percussion plays a lead role throughout in establishing the character and color of the music. Out of this inconveniencing break with orchestral habits, however, Carter creates shimmering sonorities, with hints of Debussy, Schoenberg, and Ives, that become ever richer, more varied and even ecstatic as the music ascends to its bell-saturated conclusion.

C. Composer in New York

With the String Quartet no. 3, Duo for Violin and Piano, and Brass Quintet, Carter returned to chamber music after a decade of composing for larger ensembles. All three works present Carter's "avant-garde" style in a more abstract manner. As Edmund White said of Balanchine's ballets from these same years, these three works display "a narrative impulse stripped of story, a sense of drama without exposition or denouement, everything in constant crisis."[20] In the Third Quartet and the Duo, Carter also restaged the stark opposition of psychological and clock time first heard in parts of the Cello Sonata. Now the opposition pervades the entire structure. In each work, but in quite different ways, two opposed types of temporal experience generate a field of related musical ideas, differentiated by tempo and tone color. The superimposition of these different aspects of each temporality serves to evoke a formal drama, or "constant crisis."

The Third Quartet splits its players into two duos, seated far apart, each representing a temporal category. Duo I, the psychological-time team of Violin I and Cello, presents four different ideas: Duo II, the clock-time team of Violin II and Viola, present six. Carter arranged these ten "movements" so that the breaks between movements in one duo never coincide with those of the other. Silences for each Duo allow each of the ten movements to be heard, however briefly, on its own, somewhere in the course of the piece. This strategy creates yet another kind of temporal superimposition. For the listener the music appears simultaneously as a montage of juxtaposed episodes and as an unbroken flow. If the Cello Sonata fused Schoenberg and Stravinsky, the Third Quartet married Eisenstein to Bergson.

These three chamber works extend the virtuosic instrumental writing and structural complexity of the Concerto for Orchestra even further, hard as that might be to imagine. At its premiere by the Juilliard Quartet, the Third Quartet appeared to be at the far edge of what human performers could handle. In subsequent performances, the Composers Quartet and Arditti Quartet employed click-tracks heard through headphones to make rhythmic coordination possible. Over the years, though, the audible (and visible) difficulty of the piece has made it a crowd-pleasing tour de force.

The Brass Quintet has a more smiling character even though it is more complicated in layout. Following a scheme printed in the score, Carter splintered the five performers into trios and duos, with each player involved in several different alliances. There are also five-part episodes, which Carter termed "quodlibets," and a pensive horn solo, fiercely countered by the trumpets and trombones, the one adversarial moment in the piece. The variety of colors Carter draws from these re-shuffled combinations keeps the music fresh-sounding, but the listener can also follow a two-tiered design that helps to clarify the episodic design. A sustained slow movement, heard at the very opening, serves as a backdrop to a series of faster, fleeting episodes, until it finds its *telos*, emerging as a sustained, meditative five-voice chorale. However different, these two layers, like the five musicians, seem to coexist happily.

By contrast, the Duo for Violin and Piano is Carter at his craggiest. Composed in tandem, the Duo, we might say, plays Cain next to the Quintet's Abel. Where the expressive and mathematical aspects of

Carter's art worked together in the Third Quartet and Brass Quintet, here they seem to be locked in mortal combat. The "feeling" violin sputters in anguish while the "counting" piano builds up an arsenal of ticking bombs that ultimately explode in an onslaught of pounding chords. Avoiding a geometric arrangement of episodes, and any thematic returns, the Duo simulates free improvisation, all the while exposing the alienation of its rigorously mismatched pairing. The two instruments never come together rhythmically, and for most of the piece they never share the same pitches. The few episodes in which they seem to find common ground only emphasize their essential estrangement. In his sketches, Carter described their relationship in French:

Deux caractères solitaires qui veulent se mettre ensemble sans jamais y arriver.

Like the Cello Sonata, the Duo draws on both Stravinsky and Schoenberg. Stravinsky said that his *Duo Concertant* reflected the contrast of the piano's struck sound and the violin's bowed sounds. He exploited the incompatibility of the two instruments rather than trying to disguise it. Carter, pushing the oddity of this coupling even farther, emphasized a particular dimension of this physical contrast. The piano cannot alter notes that have been struck. Its notes may resonate, but they begin to fade as soon as they sound. The violin's bow, by contrast, can sculpt and swell the sound after the initial attack, giving each note a distinctive dynamic profile. This difference in sound character also calls attention to the difference in intonation between the two instruments: the untempered, fretless violin often seems to play between the keys of the well-tempered piano. The Duo further polarizes its instruments by the division of actual pitches, a device found in Schoenberg's Phantasy for Violin and Piano, op. 47, where the two instruments play complementary hexachords of the row. In the Duo, as in the Phantasy, the division of pitches can be heard both as a barrier between the instruments and as a higher principle of unity which the two instrumental characters obey even though they seem unaware of its binding force.

Is the Duo avant-garde? It could be heard either as an interrogation of the art-work, relentlessly exposing its contradictions, or as an affirmation, since despite all its inner conflicts the work finally does have a form, however difficult it is for players to project or for listeners to perceive. Historically speaking, the avant-garde itself had moved on by the time that Carter composed this work. In some quarters the very idea seemed passé. By 1975 many of the composers who once had written similarly difficult music had simplified their styles and abandoned experimentalism. Younger composers, including many of Carter's Juilliard students, began to turn to minimalism or neo-romanticism. Carter, however, persisted. In retrospect, we might say that while the complex emotional drama of the Duo seemed worlds away from the cool consonances of minimalism (as in Steve Reich's *Music for Six Pianos*), it brought Carter closer to the tormented inscapes of the confessional poetry of Robert Lowell, John Berryman, and Sylvia Plath.

A sense of this cross-disciplinary affinity may have led Carter back to literature, a move I will discuss in the next chapter. In 1975 he completed his first vocal work since *Emblems, A Mirror on Which to Dwell*. Before extending his return to the voice in *Syringa* and *In Sleep, In Thunder*, however, he composed a work commissioned by the New York Philharmonic, which he entitled *A Symphony of Three Orchestras*. In the opening and closing sections of the work, its frame, Carter honored two of the Philharmonic's musicians, trumpet-player Gerard Schwarz and pianist Paul Jacobs, with extended dramatic solos. The title (which evokes one of Carter's favorite Stravinsky works, the Symphony in Three Movements, also commissioned by the NY Philharmonic) calls attention to the unusual ensemble, three large instrumental groups separated in space. Each of the three "orchestras" contains strings and percussion, but Orchestra I (on the left) has ten brass players, and Orchestra III (on the right) has nine woodwinds plus two horns. At the center, Orchestra II features three clarinets, piano, and an array of pitched percussion. In terms of its commission and the content he associated with the music, the work can stand as the summation of Carter's "New York period," but although he made it more practical than the Concerto for Orchestra, shorter and less difficult to play, *A Symphony of Three Orchestras* has had fewer performances than the Concerto and has yet to enter the repertory. While the Concerto has been commercially recorded three times (Bernstein, Gielen, Knussen), *A Symphony of Three Orchestras* can only be heard at present on the original recording conducted by Boulez, beautifully performed but problematically engineered.

At the time of its premiere, Carter located *A Symphony of Three Orchestras* within his renewed encounter with poetry. For many years he had considered composing an oratorio based on Hart Crane's *The Bridge*, but, despairing over what he saw as the limited abilities of American choruses, he decided to interpret the poem in purely instrumental terms. In the program notes for the premiere and in the published score, Carter wrote that the opening of the work was "suggested by the beginning of Hart Crane's *The Bridge*, which describes New York harbor and the Brooklyn Bridge." He ended his remarks by saying that "although not in any sense an attempt to express the poem of Hart Crane in music, many of the musical ideas were suggested by it and by other of his works." In addition to the opening image of a seagull dipping and pivoting above the harbor at dawn, Carter also related specific episodes in the music to the lines, "I think of cinemas, panoramic sleights/ with multitudes bent toward some flashing scene" (from the "Proem"), to the image of Rip Van Winkle sweeping a tenement on Avenue A, to "the forked crash of split thunder" in "Cape Hatteras," to the subway ride in "The Tunnel," and also to "the bells, I say, the bells break down their tower" from "The Broken Tower" a poem from *Key West: an Island Sheaf.* As he had said over thirty years earlier about "Voyage," Carter stated many times that *A Symphony of Three Orchestras* presented his thoughts about the poet's life as well as his art. Since, as we have seen, Carter had been composing a line of Crane-inspired works ever since *Pocahontas*, a return to the poet was not surprising. The overt revival of "Crane's Way" also suggests that we might hear the poet's influence in such intensely dramatic works as the First Quartet or the Piano Concerto.

Over its seventeen-minute span, *A Symphony of Three Orchestras* gradually descends in tessitura from the ultra-high notes at the opening to the deep bass thud of its close. Following Carter's suggestions, commentators have interpreted the descending curve of the work, from its bird-in-flight trumpet solo to its final pianistic plunge, as a double portrait of Crane's career as an American *poète maudit*, and, in musical slo-mo, his suicidal leap into the Gulf of Mexico. Listened to in these terms, the music can be heard to represent Crane's own poetic vision, from within, but also his life, viewed from without.

The main body of the music superimposes three streams of music, divided between the three spatially divided "orchestras," very much in the manner of the Third Quartet. Each orchestra has four types of material. Each of these twelve "movements" (as Carter called them) surfaces in iso-lation briefly, accompanied by silence, but also appears in counterpoint with one or two "movements" in the other orchestras. The flickering, multi-screened texture of this main section can be heard as a correla-tive of the stylistic and emotional collisions and cinematic references of Crane's poetry. Carter, however, surrounded this central collage with a contrasting frame, which contains some of the most atmospheric and dramatic music he ever wrote. This frame doesn't just suggest the idea of movie music, it sounds like movie music of a high order. At the beginning a dawn chorus of seagulls coalesces in a free-flying trumpet solo. At the end, huge thunder claps in the orchestra give way to the grinding ostinati of a dark satanic mill. At the very close, the piano solo encapsulates the entire downward motion of the symphony with a bravura plunge from the heights into the abyss.

While the symphony's downward motion can be heard to portray a tragic fall from an innocent state of nature to an industrial wasteland that matches some of Crane's imagery, its trajectory inverts the overall direc-tion of Crane's poem, which celebrates the modernity exemplified by the Brooklyn Bridge:

> Forever deity's glittering Pledge, O Thou
> Whose canticle fresh chemistry assigns
> To rapt inception and beatitude,—
> Always through blinding cables, to our joy,
> Of they white seizure springs the prophecy:
> Always through spiring cordage, pyramids
> Of silver sequel, Deity's young name
> Kinetic of white choiring wings . . . ascends.

Beautifully realized as it is, the descending curve of the music is thus curiously at odds with the transcendent aspirations of Crane's poetry. Despite his programmatic statements, Carter's musical design seems to sabotage Crane's optimism, his belief in ascension, his pursuit of ecstasy. Implicitly, the music seems to retell Crane's life as a "Fall of Icarus," a parable of overweening ambition and ultimate failure, a very curious homage indeed. In 1989 Carter told Enzo Restagno that he had set out to portray "the idea of the decline of youth and poetic illusion, a decline which I observed with alarming frequency in the reality of American life" (79).

A few years later, Carter distanced the music even further from Crane's vision. He told Jonathan Bernard that the connection to *The Bridge* only arose late in the compositional process and that he had decided on the gradually descending curve of the music early on and for no specific programmatic reasons. He may have envisioned the piece generically as a tragic counterpart to the vast *commedia* of the Concerto for Orchestra. When I examined the sketches for the work in Basel, I found no references to Crane's poems in them. Carter, of course, knew these poems very well and could have consulted the texts without writing in his score. Whatever role Crane's poetry may have played in the work's genesis, Carter clearly felt, after a certain point, that the close pairing he had suggested with *The Bridge* had become an unnecessary distraction, or at least a linkage that he now preferred to downplay.

Given the uncertainty about Crane's presence in the symphony, I would suggest an alternative perspective, at least for listeners who like their music with a bit of subtext. Let's rehear the music against the grain of Carter's original commentaries (and also ignoring the mind-numbingly repeated shots of Carter crossing the Brooklyn Bridge seen in Frank Sheffer's film). Where the poet celebrated the ascendant New York of the 1920s, we might imagine Carter's symphonic composition as a musical picture of the collapsing, graffiti-covered metropolis of the 1970s. Rather than hunting for hints of Crane's imagery in its dark, flickering cacophony, the listener might recall instead scenes from such quintessential "New York movies" of the era as *The French Connection, Serpico*, or *Dog Day Afternoon*, or remember the hopelessness summed up in the infamous, era-defining headline: "Ford to City: Drop Dead." (President Gerald Ford had refused to bail the city out from bankruptcy.) The headline, which put words in Ford's mouth, appeared in the *New York Daily News* on October 29, 1975, and would have been familiar to anyone who attended the Lincoln Center premiere of the symphony on February 17, 1977.

With this redrawn backdrop, let's put Crane to one side and imagine the music in terms of a diabolical counter-protagonist, far more relevant to the New York of the 1970s: Robert Moses (1888–1981), the "master-builder" of New York City, whose projects included Jones Beach, the

Triborough Bridge, the Henry Hudson Bridge, the United Nations, the Verrazano Bridge, parks, parkways, and expressways—and Lincoln Center. After the publication in 1974 of Robert Caro's devastatingly critical biography, *The Power Broker: Robert Moses and the Fall of New York City*, Moses came to epitomize the bureaucratic hubris that led to the city's decline. Caro's book was awarded the Pulitzer Prize for biography in 1975 and attracted wide attention. Even before Caro's book appeared, however, the fiasco of the 1964 New York World's Fair, the destruction of Pennsylvania Station, and the uprising against his plan to run an expressway across midtown Manhattan, had damaged Moses' reputation as an urban visionary beyond reproach. Protest against his later projects and his entire concept of urban planning was led by Jane Jacobs, Carter's Greenwich Village neighbor and author of *The Death and Life of Great American Cities*, published in 1961. By the mid-1970s the banal grandiosity of Lincoln Center, modeled on Rome's Piazza Campidoglio, as well as its many acoustical deficiencies, now seemed emblematic of a top-down, ego-driven approach to city planning. (Caro wrote that Moses, builder of the New York Coliseum, lived like a Roman emperor.) Promoted under the not-to-be-questioned banner of slum clearance, Moses's grand projects eviscerated the city they were meant to glorify.

Given the huge attention that Caro's exposé garnered in New York's intellectual community just as Carter began work on *A Symphony of Three Orchestras*, I don't think it at all bizarre to rehear it as a depiction of the life and death of contemporary New York as epitomized by Robert Moses, rather than the life and death of Hart Crane forty-five years earlier. We might therefore hear the opening trumpet solo as representing the visionary projects that brought Robert Moses fame, his soaring river crossings that dwarfed, physically but not symbolically, the Brooklyn Bridge of Crane's poem. We can hear the bludgeoning, mechanical ostinato of the coda as the devastation wrought by one of Moses' most disastrous achievements, the Cross Bronx Expressway, which reduced an entire borough of the city to a slum-surrounded escape route to the suburbs. With its dizzying collisions of grittiness and lyricism, anxiety and aspiration, *A Symphony of Three Orchestras* can be heard to evoke the urban soundscape of its decade. I don't think this reading of the piece excludes a Crane-centered interpretation. The dense polyphony of the music and its spatial sweep leave plenty of room for both narratives, one drawing on memories going back a half century, from the time when Carter first encountered modernist music and poetry, the other a less romanticized, clear-eyed picture of the present day.

However we might choose to interpret its sounds and trajectory, critical evaluation of *A Symphony of Three Orchestras* remains difficult at present because of the acoustical imbalance, apparent when I have heard the work in live performances, between the overpowering brass of Orchestra I (however evocative of traffic-clogged expressways) and the other two ensembles. This problem made it hard to follow the three-way course of events in the central section of the piece. On the only current commercial recording of the work, the middle orchestra sounds unnaturally boosted, while the other two are heard at an equally artificial-sounding remove. As with some other works of Carter, we need new performances and recordings to determine whether this apparent miscalculation is a defect or a solvable problem—or perhaps even the poetic essence. This acoustic issue, however, is perhaps secondary to a more important interpretive challenge, the connection of frame and body. If we concentrate on the lyrical material in each orchestra, it is possible to hear a through-line in the piece, an endless melody set in motion by the opening trumpet solo and then re-emerging in different guises and shapes in each of the orchestra: the descending and gradually slowing expressive song launched by the strings of Orchestra I at m. 55; the grazioso cantabile of clarinets, marimba, and solo violin in Orchestra II beginning at m. 82; and the *espressivo cantabile* in Orchestra III beginning at m. 151. These movements (which fleetingly recur) seem to converge climactically in the intense lament sounded by Orchestra II's cellos at m. 359, a last-gasp protest against the suicidal despair enacted in the piano's clattering cadenza.

Notes

1 *Copland on Music*, 177.
2 Richard Wilson told me about several private instances.
3 See Shreffler, "Elliott Carter and His America."
4 See Soderberg and Meyer in CS.
5 CPLD, 140–147.
6 Freeman, later the founder and conductor of the Chicago Sinfonietta, was completing his doctoral dissertation at Eastman at the time. For more on this topic, see Daniel Guberman, "Elliott Carter as (Anti-) Serial Composer," *American Music* 33, no. 1 (Spring 2015).
7 See Noubel, 9.
8 Carter had earlier used a similar form-stretching technique in *Holiday Overture*.

9 COM, 46.

10 Daniel Guberman's dissertation provides a wealth of details about how Carter went about getting the quartet performed both in the USA and Europe and finally recorded by the Walden Quartet, events that finally placed him on the musical map.

11 Marlowe's husband, the painter Leonid Berman, was an old friend of Nabokov. See Giroud, 56.

12 Paul Jacobs bequeathed his own harpsichord to the Yale School of Music so that it could be used for performances of Carter's sonata and the Double Concerto.

13 CPLD, 121.

14 CPLD, 140–147.

15 Carter's father also died in 1955 while the work was in progress.

16 The changed view of the avant-garde is often associated with Peter Bürger's *Theory of the Avant-garde*, published in German in 1974 and in English in 1984. Bürger claimed that "the avant-garde not only negates the category of individual production but also that of individual reception" (53). His highly theoretical study, however, makes no mention at all of music. To a musician whose work depends on a large network of people and institutions, Bürger's oft-repeated distinction between the "autonomous work of art" and the "praxis of life" seems odd, to say the least, but his restatement of the longstanding debate about the relation of art and society within the frameworks of literary theory and philosophy has been highly influential.

17 *Silence*, 268.

18 "The Orchestral Composer's Point of View," CEL, 246.

19 Carter's very odd and un-politic statement on his Berlin residency, reprinted in CPLD, 187–188 gives the impression that *he* was the victim.

20 "The Man Who Understood Balanchine," *New York Times*, November 8, 1998.

Figure 1. As Minna Lederman said many times: "There are two of them." Photograph courtesy of Ellen Taaffe Zwilich.

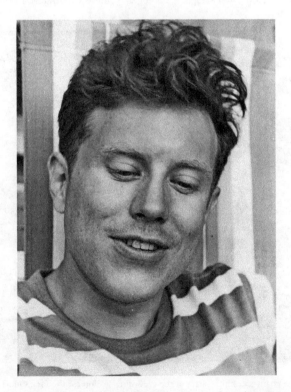

Figure 2. Young and carefree in 1939. Photograph courtesy of Amphion Foundation.

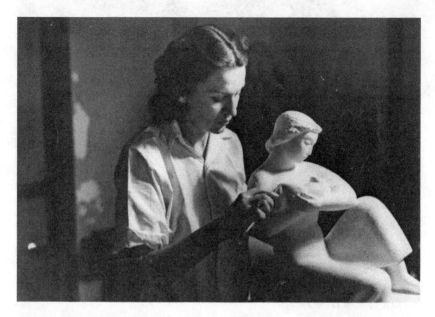

Figure 3.   Helen Frost-Jones, sculpting. Photograph courtesy of Amphion Foundation.

Figure 4.   The chain-smoking Carter at the recording session for the First Quartet, New York, 1954. Photograph courtesy of Amphion Foundation.

Figure 5. Taking command of the Concerto for Orchestra with Leonard Bernstein. Helen Carter's favorite photo. Photograph courtesy of Amphion Foundation.

Figure 6. Three giants of American music: Carter, Aaron Copland and Roy Harris, Library of the Performing Arts, Lincoln Center, 1973. Photograph courtesy of Amphion Foundation.

Figure 7. With Nicolas Nabokov and Virgil Thomson at Waccabuc, 1975. Photograph courtesy of Amphion Foundation.

Figure 8. Helen and Elliott Carter, the author, and Bruno, Waccabuc 1979. Photograph courtesy of the author.

Figure 9. With Pierre Boulez, 2008. Photograph courtesy of Amphion Foundation.

CHAPTER EIGHT

Carter vs. Poets (Round 1)

E LLIOTT CARTER HABITUALLY ENGAGED WITH SUBJECTS BY ARGUING with them. His song cycles often seem more like sparring matches with the poets than comfortable comminglings of words and music. Carter's return to the vocal medium in 1975, after almost thirty years of instrumental writing, did not spring from a renewed desire to set texts with which he had long felt a strong familiarity and connection. He had not read Elizabeth Bishop before beginning to think about *A Mirror on Which to Dwell*, nor was he familiar with John Ashbery's poetry before the poet approached him with the idea of a collaboration. Carter told me that he accepted Ashbery's proposal precisely because the poetry seemed alien to him and he hoped this distance would push him out of his comfort zone. He might have said the same for Elizabeth Bishop and Robert Lowell, even though they were closer to him in age.

The American poets Carter chose to set from 1975 onward shared his cultural milieu and were all educated in the elite Northeast colleges of the Ivy League and Seven Sisters. Many of them, however, led lives far more restless and unruly than Carter ever allowed his own to be. Elizabeth Bishop shuttled between temporary homes (and lovers) in Nova Scotia, Boston, New York, Key West, and Rio. Robert Lowell, thrice-married and chronically bipolar, spent much time in psychiatric institutions. Pursuing differences more than affinities, Carter chose poems that seemed, at least on the surface, far from his own sensibility and personality. And then he argued with them, in musical terms, sometimes in a friendly tug-of-war, sometimes in unsettling opposition.

The initial idea for a return to the voice came from Carter's acquaintance with the soprano Susan Davenny Wyner, wife of the composer Yehudi Wyner.[1] At her request he orchestrated his Hart Crane song "Voyage," which she performed at the Aspen Festival in 1974. Speculum Musicae then obtained a grant from the NEA for a work for soprano and chamber ensemble under a program that commissioned music to celebrate the American bicentennial in 1976. Carter decided that since a soprano would be singing, he would set poetry written by a woman. Robert Lowell, whom Carter knew casually (Carter's name does not appear in Ian Hamilton's biography of the poet), recommended the poetry of his close friend Elizabeth Bishop. At the time Bishop's reputation was on the rise but Lowell was still deemed the more important poet, a view that would be reversed within a few years. Today Bishop is generally considered the finest poet of her generation.

Carter wrote to Bishop in Brazil, where she lived for many years, for permission to set her work, and she happily complied, noting that, though they had never met, he was her "FAVORITE American contemporary composer."[2] Bishop, it turned out, owned two Carter recordings and admired his essay "Expressionism in American Music," which had appeared in the first issue of *Perspectives of New Music*. Her own musical tastes were broad. In the 1930s she had befriended Billie Holiday and later wrote a poem about her, "Songs for a Colored Singer." At Vassar College she took clavichord lessons with Carter's Harvard contemporary (and future *Double Concerto* soloist) Ralph Kirkpatrick.[3] She traveled with a clavichord custom built for her by Arnold Dolmetsch.[4] Her musical sophistication figures in James Merrill's delightful poem "The Victor Dog," dedicated to Bishop, which expertly imitates her style and alludes to Bix Beiderbecke, Buxtehude, Boulez, Bloch, Schubert, Ravel, Schumann, Berg, Bach, and Handel.

Carter chose six of Bishop's poems from three collections: *North & South* (1946), *A Cold Spring* (1955), and *Questions of Travel* (1965). (Several of her most famous poems, including "The Moose" and "One Art," were published only while *A Mirror* was already in progress.) As he began work on *A Mirror*, Carter wrote William Glock that he was studying the songs of Wolf and Debussy. While Carter's idiom is distant from theirs, his strategy of setting words to music is conceptually similar. Following the example of Schubert, both Wolf and Debussy would often construct a song around a single musical figure that encompassed the overall meaning of the poem but also evoked specific images and ideas. Such a strategy puts the composer in the position of reader/translator, first deciding what constitutes the poetic core and then rendering it in musical terms.

In *A Mirror*, it is easy to see how Carter pursued this approach. The vibrantly oscillating texture than runs throughout "Anaphora" springs from the line: "Where is the music coming from, the energy?" The unfolding dialogue of piano and bongos in "Argument" echoes the title, but its sonority also amplifies the image of "all that land / beneath the plane; that coastline / of dim beaches deep in sand." We can hear the buzz of the plane's propellers, the lap of the waves. In "Sandpiper" Carter not only figured the shore bird with the piping, peeping tones of the oboe, but thereby gave musical form to the bird's "state of controlled panic." In "Insomnia," the marimba suggests the silken, insubstantial qualities of "So wrap up care in a cobweb / and drop it down the well." The fragments of wind music in "View of the Capitol from the Library of Congress" figure the lines "I think the trees must intervene, / catching the music in their leaves." Finally, in "*O Breath*" the contrast of the singing style—Carter asks it to be sung as if the singer was constantly running out of breath—with the somnolent sounds of the instruments stems from the words: "Equivocal, but what we have in common's bound to be there."

In choosing the core image for each poem, Carter seemed particularly attracted to ideas that could be expressed with the musical techniques he had developed in his instrumental music, especially different kinds of superimposition.[5] The use of these idiosyncratic procedures made Carter's identity as present in the songs as Bishop's. It also threatened, at times, to obscure her words. The high vocal tessitura and dense accompaniment at the beginning of "Anaphora," for instance, renders the text virtually inaudible.

Bishop attended the premiere of *A Mirror on Which to Dwell* at a Speculum Musicae concert on February 24, 1976. Carter derived the work's title from the fourth song, "Insomnia," while also alluding to the name of the ensemble, a mirror of music. On December 28, 1976, the poet attended a second performance of *A Mirror* at the annual meeting of the Modern Language Association at the New York Hilton.

After the performance Bishop refused to take a bow when Carter tried to acknowledge her contribution. She wrote about this performance to her friend Loren MacIver on January 5, 1977:

> Did I tell you of Edna's wonderful remark after the Elliott Carter's music last Tuesday night? She was sitting by Margaret Miller, who hated it & wanted to leave & complained, etc, & asked Edna what *she* thought of the music. Edna was very canny. She said, "Well, I suppose it's good *publicity.*" I love that.
>
> (*One Art,* 610)

Poets are often dismayed by the rough handling composers give their work, especially when the words are already so full of their own music, as is the case in Bishop's poetry with its sprung rhythms, tolling alliterations, and slant rhymes (in "Anaphora": ceremony, factory, energy; bells, walls; nature, creature). At the very start, Carter aggressively asserted his own prerogatives in relation to Bishop's, setting the opening words "Each day" to the three-note motive of the Seikilos Song, his old musical signature. Similarly, he cast his own instrument, the oboe, in the role of sandpiper. The wide-ranging vocal line, demanding a soprano with Straussian strength and flexibility, pulled the music far from the speech patterns of the poems. No wonder that Bishop's friends felt that Carter had failed to capture her voice and imposed too much of his own personality on the music. He certainly did not make it easy for the singer to convey Bishop's presence, although I think it emerges most clearly in the setting of "Insomnia," which in many ways anchors the entire cycle, much as the Keats sonnet does in Britten's *Serenade.* Even in "Insomnia," though, I have yet to hear a singer who has figured out how to deliver the closing, devastating "and you love me" which Carter set as an off-hand aside, the "me" barely sounded and evaporating quickly into silence.

In choosing and ordering poems that Bishop had published over a twenty-year period and in different collections, Carter acted as a thematicizing and self-reflecting curator, much as Britten had done in his *Serenade,* or Mahler in *Das Lied von der Erde.* The poems Carter chose for his cycle present two recurring figures, the lover and the artist. Four of the poems take place in bed, though this may not be apparent either to the reader or listener. Bishop's biographer Brett C. Miller wrote that "Anaphora" expresses "the experience of coming to consciousness in the morning in bed with a lover;" set within the frame of sunrise and sunset on Key West. Bishop spent the summer of 1941 there with Marjorie Carr Stevens, to whom the poem is dedicated.[6] The lovers' bed returns as the "gentle battleground" in the second song, "Argument" (a connotation that Carter pointed out to me), more obviously in "Insomnia" (which Bishop's mentor Marianne Moore called "a cheap love poem,"[7]) and most palpably in "O breath" where the music mimics the swelling inhalations, exhalations and occasional snores of the sleeping lover. (Carter probably did not know that Bishop herself suffered from asthma.)

The counter figure of the artist appears first rather mysteriously in "Anaphora" as the weary, lampless "beggar in the park" who nevertheless "prepares stupendous studies." We see the artist again in "Sandpiper": "finical, awkward / in a state of controlled panic, a student of Blake;" and in the fifth song as a visitor to the Library of Congress, shielded from the sounds of a military band and from the power structure of the Capitol by a line of intervening giant trees (an image Bishop drew from her own experience while working at the L. of C. in 1949). The dividing line of trees reminds us of the coastline imagery of "Argument" and "Sandpiper," with their implications of permeable otherness.

The lover and the artist in these poems share a condition of negotiated alienation, a semi-disconnect even from people or objects that they describe in the most intimate terms: "see the thin flying of nine black hairs / four around one five the other nipple." In Carter's rendering this condition is the mirror cohabited by poet and composer and serves as the source of all his musical translations. If his settings sacrificed the intimate, almost whispered quality of some of the poems, they brought out the globe-spanning breadth of Bishop's poetry, which, much like Marianne Moore's, accumulates a powerful moral authority out of detailed, precise observation. Created by a "student of Blake," her poems offer instruction on how to live in an age of ceaseless motion and endless compromise. Carter's cycle brings this commanding voice to the fore.

In *Syringa*, one of his most original works, Carter staged his argument with a poetic text out in the open by adding his own countertext and giving the work the form of a vocal double concerto. The mezzo-soprano sings the words of John Ashbery's poem mainly in a *parlando* style that makes them easy to hear. The bass intones, in extravagant melismatic fashion, an assortment of texts in ancient Greek that Carter, ignoring the usual division of labor between composer and poet, assembled as a way of filling in the gaps, the "subliminal background," in Ashbery's understated retelling of the Orpheus myth. The collision of texts also dramatizes the generational gap between poet and composer. Like his fellow poets of the New York School (Frank O'Hara, James Schuyler, and Kenneth Koch), John Ashbery rejected the formalism of Carter's near-contemporaries and also their later psychoanalytic "confessional" reaction to it. Not interested in writing about "the myths, the missus and the midterms" (Koch, "Fresh Air"), they pursued the style of French surrealism in a disarmingly informal manner, like a "snapshot of whatever is going on in my mind at the time," as Ashbery described his own work.[8]

Ashbery proposed a collaboration with Carter in 1975.[9] The poet had been impressed with the newly-premiered Duo for Violin and Piano and had already emulated its non-dialogue in his poem "Litany," which is laid out in two columns "to be read as simultaneous but independent monologues." Ashbery, perhaps hoping that he and Carter would create an opera, sent him a collection of his dramatic writings. While Carter chose to set a poem (from the collection *Houseboat Days*) instead of one of the plays, *Syringa* feels operatic—and, to put my cards on the table—with a much better libretto than the one he would set in *What Next?* twenty years later.

Carter cited an early seventeenth-century quasi-opera, Cavalieri's *Rappresentazione di anima e di corpo*, as a precedent for his intrusive counter-text, but the two voices in *Syringa* replay, once again, the opposition of Dionysian and Apollonian personalities that he had sketched twenty years earlier for the unwritten Sonata for two pianos. In *Syringa*, though, Carter inverted his usual typecasting, taking on the daemonic role himself (with the still-active command of Classical Greek he had last exploited in his music for *Philoctetes* in 1931) while treating Ashbery's words as a voice of sanity, or at least of a matter-of-fact realism.

I agree with Lawrence Kramer's assessment that, with *Syringa*, Carter achieved a balance between music and poetry not found in his earlier, or later, settings: "The monolithic persona had left the building,"[10] though it might be more accurate to say that the monolithic persona had created the illusion that it had left the building. The absence of an "I" and a "you" in Ashbery's poem decreased the sense that Carter's musical devices, whether abstract or pictorial, might get in the way of a conversation. The very overtness of his intrusion here renders it more playful than antagonistic.

In shaping his *combattimento* with Ashbery, Carter came close to a formal ideal of simulated improvisation that he had pursued for years. The models he often cited for this goal were Schoenberg's *Erwartung*, which "caught fleeing dream-like, irrational changes of mood in a long, never-repeating score of music,"[11] and also some of Bartók's works from around 1920, especially the two violin sonatas. In his Third Quartet and Brass Quintet, Carter paradoxically evoked such a free continuity through carefully planned constructivist means, or, as in the first two quartets, by a double structure. Only in the Duo (the work that led Ashbery to collaborate with Carter) did the apparently unpredictable sequence and course of events mask any traces of pre-compositional geometry. With *Syringa* Carter went even further in creating a twenty-minute expanse of music that seems irreducible to any pre-existing archetype or plan. In formal terms *Syringa* is the radiant riposte to the Duo's darker design. There would be more darkness to come.

In Sleep, In Thunder, six poems of Robert Lowell for tenor and large chamber ensemble, began as a 1976 commission for an instrumental piece from the London Sinfonietta. Only in 1980, three years after Lowell's death, did Carter decide that the commissioned score would be a third vocal composition. He completed the score in Waccabuc on his 73rd birthday and Oliver Knussen conducted the premiere on October 31, 1982. Carter elected not to set some of Lowell's famous poems from the 1950s, such as "Skunk Hour," or, more topically, the poems about his short-lived political activism in the late 1960s. Tipping his hat instead to the commission's British origins, Carter chose poems from Lowell's last decade, when he lived in London with his third wife, Lady Caroline Blackwood, who had previously been married to the painter Lucien Freud and the composer Israel Citkowitz. These poems, all but one fourteen lines of unrhymed blank verse, had appeared, some in different versions, in *Notebook 1967–68* ("Across the Yard: La Ignota"), *For Lizzie and Harriet* ("Harriet"), *History* ("In Genesis," "Dies Irae," "Across the Yard: La Ignota"), and *The Dolphin* ("Careless Night" and "Dolphin"). Carter placed this last poem, with its allusion to Racine's *Phèdre*, at the head of his cycle. Lowell had explained the method of these poems in an afterword to *Notebook 1967–68* as a form of surrealism: "surrealism can degenerate into meaningless hallucinations, or worse into rhetorical machinery, yet it is a natural way to write our fictions."

As Carter would have known, these poems were controversial. Lowell, in his confessional manner, retold the story of the collapse of his marriage to Elizabeth Hardwick, and incorporated Hardwick's letters verbatim into his poems without her permission. Elizabeth Bishop, one of Lowell's closest friends, asked him in a letter (March 21, 1972), "aren't you violating a trust?" and concluded, "It is not being 'gentle' to use personal, tragic, anguished letters that way—it's cruel."[12] The appropriation soon became public knowledge. Reviewing *The Dolphin* in the September–October 1973 *American Poetry Review*, Adrienne Rich described the style of the title poem as "bullshit eloquence" and wrote that "the inclusion of the letter poems stands as one of the most vindictive and mean-spirited acts in the history of poetry."[13] Nevertheless *The Dolphin* was awarded a Pulitzer Prize.

In the published score Carter, rather than acknowledging the contentious nature of the poems he had selected, stated that "the poetry of Robert Lowell expresses some of the most important human attitudes toward our time in beautifully molded verse. Even before the poet suggested that I write music for his translation of *Phèdre*, many years ago, I had been considering setting some of his work."[14] Carter had not felt obliged to pitch the poetry of Bishop or Ashbery with such a hyperbolic apologia. He also described the cycle as a "portrait of Robert Lowell,"[15] setting up the same subject/object double perspective implied by *A Symphony of Three Orchestras* in relation to Hart Crane (whom Lowell had impersonated in *Life Studies*). This unresolvable ambiguity would appear again in *On Conversing with Paradise,* Carter's late setting of even more perplexing poems by Ezra Pound, poems that Carter said had been recommended by Lowell. We might term these three works Carter's "*maudit*" subgenre, the heart of his darkness.

Whether intentionally or not, the result of Carter's selection of poems and their order is an extended mad scene that exposes the instabilities in Lowell's poems and his life. "Across the Yard: *La Ignota*," the least troubled of the poems, can serve as an emblematic comparison with "Sandpiper" from *A Mirror*. Both poems are portraits of artists, but Lowell's down-at-the-heels diva sings "to the trash" without an audience or employer. Implying the comparison himself, Carter recycled the device of an instrumental persona for the artist, here with the solo trumpet. The setting of "she flings her high aria to the trash" as a trumpet/tenor duet recalls the earlier oboe/soprano encounter at the words "His beak is focused; he is pre-occupied, looking for something, something, something, Poor bird he is obsessed," but the trumpet solo, marked "*quasi di lontano*" seems alienated from the singing voice. Its phrases sound like pointless études, futile preparations for a performance that will never take place.

As happens in many of the other poems, Lowell turns the subject back to himself at the end, recalling a time "When I was lost and green." If Ashbery's poems avoid the "I," in Lowell it seems claustrophobically omnipresent. In his most famous poem, "Skunk Hour" (dedicated to Bishop), Lowell interrupted his voyeuristic pursuit of "love-cars" with the warnings "My mind's not right" and "I myself am Hell." His madness surfaces similarly in the poems Carter selected, first (in "Dolphin") in the clinical expression "not avoiding injury to myself, not avoiding injury to others," later (in "Harriet") with "dangerous / to yourself, more dangerous to others," then erupting fully in "Dies Irae": "this day of anger, when I am Satan's." These self-aware admissions of madness mix with others that seem unintended and symptomatic, as when Lowell suddenly projects his own terror of aging onto his daughter. At times the poems become indecipherable ravings. How should a reader (let alone a singer) interpret the terminal envoi (the specific target of Rich's charge of "bullshit eloquence") in "Dolphin": "My eyes have seen what my hand did"? Is Lowell referring to poetry, spousal abuse, or masturbation? (Carter set these words with a heroically arched phrase that could come out of the mouth of Verdi's Otello.) Two other opaque, faux-profound lines, "everything points to non-existence except existence" ("Dies Irae") and "nothing can be human without man," serve as prelude to "In Genesis" (the fifth poem among the hundred in *History* that Carter temporally inverted into a finale), which plays out the death of God/Adam/Orpheus as a nihilistic *Götterdämmerung* reduced to the suburban scale of a backyard barbecue.

Composing this cycle, was Carter acting as Lowell's willing accomplice in acts of unnecessary cruelty? Or as a sly prosecutor allowing the poet's own words to convict him of treachery? Or, somewhere in between, did he, like, apparently, the Pulitzer jury, believe that it was an artist's duty to expose and explore all aspects of human experience no matter how discomforting? I don't think that any of the available recordings of the work make it possible to sort out Carter's intensions or sympathies.

The singers, dramatic tenors who might portray Stravinsky's Oedipus, or Britten's Grimes, sound uncomfortable with Lowell's words and Carter's notes. Recordings reveal that Lowell, born a Boston Brahmin, spoke, surprisingly, with a slight southern drawl, a reminder of his years in Nashville, but also of his second wife's Kentucky origins. You would never guess this from the singers' stiff, Handelian elocution of his words, but Carter's Verdian settings of the words are also far from the vernacular. All that can be said with some certainty is that Carter felt obliged to give Lowell's Lear-like darkness a musical form, and that he would revisit this shadowland in later works. As Max Noubel wrote: "If Carter was able to penetrate Lowell's universe with such force . . . he must have found in it an echo of his own uncertainties [errances] or doubts."[16]

Even before embarking on *In Sleep, In Thunder*, Carter had signaled his interest in Lowell by describing *Night Fantasies*, his first composition for piano since the Piano Sonata, in terms of "Myopia: a Night" and its blurry-eyed "ramshackle, streaky, weird" account of a night time hovering between wakefulness and dreams. Twenty minutes in duration and written in a single movement, *Night Fantasies* could also be heard as a consolidation of the free-sounding forms of the Duo and *Syringa*. Here, though, I will discuss it as the initiation of a new phase of instrumental writing in which Carter's mature *ars combinatoria* took many forms, large and small, light and dark. After the patricidal black comedy of "In Genesis," Carter would not return to vocal music for another thirteen years.

Notes

1 CPLD, 222.
2 Letter in PSS, August 20, 1975.
3 Kalstone, Becoming a Poet, 28.
4 Miller, 81.
5 See Lawrence Kramer, "Modern Madrigalism: Elliott Carter and the Aesthetics of the Art Song," CR for a critique of Carter's practice in the Bishop songs and the later cycles.
6 Miller, 176.
7 Miller, 230.
8 Kalstone, *Five Temperaments*, 171.
9 Their brief correspondence appeared in CR.
10 Kramer 2014, 125.
11 CEL, 326.
12 Bishop, *One Art*, 562.
13 Hamilton, 433.

14 Benjamin Britten set some of Lowell's Racine translation in his last work, *Phaedra*, composed in 1975.
15 Restagno, 86.
16 Noubel, 201.

CHAPTER NINE

Macro Carter / Micro Carter (1983–1999)

I N 1989 I DESCRIBED CARTER'S RAPIDLY PROLIFERATING OEUVRE IN AN
article called "Carter's New Classicism." The title dismayed some
readers who assumed that I was branding the period as a regression, and
also seemed to displease Carter who still bristled when reminded of his
association with neo-classicism—a connection that delayed his acceptance by the European avant-garde for over a decade. In retrospect a better
label for these works might have been "Carter's new normal" because in
two highly visible ways the pattern of his composing now assumed the
form it would take for the rest of his life. In 1980, after considerable acri-
mony, he ended his relations with Associated Music Publishers and signed
with London-based Boosey and Hawkes. In the wake of this change,
most of his commissions and performances would now take place in the
United Kingdom or on the Continent rather than in the United States.

In the early 1980s Carter also initiated a series of relatively short
compositions, beginning with *Changes* for solo guitar. At first many of
these miniatures sounded like distillations of Carter's large-scale forms,
but as the list of short works grew they established aesthetic principles
of their own, which in turn recast Carter's approach to extended forms.
We might imagine that once Carter had finally achieved, in *Syringa*, his
formal ideal, he now felt free to approach form in a more playful way,
open to a variety of outcomes. This ludic turn gave rise to the new series of short (but not at all minor) *pièces d'occasion*, many written to mark
birthdays of trans-Atlantic friends such as Petrassi, Boulez, and Glock.

These short pieces gradually established their own kinds of logic, hinted at with titles like *Con leggerezza pensosa, Scrivo in vento, Gra, Fragment, Shard*, and *Figment*. Carter had been the master of the "*genre chef-d'oeuvre*" (a term Ned Rorem and Virgil Thomson tagged him with derisively.[1]) He now cultivated what I will term, not at all derisively, the "*genre bag-atelle*." His late works would form a "constellation / of patches and of pitches" (Wallace Stevens, "July Mountain"), where he stitched together even the large-scale monuments out of smaller components.

Despite Carter's objections, I still think the term "classicism" is apt for this phase of his work if we use it as an aesthetic concept rather than a historical one. Turning away, for over a decade, from his literary-related projects, Carter devoted himself to abstract forms and, after *Night Fantasies*, no longer felt the need to supply poetic programs for every piece. Similarly, he backed away from the apocalyptic dramas of the Piano Concerto and *A Symphony of Three Orchestras*. The instrumental works of the 1980s and early 1990s present themselves more as *jeux d'esprit* than *cris de coeur*. His idiom had stabilized into its own "common practice." For his own use, he had gradually compiled a "Harmony Book," a re-source which charted the components of his harmonic idiom and their interrelations. All the harmonic structures of this period derived from this still-expanding compendium.

His rhythmic practice was similarly rigorous. From the Concerto for Orchestra onward Carter began work on each new project with pre-compositional calculations for a structural polyrhythm running the en-tire length of the work and determining its tempo relationships, formal proportions, and, at times, the actual quality of its audible rhythms. All the works of this period deploy these techniques for rhythmic and har-monic organization. They might appear to verge on the kinds of system-atic approaches to composition that Carter had often criticized, but, to an audience at Brandeis University in 1986, he compared his methods to those of Bach, rather than to those of Boulez or Babbitt. Beginning in 1980, Carter mapped out the principles and full dimensions of his idiom in a Bach-like, mathematical way, constructing *Night Fantasies* on a two-voice polyrhythm; *Triple Duo* on a three-voice pattern; Quartet no. 4, four-part; and *Penthode*, five-part. Similarly encyclopedic in terms of form, these works fill in the spectrum of possible large-scale configurations. *Night Fantasies* extends the free-associative discourse of the Duo and *Syringa; Triple Duo* unfolds as a series of overlapping "movements," like Quartet no. 3; String Quartet no. 4, though played without pauses, outlines four traditional movements far more clearly than its predecessors, and *Penthode*, the most spatially and contrapuntally complex, uses the simplest formal archetype, the ternary ABA form of the Baroque aria da capo.

The instrumental works of the 1980s could be termed classical in several additional ways. Except in the area of percussion writing, where he remained an innovator for the rest of his life, Carter did not pursue new sounds, either acoustical or electronically induced, and only used extended instrumental techniques where he felt they were part of a scale of comparable sounds that could become part of the musical language.[2] At times the works of this decade also suggest a certain decorum derived from string quartets of the classical period, which were often heard as musical conversations. While retaining the systematic division of harmonic elements that he had used since the Second Quartet, he now found ways of suggesting conversation or interaction among the contrasting components of his counterpoint rather than emphasizing their irreconcilable differences. Several topical devices in these works represented cooperation far more clearly than the problematic "fusion motive" of the Second Quartet. To this end, *Triple Duo, Penthode,* and the Quartet no. 4 all make use of a *klangfarbenmelodie* technique reminiscent of the "Obbligato recitative" of Schoenberg's op. 16, no. 5, where a melodic line passes from one instrument to another.[3] In these works Carter also introduced a gradually accelerating pulse in the final third of the music, a device he said he borrowed from north Indian music, which sets up a centripetal motion, whirling the separate instruments or instrumental groups together rather than scattering them as had happened in the Second Quartet.

Perhaps because of his interest in balancing conflict with cooperation Carter also de-emphasized the spatial separation that had played such an important role in the music of the 1960s and 70s. In the Fourth Quartet, the players sit just as they would for Mozart, and even with the multi-ensemble design of *Penthode*, Carter avoided divisive, stereophonic effects. Finally, many of the works of this decade, particularly the miniatures, became "classics," entering the repertory with less resistance than many of Carter's other works had encountered. Only *Penthode*, written for a utopian orchestra of twenty soloists, remains little played, despite the fine recording by Boulez and the Ensemble Intercontemporain.

In the 1980s Carter composed five major works: *Night Fantasies* (1980), *Triple Duo* (1983), *Penthode* (1985), Quartet no. 4 (1986), and Oboe Concerto (1987). The creation of five large-scale works in one decade would have been sufficient evidence of his increasing fluency, but also he surrounded them with a series of shorter compositions:

Changes for guitar (1983)

Canon for 4—Homage to William for flute, bass clarinet, violin, and cello (1984)

Riconoscenza per Goffredo Petrassi for solo violin (1984)

Esprit rude/Esprit doux for flute and clarinet (1984)

A Celebration of Some 100 x 150 Notes for orchestra (1986)

Enchanted Preludes for flute and cello (1988)

Remembrance for orchestra (1988)

Birthday Flourish for five brass instruments (1988)

Anniversary for orchestra (1989)

Short works would continue to proliferate in the 1990s:

Con leggerezza pensosa for clarinet, violin and cello (1990)

Scrivo in vento for solo flute (1991)

Bariolage for solo harp (1992)★

Inner Song for solo oboe (1992)★

Immer neu for oboe and harp (1992★; the three★ works published together as Trilogy)

Gra for solo clarinet (1993)

90+ for piano (1994)

Figment 1 for cello (1994)

Fragment no. 1 for String Quartet (1994)

Esprit rude/Esprit doux II for flute, clarinet and marimba (1994)

A Six Letter Letter for English horn (1996)

Shard for guitar (1997)

Two Diversions for Piano (1999)

Fragment no. 2 for String Quartet (1999)

Statement—Remembering Aaron for solo violin (1999)

Fantasy—Remembering Roger for solo violin (1999)

Macros

Three large-scale instrumental works of the 80s, *Night Fantasies, Triple Duo*, and the Oboe Concerto, demonstrate the expressive range of Carter's early late style. *Night Fantasies*, simulating a state between wakefulness and sleep, presents a random sounding sequence of events. *Triple Duo* is comic in ways that suggest both slapstick and Shakespeare. The Oboe Concerto breathes the air of eternity and seems to take place in a mythical realm.

Night Fantasies, Carter's longest and most demanding work for solo piano, was commissioned by four New York pianists strongly associated with difficult new music: Paul Jacobs, Gilbert Kalish, Ursula Oppens, and Charles Rosen, and was later taken up by contemporary virtuosos beyond Carter's circle like Stephen Drury, Winston Choi, and Pierre-Laurent Aimard. Carter composed it systematically, deriving all the material from a collection of twelve-tone chords and a two-part structural polyrhythm. This approach ensured the unity of an extended composition, yet the music does not make its processes audible, the way they are in, say, Steve Reich's *Drumming*. The listener instead encounters a sequence of contrasting events of differing lengths and moods, some recurring or resurfacing, others unique and fleeting.[4] Unlike similarly abstract and atonal piano compositions like Xenakis' *Herma*, or many of Stockhausen's *Klavierstücke*, however, *Night Fantasies* does not feel like a statistical array of sounds. While just as daunting in appearance as its avant-garde cousins, Carter's score contains traditional gestural indications like *espressivo, cantabile, cantando, capriccioso*, and *recitativo collerico*. Beyond its invocations of expressive gestures, however, *Night Fantasies* is devoid of intertextual suggestions or echoes beyond Carter's allusions in program notes to Robert Lowell's poem "Myopia: a night." While the piece may recall Lowell's "ramshackle, streaky" uncertainty, it does not seem to pursue the poet's Satanic anxieties. Carter, however, proposed an alternative romantic subtext. The score's preface asks the performer to bring out the "poetic moodiness" that he enjoys in Schumann's *Kreisleriana, Carnaval*, and *Davidsbündlertänze*, but not one note in the piece alludes to Schumann in the quotation/collage manner of postmodern composers like George Crumb or Alfred Schnittke.

Perhaps more helpfully, Carter told a Los Angeles audience that *Night Fantasies* is "nothing more than his fascination with the hyperactive brain in the deep of night when nothing distracts it and nothing can stop it."[5] The exact preoccupations of this stream of nocturnal semi-consciousness, however, are hard to determine. Some listeners have speculated that the work contains musical portraits of its four commissioners, and have heard the "recitativo collerico" in particular as the voice of Charles Rosen, but this strikes me more as a party game than musical analysis. More than any other of Carter's compositions, though, *Night Fantasies* seems to mirror the sensibilities of its performers, and despite the rigor of its construction, makes widely divergent impressions when played by different pianists. Paul Jacobs, for instance, brought out its coloristic side, rooted in Debussy. Rosen, by contrast, took great care to connect up its contrasting phrases into a coherent, even Beethovenian, argument.

I still remember the impact of *Triple Duo*'s New York premiere, at the Symphony Space, the unexpected way it charmed its hard-boiled uptown audience. As we emerged from the hall onto Broadway, Minna Lederman, astute as ever, quipped: "No one warned me I'd be hearing a masterpiece." Posterity has confirmed her judgment. *Triple Duo* soon became one of Carter's most frequently performed compositions.

Carter dedicated *Triple Duo* to Fires of London "and its prime mover, Peter Maxwell Davies." This ensemble became famous in 1969 for their performances of *Eight Songs for a Mad King*, and the antic character of much of *Triple Duo* (the immediate sequel to Carter's six songs for a mad poet) may reflect that association. The first thing one notices in *Triple Duo* is the unusual (for Carter) quality of its initial sounds: raw, shrill, and raucous. We might be hearing the six "rude mechanicals" of *A Midsummer's Night's Dream*. As in Shakespeare, the warring elements of the piece gradually give way to a sense of wonder. This line of development is set in motion with the unexpected appearance of tranquil music, played by both wind and string duos, soon after the opening. Carter thereafter locates the dramatic element less in the contrast of the three duos (flute/clarinet, piano/percussion, violin/cello) than in the juxtaposition of playful, agitated, passionate, and peaceful moods, sometimes heard in simultaneous contrast, but also emerging as shared, related ideas. The three duos seem to banter rather than argue, and, in the Allegro fantastico that begins at m. 439, they converge toward a climactic accented downbeat, the only one in the entire piece, just before the ending.

The Oboe Concerto, completed in 1987, marked the beginning of two of the most important partnerships in Carter's career, with Heinz Holliger and Paul Sacher. Holliger, oboist, conductor, and composer, told me that he came to appreciate Carter's music only after he heard the Piano Concerto. Soon after that he asked his fellow Basler, conductor Paul Sacher, to commission a new concerto from Carter. As founder and conductor of the Basel Chamber Orchestra, Sacher had commissioned a long line of distinguished compositions including Bartók's *Music for Strings, Percussion, and Celesta* and *Divertimento*, Stravinsky's Concerto in D for string orchestra, and *A Sermon, a Narrative, and a Prayer*, and double concertos for oboe and harp by Henze and Lutosławski written expressly for Holliger and his wife, Ursula. Sacher also established the Paul Sacher Stiftung in Basel as an archive for twentieth- and twenty-first-century music, beginning with his acquisition of the Stravinsky estate in 1983. In 1988 the PSS acquired all of Carter's sketches and papers except for those already held by the Library of Congress.

As a one-time student of the oboe, Carter had already written some highly idiomatic music for the instrument (Sonata for Flute, Oboe, Cello, and Harpsichord; "Sandpiper") and had worked closely with such New York oboists as Josef Marx and Stephen Taylor, but his late-life association with Holliger might be compared with that of Brahms and clarinetist Richard Mühlfeld. Carter composed an impressive series of works for the multi-talented Swiss musician:

Oboe Concerto (1987)
Pastoral (1940) arranged for English Horn, marimba, string orchestra (1987)
Quintet for Piano and Winds (1991)
Trilogy (1991–1992)
A Six Letter Letter (1996)
"Òboe sommerso" from *Tempo e Tempi* (1999)
Oboe Quartet (2001)
HBHH (2007)
Figment VI (2011)

In 2009 Carter and Holliger appeared together in a series of concerts at New York's 92nd Street Y titled "Elliott Carter & Heinz Holliger: a Musical Friendship." It is instructive to contrast the joy Carter took in working with Holliger on the new concerto with his resistance to a commission for a short work from an American orchestra at the same time, one of very few American commissions he received or fulfilled during the 1980s. When an offer arrived from the Houston Symphony for the work that eventually became *A Celebration of Some 100 x 150 Notes*, Carter responded with a long list of reasons not to accept, beginning with the fact that the orchestra had never previously played his music and the conductor slated for the premiere had never led any of his works. Even after the Concerto for Orchestra and *A Symphony of Three Orchestra*, Carter still felt disconnected from the American symphonic scene. By contrast he treated the commission from Paul Sacher as a dream project that would allow him to pursue his most personal ideas without compromise.

As he had done in the Piano Concerto, Carter scored the Oboe Concerto for two ensembles. He surrounded the solo oboe with four violas and a percussionist playing timpani, vibraphone, glockenspiel, and an array of metal blocks, wood blocks, cymbals, and drums. Encircling this concertino ensemble, the main orchestra contains flute, clarinet, horn, trombone (which surfaces from time to time as the oboe's antagonist), about twenty-four string players, and a second percussionist playing on a contrasting group of pitched and unpitched instruments. This division serves an acoustic function as well as a dramatic one. Carter wanted the oboe to be audible at all times, but without scaling down the accompaniment to the dimensions of a chamber concerto. He once pointed out to me that in *L'heure espagnole*, Ravel accompanied the singers with just a few instruments, but whenever they were not singing the entire orchestra played. By splicing these two levels of accompaniment together, Ravel created the illusion of an unbroken orchestral tapestry that nevertheless allowed the voices to come through. In the Oboe Concerto the soloist's entourage of violas and percussion helps to give the impression of a continuous and active accompaniment even though much of the piece proceeds through alternating statements of the concertino and ripieno.

The otherworldly quality of the concerto appears at the very beginning, as the oboe's plaintive *cantando* line slowly descends from an altissimo A. Its character seems to arrive from a mythic sphere, far from the earthly encumbrances of the main orchestra. While the music unfolds in a single movement, there are formal milestones along the way. At m. 92, the main orchestra's agitation seems to melt away, as if finally subdued by the oboe's plangent song. The slow music that follows exudes a calm enchantment rarely found in Carter's work. When the spell wears off and unrest returns, the oboe counters with seven blasts on its lowest note. The mood then gradually brightens into a raucous celebration. In the coda, the oboe resumes the *cantando* line of the opening, rising through a halo of sustained harmonies, *poco a poco calmando al fine*, returning to its distant realm.

Micros

With the exception of two timpani studies, written as preparations for the important timpani part in the Piano Concerto, the only miniature work Carter composed between 1949 and 1983 was the one-page *Canon for 3 Igor Stravinsky in memoriam*[6] first published in *Tempo* no. 97 (1971). In the tradition of Bach's *Musical Offering*, Carter conceived it as a puzzle canon, an abstract contrapuntal structure that could be realized by different instruments.[7] Given the special role Stravinsky played in Carter's career, its form, like a secret handshake between composers, remained unique.

With *Changes*, for solo guitar, commissioned by David Starobin, who had premiered the guitar part in *Syringa*, Carter initiated a new subgenre of small-scaled works. Within a few years these works would attain an importance in Carter's oeuvre equivalent to the *Sequenze* in Berio's. Seven minutes in duration, *Changes* does not feel like a miniature, but rather like a parallel to *Night Fantasies*, scaled down to the dimensions of the guitar. Two of the earliest micro-pieces, *Riconoscenza per Goffredo Petrassi* and *Esprit rude/esprit doux*, similarly seem like compressions of earlier macropieces. *Riconoscenza*, later incorporated as one of *Four Lauds*, recalls the three interwoven musical strands of Variation 7 from the Variations for Orchestra; *Er/Ed* reduces the dialectic format of the Third Quartet to its essence. As early as the *Canon for 4, Homage to William* [Glock], however, micro-Carter became its own genre. We can see this development by comparing *Esprit rude/Esprit doux I* with *Enchanted Preludes*. In the former the listener follows the courses of two independent lines that only converge once. In the latter, constructed in a similar fashion, the gossamer texture woven by the interaction of the two instruments becomes the focus throughout. (See MEC98 for detailed discussion of all the short pieces written before 1998.)

Despite their relative brevity and the fractured connotations of many of their titles, many of the short pieces loom large. I would place the two *Fragments* for string quartet, written in 1994 and 1999, on a par with their five longer siblings. *Fragment no. 1* inhabits a ghostly sound world unique in Carter's music. All notes, both bowed and plucked, are played as harmonics, giving the music the aura of chimes from the beyond. *Fragment no. 2* was Carter's farewell to the quartet medium. It contrasts fragmentary echoes of the past quartets with two slowly moving lines played without vibrato, tranquillo and pianissimo.

Thickening the plot, Carter complicated the relation of his long and short works by publishing pieces together and suggesting, but not requiring, that they be played as suites. Three short orchestral works from the 1980s were composed and premiered separately but later published, and often performed, as *Three Occasions*. The after-the-fact suites of *Trilogy, Four Lauds, Symphonia: sum fluxae pretium spei*, and *Three Illusions* also follow this pattern. The ultimate emergence of multi-movement assemblages from works composed independently, sometimes many years apart, produces a formal uncertainty, even an element of chance, not present in Carter's earlier music. Up to this point Carter habitually composed works as a totality, mapping out the full structure before putting a note on the page. In these compilations, by contrast, the final shape only emerged slowly, often due to encouragement from performers like Heinz Holliger or Oliver Knussen, who commissioned sequels. Even after the composite versions appeared, Carter sanctioned the performance of individual movements. Would he also have approved performances of a few but not all pieces, and in a different order than their published form? Context and order make a difference in our experience of music. For a while there was a fashion for prefacing performances of Beethoven's Ninth with Schoenberg's *A Survivor from Warsaw*, giving Schoenberg's work in effect a happy ending. If the sequence were reversed the impact of the juxtaposition would be entirely transformed.

Carter's *Three Occasions* mark very different kinds of events with different kinds of music. The Houston Symphony Orchestra commissioned *A Celebration of Some 100 x 150 Notes* for its 150th anniversary, a public event for an institution to which Carter felt no attachment. A fanfare was expected, but instead Carter produced a free fantasy on the idea of fanfares, celebrating the eleven harmonic intervals by giving each one its moment in the spotlight. Extending the arts/politics divide of "A View of the Capital," Carter detached the fanfare genre from its military origins. There are just enough suggestions of the typical fanfare to allow sophisticated listeners in on the joke. *Remembrance*, by contrast, is both public and personal. A solemn trombone solo declaims a funeral oration against a changing orchestral backdrop to commemorate Carter's patron Paul Fromm. (Carter had spoken at a memorial service for Fromm.) While the piece draws its intensity from Carter's appreciation of Fromm's support, as a recognizable stylized eulogy, rising to a passionate climax in the strings, it could easily serve as a tribute to other great figures—something to play instead of Barber's *Adagio*, at least in some alternative Carterian universe.

Anniversary, a commission from the BBC, owes its title to the Carters' fiftieth wedding anniversary, and to a poem by John Donne which Carter quotes at the top of the score:

> Only our love hath no decay;
> This, no tomorrow hath, nor yesterday,
> Running it never runs away,
> But truly keeps his first, last, everlasting day.

Donne's lines place love in and out of time, but Carter's music sounds more chronometric than amorous. Carter constructed the piece on three contrapuntal lines, labeled X, Y, and Z in the score but perhaps standing for the composer, his wife, and their son. The abstract nature of all three lines does not tell us much about their personalities or experiences, but instead suggests the passing of years, minutes, seconds, a metaphysical emblem very much in the spirit of Donne's poetry.

The published ordering of *Three Occasions* moves from public to private, and, at the end of *Anniversary*, leaves the audience with a question mark in the form of an enigmatic phrase played by the tuba and bass clarinet. *Anniversary*, I believe, is the kind of piece that needs to be played twice at a concert if the audience is going to make anything of it. Perhaps it would work better as the opener, as a question which would then be answered, in two different ways, by the other movements.

All three *Occasions* share Carter's late orchestral manner, which appears more practical but is often even more challenging to conduct than the spatially divided ensembles of the Concerto for Orchestra or *A Symphony of Three Orchestras.* Carter's late period approach to the orchestra is deceptively conventional in appearance. The orchestra sits in its normal configuration, and Carter often draws on the familiar, stereotyped roles of woodwinds, brass and strings, an approach Boulez, for all his admiration for Carter, found problematic:

> His orchestral writing is well thought out and perfectly realized, but I would not say that it is the most innovative aspect of his work; I don't find his inventions in timbre equal to those in rhythm or form. You don't find special sonorities that you have never heard before. The orchestra is not used in a conventional way, but the instruments are used just as they are, the brass majestic, the winds whirling (*"volubiles"*).
>
> (Noubel, 12)

Perhaps realizing that he was imposing his own aesthetic on Carter's music, Boulez concluded by saying that "in Carter the musical idea is transcribed in a direct fashion." Since Carter's musical ideas are rarely conventional, it becomes all the more challenging for performers to project them within the routine-appearing framework of Carter's "new normal."

A Breaking Point?

In Carter's String Quartet no. 4, completed in 1986, the tensions between conventional style and innovative idea approaches a state of crisis. The quartet seems to flaunt its conventional trappings. Although performed without pauses between movements, it is the only one of Carter's five quartets to outline a classical four-movement form, Appassionato, Scherzando, Lento, Presto, without the kind of alternative structure he had deployed in his first two quartets, and would again in the fifth. Unlike the second and third quartets, the fourth does not require an unusual, spread-out seating arrangement. While the Third Quartet emphasized unusual sonorities, the Fourth Quartet avoids any devices of string writing beyond those found in Haydn or Mozart. There is a bare minimum of pizzicato and no use of harmonics. All these overtly conservative aspects of the quartet raise the question of whether Carter now saw his harmonic and rhythmic techniques as fulfilling the roles once played by classical tonal procedures—in which case the Fourth Quartet could be heard as a late life return to neo-classicism—or whether he intended its non-tonal, polyrhythmic devices to undermine its apparent classicism. In his comments, he spoke of the piece in Ivesian terms of non-hierarchic, democratic freedom, but also stressed its comprehensive organization. In a November 1988 interview in *Musical America*, however, he described the quartet vis-à-vis Ives in a surprisingly defensive way. Saying that the quartet was an interweaving of "contrasting things that makes a total piece out of it," he added: "It's said that my work derives from Ives. But Ives doesn't do this. In his Second Quartet, for example, even though there's a great deal of simultaneous material, he doesn't make it into a program that penetrates the entire work. Everyone marches together. They don't march out of phase as they do in almost all of my quartets."[8]

On its unconventional flip side, the quartet systematically keeps the four players out of phase, by giving each one its own "harmony, rhythm, and shapes of melodic figures and expression." On the page this opposition appears most obviously in cross-rhythmic ratios of 5:6:7:8 that appear in nearly every bar. While the division of the players into four distinct characters recalls the Second Quartet, the highly ornate and virtuosic writing advances beyond even that of the Third Quartet, yielding a dense welter of sounds, spread across the entire possible range of the instruments, often in an aggressive, harshly dissonant way. Carter presents the quartet's defining *objet sonore*, a fortissimo ten-tone chord, on the downbeat of the third bar. It sounds like an expressionistic "*Urschrei*." All these structural and dramatic strategies produce a surfeit of information, much harder for the listener to assimilate than the similar procedures in *Triple Duo* or *Penthode*.

To help performers and listeners navigate through this complexity, Carter used the "principal voice" designation found in Schoenberg, though, at times, in a counterintuitive way. In the opening movement, for instance, the first violin is designated as principal voice throughout, but it also moves much more slowly than the three accompanying instruments who seem to jabber behind the first violinist's back. In the second movement, by contrast, Carter broke the principal voice into fragments bounced back and forth between the four players. In the third movement the mildly jocular mood of the scherzo suddenly turns pious, as the players intone a sustained chorale reminiscent, in texture, but not harmony, of the *Heiliger Dankgesang* from Beethoven's op. 132. Around the time Carter was composing the quartet he told an audience at

Brandeis that he composed "in chorales, like Bach, but where Bach used chords with three or four pitches, my chords have six." That description matches much of the Lento. In the Presto, which explodes outward from an eight-note tone cluster, the individual character of each instrument finally emerges with an increasing frenzy that reaches a peak in a passionate dialogue between the first violin and the cello. Suddenly this "love duet" breaks off. In the mysterious final pages of the quartet, brief phrases of aggressive dissonance alternate with tranquil floating passages, a contrast recalling the slow movement of the First Quartet, but here punctuated with silences. In the last bar the four players bring their arguments to a close with a smiling sigh, followed by a wink.

On a conceptual level the Fourth Quartet is an atlas of four-way interactions, from unrelated parallel play to prayer-like convergence. After thirty years of listening to the quartet, and even with the benefit of four recordings (Composers' Quartet, Juilliard Quartet, Arditti Quartet, Pacifica Quartet), I still find its first half opaque. The assignment of roles seems formulaic, less metaphorically suggestive than in the Second Quartet. Despite its profusion of cross pulses, the music seems oddly static, notwithstanding several melodramatic "high points." Had Carter pushed his idiom past the breaking point? Apparently he did not think so. His next large chamber composition, the Quintet for Piano and Winds, which, as a lighter-weight sequel, relates to the Fourth Quartet much as the Brass Quintet had to the Third, is even more complex in its pre-compositional dispersion of harmonies, rhythms, and instrumental combination.

By 1995, when he wrote his Fifth String Quartet, Carter adopted a different course. Instead of composing an unbroken scheme that "penetrates the entire work," the Fifth Quartet unfolds as two interlaced series of miniatures, a "cooked" sequence of well-polished vignettes, and a "raw" sequence, which Carter said was meant to sound as if the players were practicing their parts, but which has always struck me as enacting Carter's own practice of sketching a piece in disconnected fragments. As if dispensing with the very idea of the "masterpiece," the Fifth Quartet is a collection of shards, figments, fragments, even illusions. With it we finally encounter Carter's late late style. Even as he approached his ninetieth birthday, however, he had not abandoned the *genre chef d'oeuvre*—quite the contrary, as we are about to see.

Notes

1 See NYT "A drenching of music but a drought of critics," October 27, 1974.
2 See the performance instructions in the score of the Oboe Concerto, where, working closely with Heinz Holliger, Carter made his most use of extended techniques.
3 See CPLD, 248–249.
4 See the table of episodes in Noubel, 192.
5 *LA Times,* April 10, 2008.
6 Reproduced in CPLD, 202.
7 See CPLD, 203.
8 Reprinted in the liner notes to the Composers Quartet recording.

CHAPTER TEN

Multi-vehicle Accidents

CARTER'S PRODUCTIVITY FROM HIS EIGHTIETH BIRTHDAY ONWARD will surely merit a place in future record books no matter how posterity may come to judge the quality of his late creations. In addition to the steady flow of miniatures, three major chamber music works, including String Quartet no. 5, two song cycles, and two concertos, the decade of the 1990s saw the premieres of Carter's two longest works: *Symphonia: sum fluxae pretium spei*, in Manchester on April 25, 1998, by the BBC Orchestra conducted by Oliver Knussen, and the opera *What Next?*, on September 16, 1999, at the Deutsche Staatsoper Unter den Linden, Berlin, conducted by Daniel Barenboim.

The size and scope of Carter's work in the 1990s is all the more remarkable given changes in his personal life, some of which were to be expected in advanced old age. With the sale of the house in Waccabuc in 1990, and a move to smaller quarters in a retirement community in Southbury, Connecticut, Carter had to dismantle and relocate one of the two studios in which he had composed most of his music. Helen suffered increasingly from chronic pain as a result of Lyme disease, a crippling ailment carried by ticks from the many deer living in the New York exurbs. As she became ever more frail, Virgil Blackwell, hired as a personal manager in 1988, took on many of the career-related tasks that Helen had undertaken in the past. Carter's hearing was becoming impaired, a condition, soon remedied with hearing aids, that first became apparent during the rehearsals for the Violin Concerto in San Francisco in 1990, when he complained frequently about not hearing details of his orchestration. (The problematic acoustics of Davies Hall, subsequently much improved, did not help.) Carter spent extended time in the hospital for heart conditions and pneumonia and was diagnosed with prostate cancer. The medication that held off the spread of the cancer for over two decades also led to weight gain, which gradually gave the older composer a genial Santa Claus-like appearance that he enhanced, in public appearances during his last years, by wearing bright red shirts and suspenders.

Perhaps because of these dislocations and medical crises, Carter altered his compositional process around the middle of the decade. Up through the composition of the Quintet for Piano and Winds and the *Symphonia: sum fluxae pretium spei*, he had continued to expand the calculations of his Harmony Book to include larger collections of pitches. With the String Quartet no. 5 (1995) he returned to the charts he had developed for the Second Quartet and *Double Concerto*, derived from the two all-interval tetrachords. He would use these charts as the basis of all his subsequent works.[1] While in conversation with John Link[2] Carter gave the impression that he was now simply putting notes on the page without much forethought or revision. The sketches indicate, to the contrary, that he continued to pre-compose, calculate, and fine-tune his music, though without the extensive scaffolding he had used earlier.

We can track the emergence of Carter's very late style by comparing works of similar genres. In contrast to the Violin Concerto (1990) and Quintet for Piano and Winds (1991), the Clarinet Concerto (1996) and Quintet for Piano and Strings (1997) are clearer in texture, more episodic in construction, and less anguished in expression. We might hear a similar contrast between the two megaliths of the decade (Carter described them to me as the "follies of my old age"): *Symphonia: sum fluxae pretium spei* and *What Next?*

Origins

While the fifty-minute lengths of these two works appear monumental in relation to Carter's typical time-scales, they also share an element of randomness, or at least uncertainty, in the ways they came into being and in their ultimate designs. As happened with *Three Occasions*, the three movements of *Symphonia* were commissioned and premiered separately, and have been played either individually or as a three-movement suite ever since. Heard as a symphony, its proportions are unusual: two twenty-minute movements, one fast, one slow, followed by a ten-minute movement whose translucent sonority Carter likened to the "Queen Mab" scherzo from Berlioz's *Roméo et Juliette.* We might interpret Carter's scherzo either as a replacement for a grandiose symphonic finale, which Carter said he was unwilling to write,[3] or as an indication that the symphony, like Schubert's Eighth or Bruckner's Ninth, is unfinished, though in this case deliberately so. *What Next?* similarly teeters between opera and anti-opera. It begins with a car crash, but its pairing of composer and librettist also stemmed from an accidental encounter.

The origins and even the genres of the two grand works of the 1990s are not clear from the published accounts. *Symphonia* emerged in stages after the New York Philharmonic cancelled a long-standing commission.[4] When I was writing MEC98, Carter told me that the idea for the work, and arrangements with three different orchestras for its commissions, were "instigated" by Oliver Knussen, but evidence for the exact sequence of events remains unclear. The Chicago Symphony commissioned *Partita* and Daniel Barenboim conducted its premiere in Chicago on February 17, 1994. The liner notes to the CSO recording of *Partita* make no mention of plans to place it in a larger symphony. *Adagio tenebroso* was commissioned by BBC Radio 3, and premiered as a stand-alone work by the BBC Symphony, conducted by Andrew Davis, at the Royal Albert Hall, London, on September 13, 1995. Near the beginning of the *Adagio* (measures 10–23) Carter reprised, in slightly altered form, a tranquillo phrase, mainly scored for flutes and violas, from measures 19–33 of *Partita.* This cross-reference, a rare event in Carter's music, and also the BBC commission for the *Adagio*, indicate that Knussen's "instigation" of the multi-movement symphony occurred only after the premiere of *Partita.*[5] The Cleveland Orchestra commissioned the third movement, *Allegro scorrevole.* Christoph von Dohnányi conducted its premiere, once again as a self-standing piece, on May 22, 1997. The three movements were finally played together as *Symphonia: sum fluxae pretium spei* on April 25, 1998, in Manchester, with the BBC Symphony conducted by Oliver Knussen. In his program note, Carter explained that the title came from a Latin poem, *Bulla* (Bubble) by the seventeenth century English Catholic metaphysical poet Richard Crashaw. He cited Phyllis Bowman's

translation of the title: "I am the prize of flowing hope." The liner note
to the recording by the Bavarian Orchestra, however, translates it rather
more darkly as "I am the price of inconstant hope." Bubbles, we might
recall from the famous painting by Chardin, often symbolized the tran-
sience and vanity of human pursuits.

Neither the sequence of premieres nor Carter's program notes make
clear the exact point at which he came to think of the three pieces as part
of a larger whole, or when he came to associate this multi-movement piece
with Crashaw's poem. In a July 1993 letter to the music theorist Jonathan
Bernard, Carter announced that he had completed the score of *Partita* and
stated that he was considering setting the Crashaw poem for voice and
piano, especially for soprano Lucy Shelton, but did not mention any link
between the poem and the orchestral piece. Though certainly obscure,
"*Bulla*" has attracted the attention of scholars of the Baroque.[6] Ultimately
Carter drew the inclusive title for the three-movement symphonic work
from Crashaw's verse and used poetry by John Hollander, written in an
updated metaphysical style, for the song cycle *Of Challenge and Of Love*.

The road to *What Next?* was full of even more unexpected twists. The
work originated in a request in 1994 from Daniel Barenboim, then musical director of the Deutsche Staatsoper Berlin as well as the Chicago
Symphony, for an opera on an American subject.[7] This was an offer that
few composers would refuse. Carter's acceptance nonetheless seems a
little surprising, beyond the obvious glee he felt at the idea of composing
his first opera in his mid-eighties. While he certainly had studied the
scores of the operatic repertory, Carter was neither a regular opera-goer
nor an opera lover. He and Helen never socialized with figures from that
glittering world. His essay on the *Gesamtkunstwerk*[8] gives much evidence
of his knowledge of opera, but little sign of a passionate enthusiasm for
the form in general, or, despite the title, for Wagner. (The operas Carter
most frequently, and positively, mentioned were by Mozart, Verdi, and
Berg.) Given his close associations with poets, however, it is equally surprising, and in retrospect unfortunate, that Carter did not turn immediately to, say, John Ashbery, for a libretto.

The question of a collaborator loomed for three years. Letters show
that on September 13, 1994, Barenboim floated the idea of engaging
Woody Allen as the librettist, but, alas, Carter said he was unfamiliar

with the comedian's writings, even though they appeared frequently in *The New Yorker*. Already imagining a surreal comedy, and, despite the commission, not particularly interested in American subjects, Carter considered adapting Ionesco's *Bald Soprano*, Jacques Tati's film *Traffic* and even Aristophanes' *The Birds*. Countering the Woody Allen idea, Carter suggested Edward Albee as librettist, but that was not pursued further. According to Paul Griffiths' journal printed in the ECM recording of *What Next?*, Carter proposed an operatic collaboration suddenly and rather casually on February 20, 1997 after running into Griffiths at a lecture at the Casa Italiana at Columbia University about Carter's old friend, the Italian composer Giacinto Scelsi. Griffiths, a British music critic then on the staff at *The New York Times*, had already written the libretto for Tan Dun's opera *Marco Polo* which premiered in Munich in May 1996 and at the New York City Opera in November 1997. There is no evidence, however, that Carter had seen the opera or read the libretto before his brief and unanticipated encounter with Griffiths at Columbia.[9]

As a critic Griffiths had written two books on twentieth-century music that treated Carter respectfully but at a clear remove from a core narrative centered on the European avant-garde. Griffiths, aware that Carter had brought up the opera *en passant*, perhaps just making conversation while waiting for a cab, wrote the composer on March 6 to make sure he was serious. The very next day, Carter wrote back to confirm the proposal. Given his age, and the fact that the offer for the commission was now three years old, he may have been concerned about time. He also may have thought that a less established librettist would be more amenable to his own ideas. Before meeting Griffiths, Carter had already decided that the opera would begin with an auto accident, and he outlined this concept in a letter to Griffiths on March 20.[10] The exact nature of the accident took different shapes in Carter's mind, sometimes involving two cars and a deer (not a freakish occurrence in Waccabuc). The image of the car crash sprang from a brief episode in Jacques Tati's film *Traffic*,[11] but Carter made no mention of this source in his letter to Griffiths and the film does not appear in Griffiths' journal. Carter's taste in comic films is reflected in the list of his favorite movies that he prepared for Frank Sheffer in 1992,[12] which begins with Buster Keaton's *Electric House* (which he recalled as *Seven Days*) and *Cops*, but also includes Billy Wilder's *Some Like it Hot*. No Tati film appears on the list. The opera, though often said to be based on *Traffic*, shows no traces of the film's story line (or Gallic whimsy) aside from the car crash. (In the First Quartet, Carter had similarly drawn inspiration from two brief moments in Cocteau's *Blood of a Poet*.)

Griffiths soon filled in the details of Carter's general vision very much in his own manner with Carter occasionally resisting and suggesting alternatives. Carter repeatedly asked for more words and objected to naming a character Zen, but Griffiths prevailed. One result of their spur-of-the-moment bi-national collaboration was that the characters in the opera, while apparently American, speak in an odd and sometimes jarring mid-Atlantic patois. American "station wagon" rather than the British "estate" rubs shoulders with "piss off" in its British usage rather than the American . . . unprintable here.

Symphonia: sum fluxae pretium spei

At the New York premiere of *Partita*, our small group of Carter loyalists cheered enthusiastically while most of the audience sat on their hands, bewildered. (The person sitting behind me asked if we were a paid claque.) The music seemed to pummel the audience with high-voltage aggression. Carter said at the time that he thought of the word "partita" in its contemporary Italian sense of a football game, an image distant indeed from Crashaw's bubble. Carter's title, however, suggests a different (and unacknowledged) Italian source, the Partita for Orchestra by Goffredo Petrassi, which Carter first heard in Amsterdam in 1933.[13] He told me many times that he considered Petrassi to be his best friend even though they rarely saw each other. He had already honored his friend with the solo violin piece *Riconoscenza per Goffredo Petrassi*, composed for Petrassi's eightieth birthday in 1984, and, while working on *Symphonia*, celebrated Petrassi's ninetieth birthday with the solo piano work, *90+*. Both works premiered at the Pontino Festival, where Petrassi served as honorary president. Carter's deep knowledge of Petrassi's oeuvre is clear in the two essays he wrote about his friend (in 1960 and 1986), whom he specifically praised for his pursuit of an "emancipated discourse," the phrase Carter used to describe his own music. In 1960, Carter lauded Petrassi's *Serenata* for flute, viola, contrabass, harpsichord, and percussion, and soon incorporated its ensemble into one of the two orchestras in his *Double Concerto*. He described the *Serenata* as "a series of explosions of the imaginative and unexpected," words that might apply equally to Carter's *Partita*.

We can interpret the homage to Petrassi implied by Carter's use of the word "partita" in terms of both overall form and orchestral practice. Petrassi's neo-Baroque suite, the work that established his reputation, is in three movements: galliarda, ciaconna, giga. The three movements of *Symphonia* resemble the sequence heard in Petrassi's *Partita*, though on a much larger scale. Petrassi's influence may be even more important in accounting for the orchestral style of Carter's *Symphonia*, which departs widely from the multi-ensemble, deconstructive strategies of the *Concerto for Orchestra* and *A Symphony of Three Orchestras*. Instead of splintering the ensemble into non-traditional groupings, Carter re-affirmed the traditional roles of winds, brass, percussion (including harp and piano), and strings (as he had begun to do in *Three Occasions*) and welded the instruments of the orchestra together through frequent doublings between different families. As he had done in *Night Fantasies*, Carter now treated the entire range of his instrument, the symphony orchestra, as an unbroken continuum. Also as in *Night Fantasies*, he defined the harmonic environment of that continuum with a family of twelve-tone chords, in this case all-interval chords that also contain the all-triad hexachord. (In MEC98 I dubbed these chords "Link" chords because they were suggested to the composer by the composer/theorist John Link.[14]) Apart from this idiosyncratic procedure, Carter would have found multiple precedents for this way of writing for orchestra, and also reassurance that it could still produce fresh sounds, in Petrassi's eight concerti for orchestra, particularly the seventh concerto, which he cited in his 1986 essay. Carter's *Partita* in particular sounds very much like a continuation of Petrassi's concerti and could easily have been titled Second Concerto for Orchestra. (Carter arrived at the title *Partita* only after considering many others, including "Windy City," which would have been a nice tip of the hat to its Chicago Symphony sponsorship.)

The structure and rhetoric of *Symphonia* also depart far from Carter's earlier orchestral pieces, again in ways that resemble qualities he praised in Petrassi. In 1960, as he was wrestling to augment his neo-modernist style with avant-garde ideas, Carter cited Petrassi's music as evidence that "adherence to traditional conceptions of detail in musical structure, such as 'chords,' 'counterpoint,' 'themes,' 'accompaniments,' or of much larger matters such as 'phrases,' 'crescendo,' and other techniques

of emphasis . . . have proved more durable than might have been expected earlier in the century."[15] The superimposition of musical streams
that Carter deployed in the 1960s and 70s tended to obscure phrase
structures because of overlaps of the different layers. *Partita* and *Adagio
tenebroso*, by contrast, unfold as sequences of clearly punctuated phrases,
like the lines of poetry. While there is hardly any literal repetition, the
music nevertheless feels thematic because of the use of a small number
of what musicologists call "topics."[16] We might list these as chaos, tranquility, melody, chorale, points, pulses, solos. Carter shuffled appearance
of these topics in an unpredictable order, but he scored them with traditional colorings (as Boulez noted) that help signal their rhetorical
function. Throughout the *Symphonia* the first violins sing out long expressive lines, as they would in Bruckner and Mahler, while the four
horns play four-note harmonies as they would, with different four notes,
in Schumann. The woodwinds scamper and cavort as in a Mendelssohn
scherzo. The percussion makes noise. These stereotyped roles, though,
coexist with an opposing traditional technique, instrumental doubling
that creates mixed timbres as they do in Brahms and Debussy. In *Partita*,
Carter guides the listener through these cross currents with a series of
woodwind solos, beginning in measure 120, with a rather enigmatic soliloquy by the English horn, followed in turn by a piccolo solo, beginning at m. 192, handed off to the flute at m. 200, a "giocoso" solo for the
E flat clarinet beginning at m. 271, and, finally, at m. 515, with a bass clarinet solo. Though widely spaced and interrupted by contrasting ideas,
these solos spotlight the quirky resilience of individual voices within the
orchestral mass.

In *Adagio tenebroso*, the central topic might be termed "fractured
endless melody." The striving for lyrical expression picks up a thread from
the last section of Partita (beginning at m. 426), where the first violins
spin out a long expressive line against a turbulent background. In the
Adagio the background is more desolate, hinting ominously at a cataclysm
that finally arrives toward the very end. At times the impulse toward song,
even in the face of disaster, spreads beyond the violins with lyrical solos
for oboe, horn, and trumpet, and somehow outlasts the deluge, though
in fragments. The movement ends with a poignant coda. Its un-Carterian
serenity recalls the closing passages of Stravinsky's *Les noces* and *Symphony
of Psalms*.

Despite Carter's stated aversion to grandiosity, the scale and rhetoric of the *Symphonia* suggest a goal that becomes apparent once we stop thinking about Crashaw and just listen to the music. However reluctantly, Carter mapped out a symphonic work with the expressive weight of Brahms' Fourth, Bruckner's Ninth, and Mahler's Ninth—or Tenth, but in a manner that reflected his own times. Of course he would never have put it that way. He did say, though, that his music "seeks the awareness of motion we have in flying or of driving a car and not the plodding of horses or the marching of soldiers that pervades the motion pattern of older music."[17]

The epic nature of this project appears in the time scales of both *Partita* and *Adagio tenebroso* which are unique in Carter's music, whether or not these are considered independent pieces. At a little under seventeen minutes in duration, *Partita* is nearly equal in length to all of *A Symphony of Three Orchestras*. That earlier quasi-symphony, as we have seen, was in three sections, and its central section contained twelve distinct musical ideas in many different tempos. *Partita*, by contrast, does not divide into large contrasting sections but is a sustained argument woven out of a small number of ideas. Over twenty minutes in length, the *Adagio tenebroso* lasts as long as the entire Second Quartet, yet it too is a unified, sustained movement, with a single tempo throughout and a small number of thematic elements.

None of the three movements resembles traditional formal archetypes at all, or even the formal strategies of earlier Carter, except for the use of Bergian climactic high points to clarify the formal and emotional arc of each piece. As we have seen, ideas—less themes than topics—recur, but in no predictable fashion, even in terms of Carter's music. In *Adagio tenebroso*, Carter untypically repeats a melodic idea, a major sixth rising from C to A, several times, as if it were an important motive, though it soon disappears. Given Carter's penchant for ciphers, which he employed to honor Boulez and Robert Mann among others, we might even suspect him of spelling out his name, but the rising sixth on these particular pitches may also be meant to recall, even more explicitly than Carter had done in the Fourth Quartet, the opening notes of Beethoven's *Heiliger Dankgesang*. While working on the *Symphonia*, Carter spent three weeks in the hospital battling pneumonia, so Beethoven's offer of thanks for his recovery may have been very much on his mind.

Although the forms of all three movements defy categorization, their contrasting expressive characters, violent struggle, tragic despair, and tentative hope, are clear and unmistakable. *Partita* explodes with energy. *Adagio tenebroso*, which Carter said drew on his memories of walking across the shell-scarred, mud-covered battlefields of northern France with his pacifist father in the early 1920s, trudges like a monumental dirge, traversing a panorama of desolation. *Allegro scorrevole* shimmers, flutters, and slowly ascends like a great mythical bird, the "gold-feathered bird" singing in the palm tree in Wallace Stevens' "Of Mere Being": "The palm stands on the edge of space. / The wind moves slowly in the branches. / The bird's fire-fangled feathers dangle down."

Or perhaps it is a mechanical bird, jet-engined. The finale, entitled with Carter's signature tempo indication, *Allegro scorrevole*, superimposes two streams of music—one, mainly for the strings, flowing at a moderate tempo, the other, mainly in the woodwinds, gurgling rapidly. The two elements do not seem opposed, however. The string melody soars untrammeled by the burdens of the Adagio, borne upward by the rushing winds, with only occasional hints of turbulence. I like to imagine that the music simulates the pleasures of modern aviation (minus all the usual indignities), particularly its sensation of simultaneous rapid motion and stillness. Although Carter called it a scherzo, the only scherzo-like movement it resembles is Debussy's "Jeux de vagues" from *La mer*, also a study in fluid motion. As in the Debussy, which is at once aquatic and erotic, Carter's evocation of flight is rich in metaphorical possibilities from aviation to philosophy. Despite its brevity relative to the other movements, it seems equal to them poetically, an ode to joy at 40,000 feet, approaching the speed of sound.

What Next?

When I first read Paul Griffiths' libretto for *What Next?*, in the London offices of Boosey and Hawkes while Carter was still composing the music, my heart sank. The six characters were painfully predictable caricatures. Every line rang false. (I even briefly considered offering to substitute a libretto of my own, but during Carter's lifetime I could never bring myself to share my reservations about the opera with him, let alone in print.)[18] I was therefore totally surprised with the impression that the opera made when I first heard it, on May 16, 1999, in a private, concert-style preview performance at the Juilliard School. It seemed charming, humane, and eminently operatic. My own reaction was shared by the composer William Bolcom. He congratulated Carter after the performance for a score whose unexpected charm and intimacy reminded him of Ravel's Iberian sex comedy *L'heure espagnole*. Afterwards I wondered how Carter had drawn such wondrous music from such an unpromising source. Or had he? Perhaps the convivial invited audience and the intimate scale of the Kaplan Penthouse at Juilliard clouded my judgment. When I heard the opera in concert performances at Orchestra Hall in Chicago its charm was less enveloping, lost in the larger space, and it had more of the feeling—that sinking feeling—of generic atonal opera. The ECM recording conducted by Peter Eöstvös, and the video of the Tanglewood production, conducted by James Levine, were even less persuasive.

As an absurdist opera buffa in a contemporary setting, *What Next?* has plenty of precedents. It descends from such early twentieth-century comic operas as Strauss's *Ariadne auf Naxos*, Ravel's *L'heure espagnole*, Busoni's *Arlecchino*, Stravinsky's *Mavra,* and Prokofiev's *Love for Three Oranges*, but also from such rarely-revived examples of the *Zeitoper* genre of the Weimar era as Hindemith's *Hin und Zurück* and *Neues vom Tage*, or Schoenberg's *Von Heute auf Morgen*, and also from more recent avant-garde musical theater like Berio's *Recital for Cathy* and Ligeti's *Le grand macabre*. This list, with a few notable exceptions, illustrates the perils of attempting comedy in modernist idioms. With its soap opera-ish family romance element (Rose is pregnant?), *What Next?* at times also recalls the plotline, but not in any way the music, of Bernstein's *Trouble in Tahiti* and its later, longer sequel, *A Quiet Place*. Apart from that tenuous relation, *What Next?* resembles no other work of American musical theater. It sounds American only because it sounds, from start to finish, like Carter. He announced his presence at the very opening of the opera, where the voices emerge from the clangorous sounds of the percussion in a way that immediately recalls the beginning of the *Double Concerto*. The allure of this opening fades quickly, however, as the first words appear: stars, starlings, starch, starkest. They sound like responses to a party game.

Paul Griffiths' libretto lists six singing characters (plus a group of non-singing road workers):

Rose, soprano; "a bride and a performer, late twenties."
Mama, soprano; "a mother and much else, late forties." She may be the mother
    of "Harry or Larry" and the ex-wife of Zen.

Stella, contralto; "an astronomer, indeterminate." Perhaps Zen's current girlfriend.
Zen, tenor; "a supposed seer and not much else, late forties or older."
Harry or Larry; "a bridegroom and a clown, early twenties."
Kid, boy alto; "a boy, twelve." In no certain relationship to anyone.

My own take on the characters is a little different: Rose acts the clichéd diva throughout. Mama is stereotypically maternal and commonsensical. Stella sings about stars. Zen poses banal riddles. Harry/Larry doesn't know who he is. Kid, the only one of the six who does not appear to be terminally clueless, doesn't have much to do but delivers the only lines in the entire opera that engage the audience.

Perhaps intentionally, Griffiths made the plot confusing, even though not much happens. The six characters emerge from a car crash, suggested in the brief all-percussion prelude, unsure about their identities or histories beyond a sense that they were going to a wedding. By the end of the opera, after a rescue crew comes by and departs without hearing or seeing them, we might think that they all actually died in the accident and we have been witnessing their surreal, post-mortal, out-of-body nattering. This interpretation would certainly explain why so many of their words sound deadly. In a more naturalistic (though equally banal) reading, the six characters emerge from the crash dazed and confused, though not otherwise injured. They gradually emerge from shock and re-establish their narcissistic everyday identities and messy relationships, even to the point of agreeing to join forces and seek help. When help fails to arrive, they revert to their habitually alienated selves, unable or unwilling to pursue any transformational possibilities created by the accident. Rose's gratuitous high C (à la Anne Truelove) ends the opera as if intoning the title's question mark.

Griffiths organized the libretto in the manner of a numbers opera, with thirty-eight very short and preciously titled episodes mixing solos and ensembles.[19] This design seems better suited to Kurtág than Carter, who repeatedly asked for more words, and as Guy Capuzzo notes in his study of the opera, is not maintained in the music. Hiding any trace of separate numbers, Carter wrote the music in a through-composed fashion, giving each character a distinctive repertory of melodic intervals in the way he had in the Second Quartet. He also associated five of the characters with an instrumental color in the orchestra: Mama with the harp; Rose with piano; Stella with vibraphone and marimba; Harry or Larry with winds; Kid with English horn.[20] This leitmotiv-like association of character and timbre also suggests a relation of the opera to Carter's instrumental practice. Diva Rose functions much like the first violin in Quartet no.2. From her point of view, the opera is really one long aria for her character from the beginning to the end.[21] Mama corresponds to the more rational second violin persona in Quartet no. 2. No instrument in Carter's chamber music, however, had ever portrayed a character as noxious as the two insufferable adult males in the opera. By comparison with them, Ferrando and Guglielmo, the two callow ninnies in *Così fan tutte*, seem models of wisdom and maturity.

In shaping the music as an extension of his own chamber music, as a vocal sextet, Carter moved it far away from the models of the numbers opera (Mozart, Verdi, Stravinsky) or the through-composed recitative-like style of Debussy. Indeed the opera contains no allusions to operatic tradition beyond Rose's impersonation of a diva. Perhaps this apparent disconnection with the past has led directors to produce the opera as a grotesque, disjointed display of absurdity. While the libretto might further encourage this alienating approach, Tati's *Traffic* has a much more benign humor, and Carter's own performance suggestions indicate that he hoped for a gentler, more compassionate view of the characters, more along the lines of Strauss' *Capriccio*.

It is possible that the charming lightweight opera I heard at Juilliard, whose characters seemed lovably silly rather than malignant, will reappear in a future production or concert more attuned to the humor in the music and perhaps even finding some in the words. The cast in such a revival might begin by attempting to pronounce the words in a way that at least suggests spoken American English rather than the artificial elocution heard on the two recordings.

Initially, at least, Carter and Griffiths were proud of their collaboration and even planned a non-comic prequel. Perhaps rethinking the dangerous potential of a false messiah like Zen, Griffiths drafted a new libretto based on the mass suicides at Jonestown, but on July 1, 2001, much to Griffiths' chagrin, Carter suddenly announced that he would not pursue the project further. Barenboim, who liked to play high-value cards, had hoped that Carter's next opera would be a collaboration with Edward Said, a close friend of the conductor, but this intriguing possibility, like the earlier idea of working with Woody Allen, never materialized.

In retrospect we might note that Carter's two large-scale "follies" of the 1990s both describe near-death experiences followed by an unforeseen second life. The first indication that Carter's music would display a parallel rebirth came with the Clarinet Concerto, composed immediately after the *Allegro scorrevole*, and premiered by Alain Damiens and the Ensemble Intercontemporain, conducted by Boulez on January 10, 1997. The buoyant, surprisingly youthful spirit of the concerto, which, unlike the Violin Concerto, was soon widely performed, presaged a new creative phase, begun as the composer entered his tenth decade.

Notes

1 See Harmony Book, 31. The charts appear in MEC and in CEL, 246.
2 CS, 44.
3 CPLD, 296.
4 See MEC98, 321–322.
5 In program notes for the American premiere of *Symphonia*, at the Juilliard School, February 2, 2008, Carter wrote that after hearing Partita, Knussen encouraged him to write the following movements.
6 See Poulet, Georges. *The Metamorphoses of the Circle*. Trans. Carley Dawson and Elliott Coleman. Baltimore: Johns Hopkins UP, 1966. Praz, Mario. *The Flaming Heart: Essays on Crashaw, Machiavelli and Other Studies in the Relations between Italian and English Literature from Chaucer to T.S. Eliot*. Gloucester, MA: Peter Smith, 1966. Stephen Guy-Bray, "'Pulchrum Spargitur Hic Chaos': Crashaw's Meta-Commentary," *Journal for Early Modern Cultural Studies* 9, No. 1 (Spring–Summer, 2009), 147–159. Carter cited Poulet's writings in other contexts and may have been familiar with the Praz book.
7 The lengthy analytic study of the opera by Guy Capuzzo does not discuss its origins in any detail.
8 CEL, 319–330.
9 Carter's colleague, Roger Sessions, had similarly solicited a libretto, for *The Emperor's New Clothes*, from a prominent local critic, Andrew Porter, rather than from a poet or playwright.
10 See CPLD, 303–304.
11 See Capuzzo, 12.
12 CPLD, 290.
13 CEL, 94.
14 MEC98, 325–327.
15 CEL, 188.
16 For a different view of thematicism in this work see Arnold Whittall, "The search for order: Carter's *Symphonia* and late-modern thematicism", in CS.
17 Notes to the Chicago Symphony Orchestra recording of *Partita*.

18 For a more upbeat appraisal see Shreffler, "Instrumental dramaturgy as Humane Comedy."
19 Capuzzo, 15.
20 Capuzzo, 13.
21 See Carter's detailed performance suggestions for Rose in CPLD: 307–308.

CHAPTER ELEVEN

Bagatelles

Caliban: the isle is full of noises,
Sounds and sweet airs; that give delight, and hurt not.
Sometimes a thousand twangling instruments
Will hum about mine ears; and sometime voices,
That, if I then had wak'd after long sleep.
Will make me sleep again: and then, in dreaming,
The clouds methought would open, and show riches
Ready to drop upon me; that when I wak'd
I cried to dream again.

Shakespeare, *The Tempest,* Act III, scene II.

MUCH OF CARTER'S LATE INSTRUMENTAL MUSIC DISPLAYS THE EN-
ergy and high spirits of a second childhood, as if fate had decided that he could be, at long last, a *wunderkind.* The abundance and
predominantly smiling character of the music owed much to the vigorous
support Carter now received from two conductors of major American
orchestras: Daniel Barenboim at the Chicago Symphony Orchestra and
James Levine at the Boston Symphony. Along with the continued encouragement from Pierre Boulez, Heinz Holliger, and Oliver Knussen,
recognition by Barenboim and Levine provided Carter with a stream of
commissions for works both large and small. Although he remained on
less happy terms with the New York Philharmonic, he was surrounded
in his home town by a group of devoted performers, most of them previously associated with Speculum Musicae. Among them were cellist
Fred Sherry, violinist Rolf Schulte, bassist Donald Palma, oboist Stephen
Taylor, clarinetists Virgil Blackwell and Charles Neidich, pianist Ursula
Oppens, and soprano Lucy Shelton. Within the protective circle of this

local, national, and international community, Carter composed as many titles after he turned ninety as in all his previous decades.

Because of the sheer size of Carter's latest-blooming oeuvre, I will focus my discussion on a subset drawn from a checklist of my personal favorites. (I will discuss the late vocal works and his final three compositions in later chapters.)

From 1983 onward Carter composed twenty-five works for solo instruments (not counting piano compositions):

Flute: *Scrivo in vento* (1991)
Oboe: *Inner Song* (1994); *HBHH* (2007); *Figment VI* (2011)
English horn: *A 6 Letter Letter* (1996)
Clarinet: *Gra* (1993)
Bass clarinet: *Steep Steps* (2001)
Bassoon: *Retracing* (2002)
Horn: *Retracing II* (2009)
Trumpet: *Retracing III* (2009)
Trombone: *Retracing V* (2011)
Tuba: *Retracing IV* (2011)
Guitar: *Changes* (1983); *Shard* (1997)
Harp: *Inner Song* (1992)
Marimba: *Figment V* (2009)
Violin: *Riconoscenza per Goffredo Petrassi* (1984); *Fantasy—Remembering Roger* (1999); *Statement—Remembering Aaron* (1999); *Rhapsodic Musings* (2001); *Mnemosyné* (2011)
Viola: *Figment IV* (2007)
Cello: *Figment no.1* (1994); *Figment no. 2* (*Remembering Mr. Ives*) (2001)
Bass: *Figment III* (2007)

[The Retracings are all derived from earlier compositions: *Retracing I* from the *ASKO Concerto; Retracing II* from the Quintet for Piano and Winds; *Retracing III* from *A Symphony of Three Orchestras; Retracing IV* from *Soundings; Retracing V* from *Gra*.]

However brief, these works display characteristics of much of Carter's late music. Their sheer number flaunts his newfound fluency. The two sub-genres labeled in series (figment, retracing) show a willingness to compose similar works in close proximity—new for a composer who, like Debussy, had always resisted self-repetition and formulas. Many of the late works pay tribute to other musicians, either composers (Petrassi, Lutosławski, Wolpe, Holliger, Copland, Sessions, Ives) or performers (including David Starobin, Heinz Holliger, Ursula Holliger, Thomas Demenga, Fred Sherry, Robert Aitken, Virgil Blackwell, Ole Bøhn, Rolf Schulte, Robert Mann, and Alexander Carter, the composer's grandson) and sometimes both in the same work, as in *Fantasy—Remembering Roger,* whose title honors Roger Sessions while the dedication is to Rolf Schulte.

4 Lauds, a collection of violin solos that had been composed for different occasions, exemplifies the larger project that Max Noubel has termed Carter's *ultima practica*.[1] The two *Lauds* that make the strongest initial impression have contrasting characters. *Riconoscenza per Goffredo Petrassi*, composed in 1984 for the Pontino Festival, was one of the first miniatures. In a simulated improvised fashion, it interweaves three elements to sketch a portrait of Carter's Italian friend: a sweetly expressive lyrical line (*dolce legatissimo scorrevole*), jagged, rapid passages with a hint of humor (*giocosamente furioso martellato*), and a slow procession of thoughtful, sustained double-stops (*tranquillo, ben legato*).

Fantasy—Remembering Roger is also made up of contrasting ideas, but in a more expansive, open-ended and bravura manner. The character of this piece may reflect Roger Sessions' unique standing among Carter's American contemporaries. Sessions, who had studied with Ernest Bloch, was one of the few American composers of his era not shaped by Boulanger, but the two master teachers had great mutual respect and admiration. In his compositions and teachings, however, he aligned with the German tradition, especially as understood by Schoenberg, with whom Sessions, again unlike Carter, developed a close relationship. Despite all these differences, Sessions was the only American composer whom Carter viewed as a role model throughout his career. Carter admired Sessions' music from his early days when he first discovered Sessions' Symphony no. 1 (1927), Piano Sonata no. 1 (1930), and Violin Concerto (1935). In 1940 Carter praised Sessions' "devotion to the purest tradition of his art"[2] as well as his "stubborn conviction" and "intransigent rigor"—qualities often later associated, usually in non-flattering ways, with Carter himself. Carter repeated and further developed his praise for Sessions in 1959 with an extended essay on the Violin Concerto and in a pair of tributes written after Sessions' death in 1985. *Fantasy—Remembering Roger* enacts the defiant spirit that Carter shared with Sessions through ninja-level virtuosity. Ironically, this celebration of idealistic resistance yielded the one *Laud* that can serve as a surefire encore.

Both *Statement—Remembering Aaron* and *Rhapsodic Musings* (a tribute to Robert Mann, founder and long-time first violinist of the Juilliard Quartet) seem more private in their manner of praise. As he would do in pieces honoring Boulez and Holliger, Carter built *Rhapsodic Musings* on a cipher, translating Robert Mann's initials into the pitches *re* and *mi*—D and E for the non-solfèged. These pitches, audibly foregrounded throughout, give the piece its spine, but the tribute-bearing cipher communicates only to score-readers or listeners with perfect pitch and a weakness for puzzles. (Carter's abiding taste for such arcana would reappear at the opening and close of *Réflexions*, where he signaled a tribute to Pierre Boulez by striking a large stone; the French for stone, of course, is *pierre*.) In *Statement—Remembering Aaron*, musical allusions also appear in disguise. Carter said that the piece referred to two early works of Copland—*Statements*, from Copland's short "difficult" period in the early 1930s, and *Ukelele Serenade*, a brilliant memento of Copland's Jazz Age style of the 1920s. Compared to the later ballet scores, neither of these works would function as an obvious Copland identifier, but Carter's echoes of them are so distant that they would escape the notice even of listeners well versed in Copland unless they had read Carter's program note. The piece serves as a reminder that overt intertextual cross-references were never central to Carter's music the way they were in Stravinsky's or Ives' or Copland's. The only piece of Carter's to spotlight an external source is *Remembrance*, where Carter recalled the most important event in his relation to Paul Fromm by quoting, in a dramatically audible fashion, his own *Double Concerto*. While some of the gestures in *Statements—Remembering Aaron* might suggest the contrasting spaciousness and syncopated spikiness of Copland's music, it never sounds like Copland. We might say, then, that the piece represents Carter's memories of the man more than Copland's music, and so, ultimately, is more of a self-portrait. This conjecture is supported by the constantly restated presence of the two all-interval tetrachords, harmonies that had been Carter's signature since the First Quartet.[3] The convoluted impulses of this short piece, perhaps reflecting the vicissitudes of a long, sometimes contentious rivalry/friendship, and fundamental disagreements about the

role of music in society, give it a gnomic quality, psychologically fascinating but hard to convey to an audience.

The issue of quotation comes up again, and in an even more fraught
context, in relation to *Figment no. 2—Remembering Mr. Ives*, for solo cello.
Again pairing tributes to a dead composer and a living performer, Carter
dedicated the piece, composed in the spring of 2001, to Fred Sherry,
with whom he had worked closely on the Cello Concerto that Yo-Yo
Ma premiered with the Chicago Symphony in November 2001. In the
published score Carter said that the music recalled "fragmentarily bits of
the Thoreau movement of the *Concord Sonata* and *Hallowe'en*," which he
cited as works he (now) loved in particular. As in the Copland remembrance, however, these allusions are not obvious. The piece nevertheless
forcefully conveys three aspects of Ives' music: its grandeur, its religious
quality, and its occasional otherworldliness. Looking through the sketches
for the piece, I found no bits of Ives' music. I also discovered that the
term "Hymnic" that appears in measure 23 was added only after an initial reading of the music, taking the place of "tranquillo." (Carter and
Fred Sherry enact this substitution in Frank Sheffer's film.) Perhaps the
first instruction did not elicit the character Carter had intended. I fear,
though, that its replacement may encourage performers to be excessively
intertextual, suddenly altering their tone to sound piously sentimental,
remembering Uncle Charlie rather than Mr. Ives. The particular quality
of the piece, an ultimate act of reconciliation, comes through even so.

In the wake of the Piano Sonata and *Night Fantasies*, Carter seemed more
stimulated in his later years by the use of the piano in ensemble works
than on its own. The later solo piano works are mostly short occasional
pieces, some very short indeed. Taken all together they add up to around
the length of the Piano Sonata:

90+ (1994) 5' Dedicated to Goffredo Petrassi on his 90th birthday
Two Diversions (1999) 8' for Ursula Oppens
Retrouvailles (2000) 2' to Pierre Boulez on his 75th birthday
Intermittences (2005) 6' to Peter Serkin
Caténaires (2006) 4' for Pierre-Laurent Aimard
Matribute (2007) 4' to Helen Levine for James Levine

Fratribute (2008) 2'40" to James Levine for Tom Levine

Sistribute (2008) 1' to James Levine for Janet Levine

For publication Carter grouped *Intermittences* and *Caténaires* as *Two Thoughts about the Piano* and the three Levine pieces as *Tri-tribute*. We might similarly pair *90+* with *Retrouvailles*, different as they are, as composer tributes. (Carter said that *Retrouvailles* could be played as the first or last of a three-movement suite along with the two *Esprit rude / Esprit doux* Boulez homages.) With the exception of *90+*, Carter's second "laud" to Petrassi (discussed in detail in MEC98), I think the short piano works are most effective when performed as a group with their siblings.

Carnegie Hall commissioned the *Two Diversions* as part of a "Millennium" project, initiated by Ellen Taaffe Zwilich, aimed at "creating an outstanding body of new work within reach of many pianists, particularly gifted young pianists." They were first published alongside works by Rzewski, Harbison, Chen Yi, Rihm, Andriessen, Babbitt, Tan Dun, Zwilich, and Hannibal. Most of these, like Carter's contributions, seem aimed more toward the "gifted" than the "many." Carter might have better titled his *Diversions* "a young person's guide to metrical modulation." They are both two-part inventions with rhythmic complexities that might be heard as a tribute to Nancarrow if they weren't also so characteristically Carterian. In *Diversion I* one "voice" moves at the rate of MM=40 (with occasional spasmodic irregularities) throughout, but this slow pulse is notated in terms of five different tempos, creating a wide range of polyrhythmic possibilities in the relation between the steady speed of the first voice and the darting, much-varied responses of the second. In *Diversion II* one line gets faster throughout while the other gets slower. At two points the voices switch from right hand to left, so that both lines cover the range of the piano.

Intermittences and *Caténaires*, composed for two top-flight pianists, present a stark contrast of disjunction and continuity, inner-directed thoughtfulness, and bravura *éclat*. We can hear these twin *ultima practica* masterpieces as articulating the background polarities of Carter's rhythmic idiom, resonance stretching into silence and stasis, and speed at the limit of digital dexterity. They also illustrate the piano's relation to the feet as well as the fingers. The title *Intermittences* derives from "*Intermittences du Coeur*," a chapter from Proust's *Sodome et Gomorrhe*. (Its musical character, though, suggests Marcel rather than Charlus.) This nocturne-like work explores the resonating aspect of the piano through a variety of pedal effects. Phrases are played *secco*, without pedal; sustained, without pedal; sustained with the *sostenuto* (middle) pedal; and sustained with the right pedal. Pitches appear as harmonics created by depressing keys without sounding them, or as resonances captured by applying the right pedal immediately after sounding a short marcato chord. This range of playing techniques produces a scale of "silences," interruptions that may contain some traces of the piano's sound, or none.

No silences inhibit the non-stop flow of *Caténaires*, a gushing ("*Jaillissant*") stream of sixteenth notes played no slower than MM=576. The score's appearance of regularity, with one meter and one tempo throughout, is deceptive, since Carter created a web of implied cross rhythms through accents. For example, in mm. 28 to 39 the right hand accents every eleventh note; in mm. 46 to 50 it repeats the pitch D every seventh note. Carter similarly refreshed the unceasing flow of notes through frequent changes in articulation and register, so that the piece becomes a glittering, go-for-broke perpetual motion toccata, a great-grandchild of the finales of Debussy's *Pour le piano* and Ravel's *Le tombeau de Couperin*.

Listening to the three little pieces commissioned by James Levine as gifts to his mother, brother, and sister, we may feel like we are intruding on a family gathering. Not knowing the sitters it is impossible to determine the accuracy of these portraits, if that is what they are, though each has its charms. The surprising member of the group, though, is *Fratribute*, which, to my ears, evokes Copland at his most elusive, the lonely Copland heard in the quiet sections of *Music for the Theater* and the third movement of his Piano Sonata.

From 2000 onward, Carter continued to extend the line of instrumental miniatures begun with *Canon for 4*:

Hiyoku (2001) for two clarinets. For Ayako and Charles Neidich.

Au Quai (2002) for viola and bassoon. For Oliver Knussen on his 50th birthday.

Tre Duetti (Duettino, Adagio, Duettone) for violin and cello (2008–2009). To Milton Babbitt; for Rolf and Fred.

Trije glasbeniki ("Three Musicians," 2011) for flute, bass clarinet, and harp. Written for an all-Carter festival held in Ljubljana, Slovenia, in November 2011; dedicated to Erica Goodman, Robert Aitken, and Virgil Blackwell.

Rigmarole (2011) for cello and bass clarinet. For Fred and Virgil.

As with the earlier miniatures, the late ones were written for friends, mostly old, a few new. We tend to think of Carter as a contrapuntist rather than a colorist but the appeal to the ear of these short pieces, which resemble each other in form and texture, springs from their particular timbres. Three of the duos derive their special character by pairing instruments of the same register: high (*Hiyoku*), middle (*Au Quai*), and low (*Rigmarole*).

Hiyoku can serve to illustrate how these late duets put the emphasis on communion (amorous rather than spiritual) rather than opposition. In a note in the published score Carter wrote that the title was suggested by Ayako Neidich because it was "a very special poetic word originally used by the ancient Chinese poet, Bi Juyi, and adopted by old Japanese authors, meaning two birds flying together with the connotation of eternal love." The note concludes with a relevant (though unattributed) poem:

. . . In the heavens we shall be two wings
Flying side by side
On earth two roots
Intertwined into one stem! . . .

The form of the piece suggests a bird taking flight with a three part design: two "wings"—one stirring, the other fluttering—surround a central "body" of tranquil music in the low register that converges on a shared middle C (concert pitch). The two clarinets are not opponents, even though they have distinctive musical identities very much like the flute and clarinet in the first *Esprit rude/esprit doux*. Each has its own repertoire of intervals and tempos. In the central section, for instance, Clarinet I sustains notes to the value of eleven triplet eighths at the tempo of quarter=96, while Clarinet II sustains notes to the value of fifteen sixteenth notes, thus producing cross-tempos of MM 26.18 and 25.6. While each clarinet in this passage maintains its musical identity, the passage emphasizes the harmonic intervals created by their combined motion. As the lines interweave, they sound all the possible intervals from unison to major seventh. Many appearances of the all-triad hexachord and the two all-interval tetrachords suggest a more covert connection between the two lines—but I leave that matter to the music theorists.

Longer Chamber Works

With the String Quartet no. 5 (1995), Carter took leave of the genre with which he was most strongly identified, but he continued to write longer works for a variety of chamber ensembles, some traditional, others not so much:

Luimen for trumpet, trombone, vibraphone, mandolin, guitar, and harp (1997), 12'; for the Nieuw Ensemble

Quintet for Piano and String Quartet (1997), 16'; for Ursula Oppens and the Arditti String Quartet

Oboe Quartet (2001) 17'; for Heinz Holliger

Mosaic for harp and ensemble (2004) 10'; commissioned by the Nash Ensemble, in memory of Carlos Salzedo; scored for harp, flute (alto flute, piccolo), oboe (English horn), clarinet in B flat (bass clarinet), violin, viola, cello, bass

Clarinet Quintet (2007), 15'; for the Juilliard quartet and Charles Neidich

Tintinnabulation for percussion sextet (2008), 9'; for Frank Epstein

Nine by Five for woodwind quintet (2009), 8'; to Joseph Polisi; for Charles Neidich and the New York Woodwind Quintet

String Trio (2011), 7'; for Rolf Schulte, Richard O'Neill, and Fred Sherry

Double Trio for trumpet, trombone, percussion, piano, violin, and cello (2011), 8'; to the Arte Musica Foundation; to Pierre Bourgie

Epigrams for Violin, Cello and Piano (2012), 12'(unfinished); for Pierre-Laurent Aimard

None of these works fills the twenty- to twenty-five-minute dimensions of Carter's earlier chamber music, but, more important, they also depart from the complex multi-layered collage forms so characteristic of Carter's style from the Concerto for Orchestra to the Quintet for Piano and Winds. Already in the Quintet for Piano and String Quartet, a two-part dialogue between the piano and the quartet takes the place of the more complicated interplay of solos, duos, and trios from the earlier quintet with winds. With several pinches of salt we might say that the Quintet for piano and winds has the heft of Brahms, while the quintet with strings has the *leggerezza* of Mendelssohn.[4]

Both written in 1997, *Luimen* and the Quintet for Piano and String Quartet followed in the wake of *Allegro scorrevole*, and share, perhaps even surpass, its lightness of spirit. *Luimen* also shares with a nearly contemporary work, the Clarinet Concerto, the stamp of Boulez's friendship. The non-standard ensemble of *Luimen*, featuring a whole family of "instruments of short duration" (as Schoenberg called them), harp, mandolin, guitar, and vibraphone, recalls the jangling sounds of Boulez's *Éclat* (1965), which used the same short-duration instruments plus piano, celesta, glocken-spiel, tubular bells, and cimbalom.

Sonority, however, is just one aspect of *Luimen* that marks it as the beginning of a new phase in Carter's music. The title, selected by the Dutch musicians of the Nieuw Ensemble, could be translated as "whimsy," a quality often found in Carter's music from the 1940s that resurfaced in the miniatures of the 1980s. The informality of *Luimen* may reflect the unusual way it was composed. For a commission from David Starobin, Carter had composed *Shard*, a short, brilliant guitar solo. In *Luimen*, he gave *Shard* a second life by incorporating it liter-ally into an ensemble piece. It appears in measures 126–197. Unless we include the multiple arrangements of the *Elegy* and the orchestrations of *Voyage* and *Pastoral, Luimen* was Carter's first "retracing." Unlike the later series with that title, however, it derives an ensemble work from a solo rather than the reverse. We can see this recycling as an erosion of Carter's earlier ideal of making each work unique, with its own idiom and form. In the late phase that notion of autonomy gives way to a looser, more forgiving aesthetic, where individual pieces appear as fragments of a larger, encompassing vision.

That change in perspective also appears in the more casual formal structures of the late works. Many of them are chains of short movements without the countervailing through-composed strategies and double-forms found in the string quartets. Though played without pauses, *Luimen* clearly falls into four sections: an introductory conversation between the instruments, a mysteriously spare slow movement, *Shard* (retraced with accompaniment), and a whirling, accelerating finale. Except for a short "preview" in the introductory section, Carter does not signal or motivate the guitarist's star turn in the third section of the piece; it just happens, leaving the listener freer than had been Carter's practice to relate the parts to the whole.

Before we rush to consign all of late Carter to the category of easy listening, we might first consider the Quartet for Oboe and String Trio (aka Oboe Quartet), commissioned by the Lucerne Festival for Heinz

Holliger. Max Noubel told me that he considered this work the "Sixth Quartet." Like String Quartets 2, 4, and 5, it assigns each of its players a distinctive repertory of intervals, though, as in other late works, the clearly-etched individuals are not antagonists. The work presents a great variety of textures and moods within a seventeen-minute span. Like its fellow late long-form works it is a sequence of miniature movements, highlighting different groupings of instruments. In his liner note for the 2008 recording by the Swiss Chamber Soloists (supervised by Holliger), Noubel identified these as following:

1. Moderato (exposing characterizing material of each instrument)
2. Maestoso (violin and viola)
3. Moderato leggiero (oboe and viola)
4. Andante appassionata (oboe and cello)
5. Tranquillo (oboe, violin, viola)
6. Allegro agitato (viola and cello)
7. Andante (violin and cello playing legato; oboe and viola, staccato and pizzicato)
8. Allegro fantastic (oboe and violin duet)

There is also an element of recurrence in the score. The oboe brings the Allegro agitato to a halt by re-sounding the repeated G heard at the outset of the work; the Allegro fantastic, with its giddy, quasi-operatic pairing of the two soprano instruments, ends with a coda that recalls many of the previous movements.

Mosaic

One of the skills that Carter learned in his studies with Nadia Boulanger was the ability to imagine all the possibilities of a particular instrument just from looking at fingering charts and orchestration books. (Carter recommended those by Casella and Koechlin to his students even though they had never been translated into English.) He preferred formulating the abstract potential of an instrument in schematic form to the study of repertory. With the harp, for instance, most composers would follow the examples of Ravel and Britten. Rather than steeping himself in older repertory, Carter composed the elaborate guitar part of *Syringa*, for example, on the basis of a beginning how-to-play manual he bought at a Woolworth's five-and-dime a few blocks from Juilliard. No single instrument engaged his imagination, however, more than the harp—a fascination that went back to his discovery of Carlos Salzedo's *Modern Study of the Harp*, published in 1921 and still in print.[5] This interest bore late fruit in *Bariolage, Immer Neu, Mosaic*, a concertino for harp and seven players that Carter dedicated to Salzedo's memory, and *Trije glasbeniki*.

On several occasions Carter groused that, ever since he composed the brief but challenging harp solo in his *Variations*, no two harpists could agree on what passages in his music were unplayable, or merely difficult, or on how to correct problematic spots. Heinz Holliger told me that when Carter was composing *Mosaic* he asked Nancy Allen, harpist of the New York Philharmonic, if he could borrow her instrument for an hour, and, even though he had no training as a harpist, tested out various effects on his own. As the title suggests, *Mosaic*, though composed in 2004, reverts to Carter's earlier cut-up method, but in two different respects. Even more than in the two pieces he had written for Ursula Holliger, Carter endeavored to include every special effect associated with Salzedo and juxtaposed them throughout. Older harp techniques like harmonics and "*près de la table*" alternate with such Salzedo inventions as xylophonics, rustling glissando, slap pizzicato, snare drum effects, whistling sounds, string noise, and "thunder." In form the work similarly juxtaposes strophes for different combinations of instruments, often, but not always, treating the harp, winds and strings as separate elements. As in much of Carter's late music, however, a central, sparse slow movement holds the greatest interest. Here long held notes in the strings convey a sense of timelessness, punctuated by firefly flashes in the winds and harp.

Tintinnabulation

Given the influence that both Henry Cowell and Edgar Varèse exerted on the young, impressionable Carter through their ideas, music, and friendship, and also given his later friendship with Lou Harrison, it is curious that Carter did not pursue their development of percussion music until the *Double Concerto*. Even there his approach was closer to that of European composers like Stockhausen and Xenakis than to the Americans whom Virgil Thomson dubbed the "rhythmic research boys." From his work on the *Double Concerto* onward, however, Carter never lost his fascination with the resources of percussion instruments. Every time he wrote for percussion he introduced an instrument or a method of playing that he had not used before. Nevertheless, he did not write a piece for percussion ensemble until his one-hundredth year. *Tintinnabulation* premiered on December 2, 2008.

Composed for the New England Conservatory Percussion Ensemble, *Tintinnabulation* calls for six percussionists who play sixty-seven instruments with fifteen different beaters, including brass-headed mallets, metal knitting needles, and a Mahler Hammer (as in the blows of fate in the Sixth Symphony). As the Poe-inspired title would suggest, bell-like metal percussion is particularly important to the sound of the work, although wood and skin instruments are given their due. Conspicuously absent are pitched percussion instruments like timpani, marimba, or glockenspiel. The challenge to the composer was to shape six minutes of music without the resources of melody or harmony. The piece also challenges listeners to attune their ears to a musical argument based solely on timbre and rhythm.

Historically, most European and American percussion music had its roots in exotic idioms, beginning with the "Turkish" music of the classical period, which associated percussion with military music—a link still audible in Varèse's *Ionization*, whose main theme is a swaggering *marche militaire*. The American percussion music of Cowell, Cage, and Harrison was greatly influenced by the Balinese gamelan, while Steve Reich's *Drumming* derives from his study of West African music. Following the ideas of the Futurists, some twentieth-century European percussion music, and, most famously, George Antheil's *Ballet mécanique*, used percussion to suggest the noises of factories or battlefields or airplanes.

Tintinnabulation, by contrast, is neither noise-music nor, despite the globe-spanning variety of its instrumentation, "world music." Rather than treating the percussion as an Other, it shapes its argument by articulating different scales of values, filling time and space with sounds that range from very low to very high, slow to fast, soft to loud, short or extended (either by being allowed to resonate, or by being rolled). The precise way that Carter imagined every individual sound through fresh pairings of instrument and beater would be remarkable for a fifty-year-old composer. At nearly twice that age this acuity is astonishing.

We might hear *Tintinnabulation* as a didactic work, designed to heighten the listener's awareness of subtle shadings in sound. The episodic form spotlights each family of percussion, wood, metal, and skin,

in its own "movement." As in much late Carter, these movements alternate with ritornelli.[6] The music begins with a fanfare-like barrage of
short notes for all three families. The next section features wood percussion: wood drum, maracas, wood blocks, temple blocks, claves, shaker, log
drum, climaxing in an extended solo by the fifth percussionist on temple
blocks and wood blocks. After a second section for all three families—
a conceptual ritornello—there is a slow movement for metal percussion: tamtams, cymbals, gongs, Almglocken (Alpine cowbells), Chinese
nipple gongs. After a climactic Almglocken solo, the slow movement
echoes on in a shadowy, barely audible rustle of rolled snare drums. The
mixed-family ritornello then reappears, leading, via a solo on the congas
and bongos, to a section for skin percussion: tomtoms, snare drums,
bongos, congas, and Carter's old friend, the North African darbouka.
A closing coda again reunites the families in a way that recalls the very
opening but introduces a few instruments not previously featured: large
ratchet, brake drum (played with a steel hammer), and, most sensationally,
Chinese opera gong.

Most of the works for large ensembles composed after the *Allegro
scorrevole* are concertante in character. We can divide them into three
groups; space will only permit extended discussion of one or two works
from each group:

    Ensemble concertos:

ASKO Concerto (2000) Dedicated to the ASKO Ensemble NL; 15'
Boston Concerto (2002) Commissioned by the Boston Symphony Orchestra; ded-
    icated to "my wife Helen"; 19'

The *ASKO* and *Boston* concertos are similar in form, quite different in
sound. The first is scored for a chamber orchestra with sixteen players;
the second, for large orchestra. Both pieces alternate ritornelli for
the full ensemble with episodes for smaller groups of instruments. In
ASKO the ritornelli are *maestoso* in character, somewhat suggestive
of the granitic Yankee seriousness of Carl Ruggles. The contrasting
episodes are played by oboe, horn, and viola (*giocoso*); clarinet and bass
(*Allegretto lyrico*); bass clarinet, muted trombone, and cello (*Tranquillo*);
trumpet and violin (*con intensità*); piccolo, xylophone, celesta, and harp

(*leggierissimo*); and, finally, bassoon (*con umóre*). (Carter recycled the bassoon solo in his first *Retracing*.) This carefully planned variety of timbres keeps the sound fresh without resorting to any "new sounds." Although it was written for a Dutch ensemble, the tough, uncosmetic mien of the piece exemplifies the aesthetic priorities of the Uptown New York scene.

By contrast the *Boston Concerto* displays Carter's under-appreciated orchestral wizardry. Composed in 2002, it was the fourth and final work that Carter dedicated to his wife Helen; she died six weeks after the premiere on April 3, 2003. (Previous works dedicated to Helen were the Symphony no. 1, *Duo*, and *Anniversary*.) At the front of the published score Carter placed a quotation from William Carlos Williams:

As the rain falls
so does
    your love
bathe every
    open
Object of the world—

The evocation of falling rain forms the ritornello thread that binds the episodes of the piece. Drawing on a whole palette of short-duration sounds, Carter mixed pizzicato strings, flickering woodwinds, staccato, muted brass, wood percussion, piano, and harp in ever-changing combinations in seven statements spread across the entire piece. The intervening episodes seem, at first, to follow a concerto for orchestra logic, spotlighting different sections in turn: flutes and clarinets; vibraphone, piano and harp; violas and basses; the brass choir; double reeds; violins and cellos. The juxtaposition, however, has a more important dramatic function. In contrast to the rapid patter of the "rain music," the episodes are mainly slow and meditative, but whereas the "rain" ritornelli exist in the moment, always changing yet always the same, the episodes gradually increase in their emotional intensity, building to an expressive climax worthy of Mahler in the Maestoso movement for violins and cellos. As the warmth of these episodes slowly increases so too does the pathos of their contrast with the "rain music" whose glistening beauty transcends emotion. The concerto slowly reveals itself as a heart-felt *tombeau*.

Between 2003 and 2012 Carter composed six works for piano and orchestra:

Dialogues (2003) commissioned by the BBC; dedicated to Nicholas Hodges; 14'
Soundings (2005) dedicated to Daniel Barenboim; 10'
Interventions (2007) commissioned by the Boston Symphony Orchestra and the
   Staatsoper Berlin; dedicated to Daniel Barenboim and James Levine; 15'
Conversations (2010) for solo percussion, piano and orchestra; dedicated to Colin
   Currie and Pierre-Laurent Aimard; 7'
Two Controversies and a Conversation (expanded version of Conversations, 2011);
   Commissioned by the New York Philharmonic; 11'
Dialogues II (2012) commissioned by Teatro La Scala and by Staatsoper Unter
   den Linden, Berlin "For Daniel Barenboim on the occasion of his 70th
   birthday"; 5'

While clearly creations of the same composer, the late works for piano and orchestra vary widely in sound and mood. Carter scored the two *Dialogues* for small orchestra without percussion. *Soundings* and *Interventions*, both for large orchestras, were composed largely as alternate passages for piano and orchestra so that they could be conducted from the keyboard. The two versions of *Conversation(s)* pair the solo piano with an alter-ego solo percussionist.

We can see the range of mood in these works by comparing *Dialogues I* and the unfortunately titled *Interventions*. If I had the power I would re-name both pieces. *Dialogues I* feels like a one-movement concerto. If Carter felt reluctant to call it his second piano concerto, because it is so different in every way from his first, he might have followed Stravinsky's example and named it "Capriccio." However dialogic the format of the piece may be in its interplay of piano, winds and strings, the piano easily dominates the conversation—in a good way. It all begins rather grimly with the tempo indication "*Mesto*," a rare usage for Carter (more familiar from Bartók's Sixth Quartet), and a mournful English horn solo (recalling the one in *Partita*). Carter began to compose the music shortly after Helen's death, so its dark tone is what we might expect, yet the mood of sadness does not prevail. With its entrance, the piano expands and extends the English horn's terse eulogy, and, in no short time, transforms the sound of grief to celebration. The charm of the piece is its mercurial unpredictability from phrase to phrase. Moving away from the episodic form of the preceding clarinet, cello, *ASKO*, and *Boston* concerti, Carter once again achieved the emancipated, free-associational continuity he had pursued twenty years earlier in the *Duo*, *Syringa*, and *Night Fantasies*, but with much more lucid textures and a simpler thematic process. Its variety of events all stem from a small set of ideas, beginning with the English horn's opening exposition of the all-triad hexachord.

If *Dialogues I* quickly moves away from its initial sadness, *Interventions*, which premiered a few days before Carter's hundredth birthday, reverses that course soon after a deceptively humorous beginning. A kerfuffle between orchestra and piano on the pitches A and B♭ (A and B in German) that might be a whimsical nod to the two maestros named in the dedication, soon emerges as an existential question—"A or B?"—that prompts extreme, dramatic mood swings between Carter Light and Carter Dark. (Since Xenakis had already used the apt title "Morsima/amorsima," perhaps a title without the distracting contemporary connotations of "interventions" could be found in *King Lear* or *Paradise Lost*.) The music throughout has a spacious, monumental character. Like *Soundings*, it can be conducted from the keyboard and is built in alternating phrases for piano and orchestra. Here the piano is aided by two trios of solo instruments: flute, bassoon, and trumpet; oboe, clarinet, and horn. But while *Soundings* contrasts the piano's statements with different subgroups of the orchestra (most sensationally with a trio of piccolos), *Interventions* pivots between fast, textural music and slow, wide-ranging expressive melodies intoned at different times by the piano and its entourage and by every member of the orchestra. Two essential aspects of human existence, which we might term energy (*élan vital*) and pathos (*lacrimae rerum*), are spread out before us; which to choose? The ending, returning to A and B♭, now trilled by the entire ensemble, suggests that they are finally inseparable.

In his late late period Carter composed five non-keyboard concertos:

Clarinet Concerto (1996) dedicated to Alain Damiens and Ensemble Intercontemporain on its 20th anniversary; 18'

Cello Concerto (2000) commissioned by the Chicago Symphony Orchestra; dedicated to Fred Sherry; 18'

Horn Concerto (2006) commissioned by the Boston Symphony Orchestra; dedicated to James Levine and James Sommerville; 12'

Flute Concerto (2008) dedicated to Elena Bashkirova (wife of Daniel Barenboim); 13'

Concertino for Bass Clarinet and chamber orchestra (2009) dedicated to Virgil Blackwell; 9.'

Clarinet Concerto

For his Clarinet Concerto Carter broke the orchestra into six small groups. Each small ensemble dominates one of the first six movements in turn (the seventh brings all together) and in the course of the work the clarinetist can wander from one group to the next. This format pays homage to Boulez, who commissioned the concerto. The French composer had done something very similar in his own *Domaines* for clarinet and six instrumental groups (composed between 1961 and 1968). The two works don't sound anything alike, however, and exemplify the profound differences in aesthetic sensibilities between the two composers, who nevertheless expressed the greatest admiration for each other's music. Putting it crassly, we might say that Boulez's highest priority was sound while Carter's was form. With a bit more nuance, we might observe that through his experiments with mobile forms (the episodes in *Domaines* can be played in different orders) and his habit of extending older pieces to create new ones, Boulez challenged assumptions about musical unity and the relationship between composition and performance. Carter's preference for ordinary sounds over unusual ones, on the other hand, allowed him to use a much greater range of colors, from the sensuous to the painful, than Boulez usually deployed. I think Carter underscored that point with the long solo for contrabass clarinet in his last big tribute to Boulez, *Réflexions*. Far from our usual sense of musical beauty, it sounds like a strange creature emerging from the ocean's floor.

The Clarinet Concerto established the formal model Carter would follow in most of the subsequent concertante works. There are six short movements, each played by the clarinet with one of the orchestral subgroups. These are linked by brief interludes that presage a closing *Agitato* movement that finally pits the soloist against the entire orchestra. An outline of the form can show how this format produces a wide range of moods within a short time span:

1. *Scherzando*: for clarinet, percussion (mainly pitched), harp and piano
2. *Deciso*: clarinet and non-pitched percussion
3. *Tranquillo*: clarinet and muted brass
4. *Presto* (as fast as possible): for clarinet and woodwinds
5. *Largo*: clarinet and strings
6. *Giocoso*: clarinet and open brass
7. *Agitato*: clarinet and tutti

Throughout the piece we hear brief entrances of the instrumental groups not featured in a particular movement. These passing appearances create the impression that six kinds of music are actually unfolding throughout, their separate, submerged streams finally surfacing and converging in the last movement.

The concertos for cello, horn, flute, and bass clarinet each contain passages resembling movements from the Clarinet Concerto, especially its second and fifth movements. The Cello Concerto seems to retrace its predecessor's seven movement structure. These recurrences might appear formulaic, but they are consistent with Carter's willingness, in his *ultima practica*, to compose works whose overt similarities allow the listener to concentrate on less obvious differences. The clarinet and cello concertos sound like siblings, but where the first was written for a compact new music ensemble, the second was commissioned by a great orchestra for a premiere by a star soloist, Yo-Yo Ma.

We might detect in the Cello Concerto a certain ambivalence about this liaison to the musical establishment, but Carter used this unease to shape the work's narrative line. The opening and closing sections recall the cello concertos of the standard repertory, an echo Alisa Weilerstein amplified when she recorded (with the Staatskapelle Berlin under Barenboim) Carter's concerto alongside Elgar's. The two works begin with similar-sounding recitatives that announce the weightiness of their protagonists' musical characters with echoes of Bach's solo suites. At the end of Carter's concerto, the orchestra interrupts a lightly scored fast movement with a fortissimo twelve-tone barrage. However dissonant, this passage announces a coming cadenza, serving the same function as a second-inversion tonic triad in older concertos. The soloist obliges with a final display of virtuosity that recalls the quadruple stop chords of the opening recitative and the rapid-fire passage-work of the last large section, Allegro fantastic. At other places, however, the concerto's relation to tradition takes more ironic forms. In the Allegro appassionato that follows the opening recitative, the cello sings out an intense lyrical line but gets little encouragement or support from the orchestra which counters the cello's legato with a sporadic, staccato filigree that occasionally converges in hostile-sounding clouds. The Giocoso that follows pits the soloist against unpitched percussion, as in the second movement of the Clarinet Concerto. Here, though, the cello's syncopated sixteenth notes suggest that it would rather be playing at a jazz club than at Orchestra Hall. In the central Maestoso movement, the brass takes on the countercultural role of the percussion in the Giocoso while the soloist reasserts its classical side with a return to the recitative style of the opening. In the two slow movements, one written in the cello's lowest register, the second in its highest, the orchestral mass seems to vanish altogether, the accompaniment reduced to barely audible, nearly motionless wisps for string harmonics and low winds. These meditative movements, which have their counterparts in the clarinet, flute, and horn concertos, are the particular glory of Carter's late style. In the dramatic context of the Cello Concerto we may hear them as the opposite pole to the opening and closing, a private sphere far from the public-facing gestures of the work's frame.

In his last decade Carter also composed a short list of non-concertante pieces for large ensembles:

Réflexions (2004) composed for the Ensemble Intercontemporain; dedicated to Pierre Boulez on his 80th birthday "*avec mille souhaits amitié affection et admiration*"; 10'

Sound Fields for string orchestra (2007); commissioned by the Tanglewood Music Center; dedicated to Ellen Highstein; 4'

Wind Rose for wind ensemble (2008); commissioned by the BBC; dedicated to Oliver Knussen; 6'

Three Illusions for Orchestra; commissioned by the Boston Symphony Orchestra[7]:

    1. *Micomicón* (2002); dedicated to James Levine; 3'

2. *Fons Juventatis* (2004); dedicated to James Levine and the Boston Symphony Orchestra; 3'

3. *More's Utopia* (2004); dedicated to James Levine and the Boston Symphony Orchestra; 3'

Instances for chamber orchestra (2012); commissioned by the Seattle Symphony; dedicated to Ludovic Morlot; 8'

Perhaps the most unexpected of these was *Sound Fields* for string orchestra, inspired by the Color Field paintings of Helen Frankenthaler. Working without a primer, Frankenthaler let her pigments soak into the canvas. Free of the agitated surface of much abstract expressionism, the resultant glowing colors became the essence of her paintings. At the same time her paintings were strongly evocative of the natural world. In emulation of these paintings, Carter restricted the dynamic of *Sound Fields* to a uniform mezzopiano and limited the articulation entirely to bowed notes played without vibrato and with only a few notes slightly emphasized with a tenuto indication—never accented or *sforzando*. In this meditative study in sonority, there are no short or rapid sounds at all. At its Tanglewood premiere many in the audience heard echoes of the strings in Ives' *Unanswered Question*, while others related its mood to the un-Carterian sound world of Morton Feldman, though Copland's *Quiet City* and Schoenberg's "*Farben*," op. 16, no. 3, might also come to mind. Never before had Carter composed music so lacking in rhythmic and rhetorical contrast, so intently focused on a particular timbral sphere. *Sound Fields* made such a powerful impact that Oliver Knussen asked Carter to compose a companion piece for wind instruments, and on December 16, 2008, Knussen conducted the premiere of *Wind Rose* in the Barbican Hall, London. Carter scored the successor for a Mahlerian twenty-four-piece woodwind section: piccolo, three flutes, two alto flutes, bass flute, three oboes, two English horns, clarinet in E flat, three clarinets in B flat, three bass clarinets, contrabass clarinet, three bassoons, and contrabassoon. Heard back to back, the two pieces display intriguing similarities and differences, all presented as if on the verge of eternity. I would propose, though, a larger gallery for the diptych, which might bring out their special character even more: a five movement suite of *Sound Fields, Tintinnabulation, Wind Rose,* either *Soundings* or *Instances* (which I'll discuss in the penultimate chapter) and then a reprise of *Sound Fields.* Just saying. . . .

Notes

1 The published score prints the four pieces out of chronological order without explanation. Since Carter termed *4 Lauds* a collection rather than a suite, the printed order does not indicate a preferred performance order, but rather serves to facilitate page turns within each individual piece.

2 CEL, 50.

3 For the role played by these tetrachords see the analysis by Brendan P. McConville in *iSCI: The Composer's Perspective* 1, no. 1.

4 In my reading of the score I can imagine it performed somewhat more playfully, less aggressively, than on the Oppens/Arditti recording.

5 CEL, 82.

6 See Marguerite Boland's discussion of ritornello form in CS, 80–109.

7 For an extended discussion of *Three Illusions* see Max Noubel's analysis in CS.

CHAPTER TWELVE

Carter vs. Poets (Round 2)

No poet, no artist of any art, has his complete meaning alone. His significance, his appreciation, is the appreciation of this relation to the dead poets and artists.

—*T.S. Eliot, "Tradition and the Individual Talent" (1919)*

I N THE FINAL YEARS OF CARTER'S LIFE, AND RIGHT AFTER HIS DEATH, many critics who previously had been hostile to his music praised the very late works for achieving, at long last, an engaging lucidity. They had not yet taken into account, however, the weightier and darker pursuit of his last decade, seven works for voice and large ensembles to texts by the founding generation of American modernist poetry. As rich and varied as the late instrumental works may be, these vocal cycles, about 90 minutes of music altogether, have the appearance of a final testament, though their full significance may only become clear once recordings for all become widely available. The works, in chronological order:

Of Rewaking Three Poems of William Carlos Williams for mezzo-soprano and
    orchestra (2002); dedicated to Daniel Barenboim; 17'
      I. The Rewaking
      II. Lear
      III. Shadows

In the Distances of Sleep for mezzo-soprano and chamber ensemble (2006); poems
    by Wallace Stevens; dedicated to James Levine; 15'
      I. Puella Parvula
      II. Metamorphosis
      III. Re-statement of Romance
      IV. The Wind Shifts
      V. The Roaring Wind
      VI. God is Good. It is a Beautiful Night

On Conversing with Paradise for baritone and chamber ensemble (2008); poetry by Ezra Pound: Pisan Canto 81 and an excerpt from Canto 120; dedicated to Oliver Knussen; 12'

What are Years 5 poems of Marianne Moore for soprano and chamber orchestra (2008–2009), dedicated to Pierre-Laurent Aimard; 14'
>   I. Like a Bulwark
>   II. That Harp You Play so Well
>   III. The Being So-Called Human
>   IV. To an Intra-Mural Rat
>   V. What Are Years

A Sunbeam's Architecture, 6 poems of e.e. cummings for tenor and chamber orchestra (2010); dedicated to Daniel Barenboim and "to my son, David, and Carol Parks"; 11'
>   I. your little voice
>   II. no man
>   III. my sweet old etcetera
>   IV. love
>   V. it's jolly odd
>   VI. somewhere

Three Explorations drawn from T.S. Eliot's *Four Quartets* for baritone, winds and brass (2011); dedicated to Henri Dutilleux; 10'
>   I. The River
>   II. Time and the Bell
>   III. The Fire and the Rose

The American Sublime Five Poems of Wallace Stevens for baritone and large ensemble (2011); dedicated to James Levine, 14'
>   I. The American Sublime
>   II. The Woman in Sunshine
>   III. This Solitude of Cataracts
>   IV. Life in Motion
>   V. This is the thesis (from "Ésthetique du mal")

Carter's interest in these poets went back to his high school and college years. All six had published a literary landmark well before Carter graduated from Harvard:

e.e. cummings: *Tulips and Chimneys* (1923)
T.S. Eliot: *The Waste Land* (1922)

Marianne Moore: *Observations* (1924)
Ezra Pound: *Personae* (1926)
Wallace Stevens: *Harmonium* (1923)
William Carlos Williams: *Al Que Quiere!* (1917)

Why did Carter undertake this epic project? One possible answer might simply be nostalgia—a very old man recalling the literary enthusiasms of his youth, eighty years earlier. In returning to these poets, however, Carter did not limit himself to poetry from that time. Many of the poems that he chose were written later, some as late as the 1960s. A nostalgic intent seems more obvious in the instrumental pieces remembering Ives, Copland, and Sessions—artists with whom, unlike any of the six poets, Carter had important personal connections. The vocal works, by contrast, are far more complicated in their relations to the dead.

Listening to all seven cycles (actually six cycles and a dramatic *scena*), it becomes clear that they face both the past and the future, raising questions about both origins and legacies. At several points earlier in his career, Carter had attempted to locate his work within a constructed tradition. Previously he had emphasized his role as a successor to both European modernist composers (Debussy, Stravinsky, Schoenberg, Bartók) and American ultra-modernists (Ives, Varèse, Cowell, Nancarrow). With these late song cycles, however, Carter reconfigured his own artistic origins by designating poets rather than composers as his true precursors. In returning to the poets he had read at Harvard, a time when he was not yet a seriously committed musician, he separated the story of his creative impulses from that of his musical education, portraying the latter as a means to realize the former. This group of poets, moreover, provided him with precedents for difficulty independent of specific musical techniques.

Carter made the future-facing aspect of these works clear by his choice of texts. Many of them are retrospective crisis poems that struggle to make sense of a life's work in the face of mortality and with an eye to the judgments of generations to come. They are poems about legacy. Whether in secular or religious term, they confront Last Things, albeit mainly in a non-religious fashion. Moore asks: "What are years / What is our innocence / what is our guilt?" Pound responds: "What thou lov'st well is thy true heritage." Eliot foresees "A condition of complete simplicity / (Costing not less than everything)." Williams declares: "Sooner or later / we must come to the end / of striving." Stevens asks: "how does one feel?" And answers: "the sublime comes down / To the spirit itself, / The spirit and space, / The empty spirit / In vacant space." These questions and answers make the seven cycles Carter's expansive equivalent to the Four Serious Songs of Brahms.

As with *In Sleep, In Thunder*, Carter's late cycles are open to contradictory readings. An ambiguity is built into their very structures. In two of the cycles he respected the poet's intentions by setting complete poems, not excerpted lines, but in the others he aggressively refashioned the original poems. In all seven cycles he ignored the chronological order of publication, or groupings created by the poets, shuffling early poems and late ones, poems that are familiar with others that are obscure. Uniting, framing, and sometimes abbreviating disparate texts, the cycles lay out thematic narratives of Carter's making. Taken as a summation of Carter's work, the seven cycles can be interpreted ultimately as an epic self-portrait, with each of the six poets serving in turn as a persona. Carter presented his "many selves" behind six very different masks. Some fit better than others.

Because they have few precedents in American music, Carter's late cycles present great challenges to the singers even beyond negotiating the bits of Greek, Italian, and Middle English in the Pound cycle, or deciphering lines in Stevens like "Ruffling its common reflections, thought-like Monadnocks." All six poets exercised their right to be inscrutable, a modernistic form of poetic license that Schubert and Mahler never had to face. The English language itself, with its diphthongs, abundance of schwa-sounds, and colliding consonants can appear more awkward to sing, at least in a high-register classical manner, than Italian or German. And Carter did not help with occasional infelicities like setting "different" as a three-syllable word (just as he had done with "chocolate" in *What Next?*). Although he made a point of limiting his project to American verse, he did not instruct singers to use an American inflection. Some of the recorded performances, with rolled r-sounds and British-sounding vowels, make no effort in this direction. To my ears, Nicholas Phan's recording of *A Sunbeam's Architecture* provides a model of how to get the words across clearly and without affectation, as does Lucy Shelton's recording of the Zukofsky songs.[1]

Of Rewaking, for mezzo-soprano and medium-size orchestra, the first
cycle, already presents some of the conundrums and pleasures that will
reappear in the subsequent cycles. Rather than setting such signature
early Williams poems as "The Red Wheelbarrow" or "This is just to say,"
Carter chose instead three lesser-known later verses, beginning with the
last poem from *Pictures from Brueghel*, Williams' last published volume. In
setting them, however, Carter chose to ignore one of the most defining
aspects of Williams' style: line breaks. On the page the first stanza of "The
rewaking" takes this form:

> Sooner or later
> we must come to the end
> of striving.

The line breaks clarify the accentual metrics of the poem with two
stresses in the first line, three in the second, one in the third. They also
call attention to the word "end," placed before a line break. In the music,
however, Carter set the first two stanzas as a single continuous phrase
without any indications of the line breaks, fusing the lines and stanzas as
if they were prose. Imposing a musical design that overrides poetic meter,
Carter smoothed over Williams' gapped verse to focus on a central theme,
the revival of life through the power of love.

Carter solidified Williams' fractured forms as well. Rather than
preserving the cubist appearance of the poem, the song outlines the form
of the Baroque aria da capo, ABA'. After the short orchestral introduction, the singer intones a sensuous, tripartite melody against a drowsy
instrumental countermelody surrounded by an early-morning haze. The
first phrase is accompanied by the strings, the second by the winds, the
third by both, with occasional punctuations throughout by piano, harp,
and percussion. The agitation of the middle phrase, something we expect in an ABA design, here takes on a suggestion of sexual arousal in
the image of "the violet, the very lady's slipper." In relation to the entire
cycle, then, "The Rewaking" might be termed an erotic aubade, hinting
at the more disruptive visions that follow.

"Lear" comes from *The Clouds*, published in 1948 and reflects the
war years, "when the world takes over for us / and the storm in
the trees / replaces our brittle consciousness." The poem's densely-
packed, ambiguously un-punctuated argument unfolds on three

levels. One concerns the poet's identity in the fact of violence: "Was it I?" The second pictures Lear on the heath, raving against the storm, as the poet's imagined predecessor who perhaps should have "yielded earlier" to the storm's overwhelming power. The third level, harder to connect neatly to the others, but ultimately the core, involves images of women and ships "female to all seas." (Ships belong to the small class of inanimate English nouns assigned a grammatically feminine gender.) The return of the storm "makes wives" (battered wives?) of everyone, and as "Wife" to the storm's power, Lear, the poem says, should have submitted to it and adopted a wise passivity symbolized by the "figures of women at repose" that confront the waves lashing a ship's bow. At the very end Williams suddenly overturns the troubling sexism of the poem, flipping passivity into power by saying that these female figures "signify the strength of the waves' lash." Returning to the figure of the poet, the I of the poem, we might associate that passive strength with the "negative capability" that Keats found in Shakespeare.

Many people would assert that music cannot possibly do justice to such a complex literary argument, but evidently Carter disagreed. His setting, though, brings up an aspect of many of the late cycles that has perplexed critics, the overly-obvious translation of image into sound that musicologists refer to as "madrigalism" or "Mickey-Mouse-ing." At many times in all of the late cycles Carter mirrored a verbal image in a musical color or melodic shape. In "Lear," for instance, he tagged the mention of "smoke from the bonfires" to cymbal-clouded filigree on the marimba and harp.[2] Because of their jarring immediacy, the way they jump out of the music, we might interpret Carter's apparent literalisms as deliberate provocations that expose the interpretive possibilities in the text rather than narrowing them. At first hearing, Carter's setting of "Lear" may sound like the stereotyped storm music of a movie soundtrack. On rehearing, though, we notice that the contrast of voice, pattering percussion, and stabbing chords played by the whole orchestra mirror the three levels of the poetic argument. The music maps out the poem more than it illustrates it. It does not read the poem for us.

The third song, "Shadows," is the longest and most complex. Formally it functions as the varied reprise in a large ABA' design, revisiting the images of "The Rewaking." The poem was published in 1955 in *Journey to Love*, a volume in which Williams experimented with lines grouped in threes by indentation:

> Shadows cast by the street light
> under the stars,
> the head is tilted back.

As in the "The Rewaking" Carter's setting does not preserve the poem's line breaks or stanza format in the music, but it does mirror, dramatically, its two halves, one nocturnal, one diurnal. This division frames the theme of the poem, its two worlds "one of which we share with the rose in bloom / and one, / By far the greater, / with the past, / the world of memory, the silly world of history, / the world / of the imagination." Placing his own aesthetic squarely before us, Williams celebrates "the instant / trivial as it is" as the site of renewed inspiration.

Carter, however, twice emphasizing the word "imagination," does not seem to have shared my interpretation of the poem. I read "by far the greater" as an ironic statement, signifying the weight of the past, the collective burden of memory, "silly history," and imagination, an unexpected bracketing from which Williams hopes to escape. The prominence Carter gave to the word "imagination" implies an aesthetic more typical of Stevens than Williams. Carter's setting similarly displays a grandiosity at odds with Williams' attentiveness to apparent trivia, "the little dog in the snapshot," or "refractive / surfaces / and rotting things." In the second half of the song the vocal line swells and swoops melodramatically with high notes that seem incongruent with Williams' ideas or style. Whether we think of it as an argument with Williams' famous mantra "no ideas but in things" or just as a misreading, Carter's cycle has its own thematic coherence. Instead of the retrospection of old age, it presents a story of artistic arousal, crisis and renewal. Through Williams' words, the 94-year-old composer gave musical form to his own re-beginning.

With *In the Distances of Sleep*, Carter turned to the more like-minded spirit of Wallace Stevens. Much of the music attains a transparency not found in *Of Rewaking*, but only after a bumpy start. The opening poem "*Puella Parvula*," from the late collection *The Auroras of Autumn* (1949), makes an argument even harder to convey in its gendered language (contrasting the submissive *Puella* with a "wild bitch") than the one in

"Lear." As is often the case with Stevens, an apparent conversation turns out to be a soliloquy with an "interior paramour." The young girl of the title is not a person but an aspect of Stevens' psyche, as is the "wild bitch." At the opening of the song, Carter originally had the singer speak the words, not found in the poem, "little girl, listen to me," thereby creating the entirely misleading impression that we are about to hear a poem for children. In a rare instance of second-guessing, Carter later made performance of the spoken phrase optional.[3] Once we get past that momentary uncertainty, we can read Carter's placing of this oddly figured crisis poem on the cycle's prow (like Williams' strong women in repose) as another deliberate provocation, shaking the listener out of the clichéd picture of Stevens as a solipsistic aesthete. Instead we hear the older Stevens, and the even older Carter, anxiously looking back on a lifetime's work, seeking to recover child-like clarity from inner turmoil—"the mind gone wild"— struggling as they near life's endgame to find order in chaos and to raise their art to ever higher levels. The pursuit of this goal, the "*summarium in excelsis,*" will become the through-line of the entire cycle.[4]

As its title forecasts, most of *In the Distances of Sleep* is nocturnal, set in a near-total darkness, literal and metaphorical, lit only by an occasional street lamp until the brown moon rises on the final song's beautiful night. A second thread of imagery evokes the wind, a force that dissolves Gibraltar, spells out September, swings the dangling street lamps to and fro, shifts suggestively, and finally speaks. A third thread, source of the cycle's pathos, is the autumn. The poems take place well past the midpoint of life, when "every thread of summer is at last unwoven," where "summer is in bones," only a "stump."

In the longest poem in *Harmonium*, published in 1923, Stevens had portrayed himself as a "comedian," a category that would include both Chaplin and Dante. The second poem of the cycle, "Metamorphosis," from *Parts of a World* (1942), is at once jocular and cosmic, charting the passage of time, the dissolutions of autumn, in an increasingly whimsical, increasingly nihilistic naming of months: "September . . . Otoout-bre . . . Niz-nil-imbo." Carter scored his setting for an unusual ensemble—two flutes, alto flute, marimba, and metal pipes, with a few wisps of sound in the strings—that immediately evoke the way "the rude leaves fall," but, before we call out the "madrigalism" police, they also evoke the fleeting, insubstantial, passage of time. The setting conveys both the apparent lightness and the encroaching weight of the poem, taking an unexpected dramatic turn as the apocalyptic Niz-nil-imbo arrives.

The third poem, "Restatement of Romance" from *Ideas of Order* (1935), is a meditation on love with a characteristic Stevens ambiguity. It pictures an I and a You who interchange "each in the other what each has to give." Are they man and woman, or poet and reader? The poem leaves the question unanswered. The music, some of the simplest and most directly expressive Carter ever wrote, figures the communion and separateness of the poem in a counterpoint of two melodic lines, one for the singer, espressivo, the other, tranquillo, curling around the vocal line and played as a *klangfarbenmelodie*, handed off, one or two notes at a time, from one string section to another. While Stevens' poem can be read as either a sexual or literary encounter, Carter's setting brings out its sensual side, its spare texture conveys a feeling of physical intimacy even beyond that heard in "*O breath.*" As the third of five movements, this song is the cycle's heart.

The fourth and fifth poems, "The Wind Shifts" (1917) and "The Roaring Wind" ("To the Roaring wind") (1916), both from *Harmonium,* share a single wind-swept movement, the first poem accompanied by winds and percussion with the strings joining in for the second. We might term this two-poem movement the scherzo of a symphony in song, a prophetic scherzo that ultimately speaks in fiery tongues. Since Carter had earlier based one of his grandest compositions on a poem ti-tled *Vents*, his choice of poems and manner of illustrating them should not surprise us, but the wind in Stevens' poems has a different lineage. As Harold Bloom pointed out, it evokes Shelley's *Ode to the West Wind.* That poetic predecessor announces, in its very opening, much of the imagery of the Stevens poems that Carter gathered for his cycle:

O wild West wind, thou breath of Autumn's being,
Thou, from whose unseen presence the leaved dead
Are driven, like ghosts from an enchanter fleeing. . . .

More important, Shelley's ode also establishes the symbolic framework that Stevens would adopt for his own purposes:

Be thou, spirit fierce,
My spirit! Be thou me, impetuous one!

Drive my dead thoughts over the universe
Like wither'd leaves to quicken a new birth!

That fierce spirit leaps out in the ecstatic vocalise, a rarity in Carter's sung music, that takes up most the setting of "The Roaring Wind".[5]

Like the Williams cycle, *In the Distances of Sleep* ends with a knotty speculative poem, in this case "God is Good. It is a Beautiful Night" (1942) from *Transport to Summer.* The title, which is not sung, might lead us to expect a simple expression of faith. but the word "God" does not figure in the poem. Instead, its central image is a "brown moon, brown bird." Like many other late Stevens poems, this one has provoked speculation about his ultimate spiritual state. Scholars have debated whether Stevens had a deathbed conversion to Catholicism, as was reported by a single witness, Father Arthur Hanley, a priest with whom Stevens discussed theology in his last years.[6] The ambiguity looms in the first three words of the title. They can be read as a statement of Christian orthodoxy or as its polar opposite, an identification of God and the universe stemming from Spinoza.

The argument of the poem, however, is less obscure than it might first appear. The six three-line stanzas describe two different kinds of motion, a circle, and a rising line that eventually pierces the circle. The moon travels in a circular orbit, symbolizing the recurrences of nature. But, like a bird, it appears to rise, and the poem traces a motion upward from "the head and zither / on the ground" and "the book and shoe, the rotted rose." The head reads the book and, turning to the rose, squeezes "the reddest fragrance from the stump / of summer." It picks on the "rustiest string" of the zither (mirrored momentarily with a buzzing *sul ponticello* tremolo on the violin), raising it to a "venerable song," "The song of the great space of your age." The music, contrasting floating and fleeting sounds, begins and ends with barely audible halo-like chords in the strings and gradually fills that great space as the vocal line attains its "celestial rendezvous" in a high A flat on the final word, "night."

As if taking a deep breath before continuing his survey of modern poetry's old masters, Carter returned, after sixty years, to the a cappella vocal genre of his two Emily Dickinson madrigals. For a commission from the Tanglewood Music Center, he composed *Mad Regales*, a setting of poems by John Ashbery for six solo voices, in 2007. It premiered as part of the week-long celebration of his centenary held at Tanglewood in July 2008 and Carter dedicated it to the Center's director, Ellen Highstein. In Ashbery's poetry, as in the poems of Louis Zukofsky that Carter set a year later, we seem to hear the language speaking, not the poet, a welcome respite from the strong personal presences looming in the large cycles. At the premiere of *Mad Regales*, I sat right behind the poet, who did not hide his delight in Carter's ingenious dispersal of his words between the members of the vocal sextet. Like *Caténaires* and *Sound Fields*, which were also played at the festival, it was an instant crowd-pleaser.[7]

On Conversing with Paradise is a powerfully disorienting puzzler rather than a pleaser. Returning to his larger project, Carter took on the challenge of setting difficult poetry by a supremely problematic poet, and thus waded deep into the controversies surrounding Ezra Pound's art and life. More compressed and dramatic than its two predecessors, it is not a song-cycle, but a twelve-minute-long (not the twenty minutes indicated in the score) *scena*, a mad *scena*, for baritone and a chamber ensemble of flute (piccolo), clarinet, bass clarinet (contrabass clarinet), French horn, five percussionists, piano, and a small string section of at least ten players. Except for a short closing section that sets half of Pound's Canto CXX, its text is drawn from Pisan Canto 81, much of it written in 1948, when Pound was confined to a cage at a US Army base near Pisa but was, at times, allowed to use a typewriter. The published score confusingly prints the texts as excepted by Carter without indicating that there are significant omissions from the original poems, or identifying these cuts. (Assuming the role of *il miglior fabbro*, Carter cut line 2, half of line 3, lines 4–112, 170–173, and 187–188.) He may have felt that the multi-lingual Babel of the first half of Canto 81, along with its myriad obscure references to historical incidents, private encounters, and little known texts, was simply too arcane to impose on a singer or an audience. His cropped version of the text, however, also opens him up to accusations of intentionally covering up, or aestheticizing, the disturbing elements in the poems.

In choosing to set Pound's Pisan Canto 81, Carter presented the questions of retrospection and legacy in their most controversial form. Pound's career fell into three phases. Up through the early 1920s he was the self-styled instigator and promoter of modernist innovation.

His friend T.S. Eliot wrote that he was "more responsible for the xxth Century revolution in poetry than is any other individual." He helped advance the careers of Hilda Doolittle (H.D.), William Carlos Williams, Marianne Moore, Wyndham Lewis, and Ernest Hemingway, and played crucial roles in the publications of the two greatest literary landmarks of English-language modernism, T.S. Eliot's *The Wasteland*, and James Joyce's *Ulysses*. Soon after the end of the First World War, Pound settled in Rapallo, Italy, and quickly took an interest in the fascist politics of Mussolini. That attraction rapidly intensified into a passionate admiration. In the 1930s Pound also adopted ideas from the "Social Credit" theories of C.H. Douglas, interpreting them as showing that usury was undermining the values of politics and culture. By the late 1930s his poems and letters became crudely anti-Semitic. Pound remained in Italy during the Second World War and made propaganda broadcasts in support of the Axis powers. On April 27, 1943, for instance, he said on Radio Roma that "it might be a good thing to hang Roosevelt and a few hundred yidds IF you do it by due legal process." He continued his propaganda efforts even after the Nazis had set up a puppet government.[8] On May 3, 1945, four days after Mussolini was executed by Italian partisans, American soldiers took Pound into custody. He was held, in a cage, at the detention Training Center in Pisa. Here he wrote his Pisan Cantos.[9] When they first appeared, some critics read them as a rejection of his former politics. Robert Fitzgerald found in them "a personal desolation and a kind of repentance." This view encouraged readers to separate the poetry from the poet's life. Others have read the Pisan Cantos as an unrepentant, thinly veiled self-justification that retracts nothing. Pound's final addition to the poems, Canto 84, was a farewell to Mussolini. For the rest of his life and even until today, critics have debated whether Pound was a traitor and/or insane, and to what extent either of these possibilities needs to figure in a reading of his poetry. Carter knew this history very well before choosing to set Canto 81.

In her nuanced and informative discussion of the cycle,[10] Rachel Blau Duplessis concluded that Carter's approach to Pound amounts to a retrograde re-aestheticization, walling off politics from art. She termed the cycle "an elegant, high-minded, and richly modernist erasure of politics and the social meanings of the poetic act." Her view finds troubling support in Carter's anodyne and historically inaccurate introductory note which states that Pound "was occasionally allowed by the Fascist-controlled radio to broadcast in English his rather fanatical views that the American bankers and banking systems were destroying the US, a country he loved." As Duplessis noted, Pound paid for those broadcasts, all 120 of them, himself. Pound continued to defend Mussolini and Hitler after the war and "never qualified his sociopolitical anti-Semitism." Nevertheless, he was awarded the Bollingen Prize in literature in 1948, and, while he was at St. Elizabeth's psychiatric hospital was visited by such important American poets as Marianne Moore, Elizabeth Bishop, Robert Lowell, and Charles Olson, as well as by an assortment of neo-fascists and "KKK-associated racists."[11]

If we put aside, for the time being, Carter's introductory note, strikingly similar in its tone to the one he wrote for *In Sleep, In Thunder*, I would suggest, cautiously, that the musical setting may paint a darker view of Pound than the complicit, airbrushed portrait that Duplessis describes. While I agree with her description of the work as a "closet opera" I don't think we have to jump genres to disentangle Carter from Pound. Setting a text in itself is no sure proof of identification or even of sympathy. The "on" of Carter's title already situates Pound as an object of scrutiny, described from without. (The title itself comes from Blake, not Pound.) There are plenty of precedents in the art song repertory for distance between the dramatic persona of the singer and the perspective of the composer. An obvious one would be Mahler's *Kindertotenlieder*, also a "closet opera," and, as a psychodramatic monodrama, a model for Schoenberg's *Erwartung*; but going back further I think it would be naïve to identify Schubert with the Miller or even with the protagonist of *Winterreise*. Both Pound and Eliot adopted the dramatic monologue genre of Browning (e.g. "My Last Duchess"), in which speakers unwittingly reveal the darker aspects of their character. We might consider placing *On Conversing with Paradise* in this category, hearing it as Pound's self-incriminating testimony rather than an as Carter's endorsement or apology, let alone as his "artistic testament" as Bayan Northcott has claimed.[12] In pursuing this interpretive angle there is the danger of letting Carter off the conspiratorial or enabling hooks too easily, but let's see, if it is possible, which reading is best supported by the music.

The music, even more Lear-like than the setting of Williams' "Lear," begins by framing the poet's voice, as impersonated by a blustering horn solo, with the schematically bi-polar contrast of savage, fortissimo percussion (Goneril and Regan; the *Inferno*) and serene, nearly inaudible harmonics in the strings and vibraphone (Cordelia; *Paradiso*). The melodramatic efficiency of this prelude—the stereotypical, even crass, nature of its sound imagery—once again raises Lawrence Kramer's accusation of a retrograde "mimetic/expressive" approach to the text. If we hear the music in operatic terms, however, we can interpret it as a theatrical depiction of the poet's state of mind, not the composer's.

Carter organized the monodrama around three repeated phrases in the poetry: "Lawes and Jenkins guard thy rest / Dolmetsch ever be thy guest;" "what thou lovest well"; and "Pull down thy vanity." The first phrase refers to the revival of English Renaissance music, such as the lute-accompanied songs of Waller and Dowland, by Pound's friend, the instrument-maker Arnold Dolmetsch (1858–1940). While many composers would have jumped at the opportunity to write a Dowland pastiche, Pound's invocation of early music finds no stylistic echoes in Carter's accompaniment. Instead, he once again resorted to a deceptive literalism, accompanying the words "Has he curved us the bowl of the lute?" with an inverted bowl-shaped figure in the clarinet and strummed pizzicato in the strings, but also with the alien, uneasy presence of tomtom, log drum, and guiro. By mirroring the words while at the same time clouding the reflection, the music suggests the tension between Pound's invocation of the past and his modernist agenda, exposing the seductively lyrical refrain as a rhetorical ploy that masks self-justification. In Carter's tight abridgment of the poem, the refrain is the first stage of an extended apologia that proceeds from aesthetics to emotions to moral judgment. Significantly for the monodrama's portrayal of Pound's character, Carter separated the first two phases of the apologia with an oddly peaceful section of incoherent ramblings. From *"Ed ascoltando"* to "half-mask's space," the music recalls the "paradisal," floating string chords of the opening, stretching out the syllables almost to the limit of a singer's breath, as if Pound were lost in his own thoughts. This uneasy slow movement is the calm before Lear's storm. Thundering percussion returns to frame the self-inquisition of "Pull down thy vanity," growing more violent with every repetition of the phrase. Like other would-be penitents, Pound lapses into self-pity and victimhood: "Thou art a beaten dog beneath the hail, a swollen magpie in a fitful sun."

A cataclysmic cloudburst from the entire ensemble frames the climactic final statement of "Pull down thy vanity" with a diabolic intensity that recalls Iago's "*Credo*" in Verdi's *Otello*.

Does this dramatic apex lead to self-understanding or to more delusional special pleading? The setting of the end of Pisan Canto 81 and the first half of Canto 120 returns to the tripartite sound-imagery heard at the very opening of the cycle: assertive horn, rattling percussion, hovering strings. The serene vibraphone chords that usher in the Coda suggest that Pound, Carter, performers, and listeners are on the verge of some kind of Paradise, but, as with the entrance of the gods into Valhalla at the end of *Das Rheingold*, the appearance of resolution is uncertain. With an ultimate stroke of madrigalism, Carter figures the closing lines "Do not move / Let the wind speak / That is paradise" with an orchestral tremolo marked "(*fpp subito sempre non cresc. /non dim.*)" that can be heard as an affirmation, or as a question mark.

Since many have said that *On Conversing With Paradise* is a "closet opera," why not take it out of the closet and put it on the stage? Just raising that possibility shows us how inhibited the concert hall remains compared to the opera house in the age of "director's opera." Imagine a dramatic performance of the cycle with the singer placed in a metal cage, alone with his typewriter, surrounded by military police. Instead of burying salient background information in program notes, projected images could show Pound with both poetic and political associates, interspersed with texts from his wartime broadcasts. This style of production would uncage Carter's fiercely dramatic music from the irrelevant decorum of the song cycle genre.

In the fall of 2008, on the rebound from wrestling with Pound and perhaps from the increasingly heavy thematic burden of the large song cycle, Carter rapidly set nine poems by Louis Zukofsky for soprano and clarinet. The Zukofsky cycle is actually longer than *Conversing* and, however whimsical it feels at times and despite its pared-down forces, has its own weight. Zukofsky is often described, outside the literary world, as a kind of adjunct—Pound's Jewish friend, violinist Paul Zukofsky's father. In his own right he loomed very large as the founder of what is known as Language Poetry. His poems and ideas continue to exert a vast influence on American poetry today, far more than Pound's,[13] and I would add here that through Zukofsky's short poems Carter discovered a new aphoristic manner, which would return in his last work, *Epigrams*.

Carter's next large-scale song cycle, *What Are Years*, sets five poems by Marianne Moore written between 1915 and 1956.[14] Composed in 2008–2009 for the Aldeburgh Festival and dedicated to the festival's director Pierre-Laurent Aimard, the cycle is scored for soprano and twenty-piece chamber orchestra.

Just as Carter steered clear of the much-anthologized early poems of Williams and Stevens, he mainly avoided the extensive menagerie of "creature" poems so strongly identified with Moore. The poems Carter chose, and their ordering, emphasize the way Moore used her observations of nature to comment on human behavior and interactions. Her rat in the walls, scuttling quickly by in Carter's setting, reminds the poet "of many men / Once met, to be forgot again. . . ." In a parallel inversion of expectations Carter foregrounded the commanding moral voice of Moore's poetry, equal in its wide-spanning authority to the similar tone found in Yeats and Auden, rather than her much more celebrated attention to natural minutiae.

What Are Years has a five-movement structure that resembles the arch forms of Bartók's fourth and fifth string quartets. Movements one, three, and five set poems written after Moore was fifty. They portray the human species at times in intimate physical terms, at other times *sub specie aeternitatis*. They are Moore's equivalent of Alexander Pope's *Essay on Man* and form a progression beginning with the protective armor, "like a bulwark" that as "a paradox" may be a sign of weakness or of strength. The Cold War subtext hidden in the phrase "thrust of the blast" flares out at the end of the song with the image of an American battleship flying "Old Glory full mast." "That Being So-Called Human" contrasts the mammalian facts of bodily existence— "warm blood, no gills, / two pairs of hands and a few hairs"—with the soul's unaccountable optimism. The "serge-clad, strong shod" individual who greets the sun resembles the assenting beggar in the park in Elizabeth Bishop's "Anaphora." In the concluding title poem, written as the United States entered the Second World War, we arrive at a moral reckoning. Characteristically Moore finds the answer to the title's question in a bird's song that proclaims "satisfaction is a lowly / Thing, how pure a thing is joy." The second and fourth poems, both written early in Moore's life and published in her first book, might be termed intermezzi. In "That Harp You Play So Well," scored just for voice, cello, and, inevitably, harp, the young Moore envisions a life's work devoted to creating, like David, Blake, Homer, and Job, "stout continents of thought." "To an Intra-mural Rat" originally greeted readers on the first page of Moore's *Observations*. Counterbalancing the monumental intentions of the psalmist, it reminds us of life's ephemera and indignities. Carter scored his setting, just nine measures long, for scampering woodwinds, percussion, and solo strings, which may picture the hidden rodent or its human equivalents.

Marianne Moore's low-pitched, slightly raspy, unmistakably American speaking voice sounded very much like Helen Carter's, though a bit more down to earth, but I don't hear either voice in *What Are Years*, and not simply because neither was a soprano. Despite its clearly thought-out thematic structure I am not yet convinced that the cycle captures Moore's distinctive qualities. So much of its musical imagery sounds casually repurposed from the previous cycles, right down to the paradisal vibraphone at its conclusion. As in the Williams cycle, the expressive registers of poet and composer do not readily align. Moore began her early *ars poetica* with the famous escape clause "I, too, dislike it." Her wariness of poetry gave her access to kinds of language usually associated with prose, from science or philosophy or theology. Read aloud, "What Are Years" can sound at first more like a Donne sermon than a Donne sonnet, however holy. But then we begin to notice rhymes, some straight, some slant: innocence and whence, others and stirs. These rhymes and their odd placement in relation to both grammar and lineation create rhythms. Suddenly we realize that we have been reading poetry all along. This hovering between poetry and prose finds no equivalent in Carter's grand style, and his dialectic of *leggerezza* and *gravitas* does not illuminate Moore's verse, which always displays a stern yet generous impersonality, a fundamental even-mindedness. I don't sense here the deliberate reading against the grain that I hear in *On Conversing With Paradise*. Perhaps the gap between Carter and Moore is less a question of disagreement than of orientation. Whether describing animal species or baseball player, Moore wrote as a public poet. Her poems are about us. Carter's music, so much of it written for chamber ensembles, is more private, looking inward or conversing with a small circle of friends.

While it is not surprising, given his habit of introspection, that Carter ultimately found his closest affinity with Stevens rather than Moore, a far less predictable alter ego turned out to be e.e. cummings. *A Sunbeam's Architecture: 6 poems of e.e. cummings*, strikes me as the most humane and spontaneous sounding of all the cycles, the most emotionally grounded. Carter scored this cycle for tenor and nineteen players (though the minimum ten-person string section can be expanded). The physical and psychological vulnerability portrayed in these songs arises from the particular time frame of the texts in cummings' life and in Carter's as well. Carter wrote: "The choice and ordering of these poems by E.E. Cummings was made to show the poet in a period when the telephone was still a novelty and the First World War (1914–1919) was raging. It begins with a personal expression, then goes to his calling . . . poetry (A Sunbeam's Architecture), that is interrupted by the war and ends returning to his personal life." Carter's commentary is slightly misleading, as is the cycle's subtitle. Carter set five poems; the brief fourth movement, performed without a break after the third, repeats lines from the second. While three of the poems appeared in the 1920s, others were written later:

1. your little voice (from *Tulips and Chimneys*, 1922)
2. no man (from *1 x 1*, 1944)
3. my sweet old etcetera (from *is 5*, 1926)
4. love (a reprise of two lines from the last stanza of "no man")
5. it's jolly odd (from *is 5*)
6. somewhere (from *W (Viva)*, 1931)

Throughout his life cummings portrayed love in daringly embodied and intimate terms. In Carter's sequence, the course of love—first kindled by a voice heard over the telephone—supports the poet's god-like artistic calling, amplified by the trombone, to "solve the depths of horror to defend / a sunbeam's architecture with his life," and survives the wartime jingoism of his family: "my / mother hoped that / i would die etcetera / bravely of course," and even the "jolly odd" shellshock of the battlefield. In the final poem cummings celebrates the power of love, "beyond / any experience," and its "intense fragility." Carter suggests this wide spectrum in the instrumental accompaniment. The first song is scored for piano and solo strings, suggesting the intimacy of chamber music. The fifth, scored just for percussion, depicts the wasteland of trench warfare. The other movements draw a grander orchestral sonority from the ensemble with the trombone playing a dual role as the tenor's instrumental partner and acoustically as the fundamental tone for the ensemble. Carter also exploits the trombone's historically protean character, its religious and heroic connotations (Monteverdi, Schütz, Wagner), and the jocular speech-like character it often displays in jazz ("Tricky Sam" Nanton). At the very opening of "my sweet old etcetera," the cup-muted trombone speaks the title with a playful glissando—while at the same time stating the pitches of Carter's signature all-triad hexachord. Both the glissandi and the hexachord return, transformed in the last movement's spacious setting of cummings' most famous love poem. The sliding gesture now appears in the strings as a finger stroke, an instrumental caress evoking intimate physical contact. The trombone's six-note joking gesture of "my sweet old etcetera," which finds its payoff in the song's hilariously carnal climax, returns, as a quietly amorous near-whisper in the vocal line at the cycle's conclusion: "nobody, not even the rain, has such small hands."

When I began work on MEC83 Carter told me that Andrew Porter, who had already instigated *A Symphony for Three Orchestras* with the suggestion of an oratorio based on Hart Crane's *The Bridge*, had persisted in his frustrated hopes for a major choral work and proposed an even grander and, at the time, far more prestigious text, T.S. Eliot's *Four Quartets*. While the title of Eliot's poem already sounds like an apt invitation for Carter (who at the time Porter sprang the idea, had written three quartets), Carter refused to pursue the project. He told me that he could not set Eliot's canonical poems because they were deeply Christian in character and he did not consider himself to be a Christian. A lot can happen spiritually over three decades, however. Carter's decision to set excerpts of Eliot's poem as *Three Explorations drawn from T.S. Eliot's Four Quartets*, for solo baritone, winds, and brass, in the fall of 2010 as he neared his 102nd birthday was, to say the least, unanticipated, and he never explained his change of mind, let alone whether it indicated a return to some kind of religious faith. Aside from the fact that Carter set a small fraction of Eliot's text and passed over the second poem, "East Coker," entirely, his settings display no signs of irony or distance. However we might speculate on Carter's end-of-life beliefs, we can say with certainty that Eliot's poems inspired him to use one of the most extraordinary-sounding ensembles in all of his music: three flutes, three clarinets, three trumpets, and three trombones; the middle movement uses only the six woodwinds. Carter said that he was influenced by the instrumentation found in the religious music of Heinrich Schütz, but the seventeenth-century master never employed or encountered either the alto or bass flute, or any variety of clarinet, and Carter's wind writing is neither early Baroque in character nor organ-like; it is the work of a twenty-first century orchestrational master.

Eliot wrote the first two of what eventually became the *Four Quartets* in the late 1930s; the last two were written during the war. The final poem, "Little Gidding," famously depicts, in stanzas of terza rima, the poet as an air-raid warden during the Blitz, pursued by the spirit of the recently departed W.B. Yeats, much as Dante was by Virgil in the opening of the *Divine Comedy*. Following the practice of his earlier cycles, Carter excerpted only a small part of the poem, two pages out of nearly forty, and also re-ordered Eliot's text, beginning with an excerpt from the third poem, "The Dry Salvages." Here the poet, who had lived abroad for most of his life, returned in his imagination to New England and to his native St. Louis, Missouri. The poem is saturated with American images. The "strong brown god" evokes both the muddy Mississippi River and Mark Twain's character, Jim, Huck Finn's black companion on that river. The "April dooryard" immediately suggests Walt Whitman's elegy for Abraham Lincoln. Carter, who had little contact with the Mississippi, nevertheless summons up this great "useful, untrustworthy . . . conveyor of commerce," drawing sounds suggestive of river-borne tugboats and barges from his small wind ensemble.

By placing "The Dry Salvages" first, Carter in effect brought the poet home. Eliot's nostalgic scenery, however, was more symbolic than geographical, and his journey, like Dante's, was spiritual. The poem's title, unlike those of its three companions, which name places in England, refers to "a ledge of rock off Cape Ann which acted as a seamark when Eliot, as a boy, used to sail out of Gloucester [Massachusetts] harbor."[15] Eliot says that it rhymes with "assuages," and its sound thus suggests both savagery and salvation—themes that will reappear refigured as "the fire and the rose" at the end of "Little Gidding" and of Carter's cycle. The river is a symbol of time, as it is, in a different way, in Wallace Stevens' "This Solitude of Cataracts," the central poem in Carter's next and final cycle. *Four Quartets*, with its recurrent leitmotivs of the present and the past, beginnings and endings, seeks an escape from time to "the still point in a turning world" within a Christian symbolic framework derived from both the Bible and Dante. "Tongues of flame" refers to the Pentecost; the image of the rose comes from the "*rosa sempiterna*" in Canto XXX of Dante's *Paradiso*. We might expect that Carter's selections would emphasize the theme of exploration, the continuing process of self-understanding, more than a leap out of consciousness, out of time, back to "complete simplicity"; but they balance journey and arrival. The transparent texture of "Time and the Bell," and the translated tintinnabulation in the flutes that illuminates "the still point of the turning world" fuse the poetry and the music.

The last song, "The Fire and the Rose," mirrors Eliot's image of an ultimate unity with an orchestral device that subtly surrounds the words with a cathedral of sound. By opposing the choirs of wind and brass instruments, alternating their statements until they converge in the last phrase, Carter recalls the polychoral musical styles that the Venetian composers Andrea and Giovanni Gabrieli developed for the resonant acoustics of San Marco, and which Stravinsky imitated in his late *Canticum Sacrum*, composed specifically for performance in that Byzantine Venetian setting. The Eliot/Stravinsky link brings to mind a photograph taken far from the sacred space of San Marco. Stravinsky, gripping a Scotch on the rocks and grinning broadly, stands to the left of his radiant wife Vera, while to their right we see an equally delighted Valerie and Tom Eliot. With *Three Explorations*, Carter put himself right in the middle of the convivial modernist cocktail party.

In my well-worn college volume of Eliot's poems and plays, I found the note "showing what it feels like to believe," a helpful suggestion for how a non-believer might share in Eliot's explorations. We might apply that wisdom beyond *Three Explorations* to all seven of Carter's cycles. Each one traces an exploratory path to a final affirmation whether in the "scent of the rose" (Williams), or "the fresh night" (Stevens), or "paradise" (Pound), or "such small hands" (cummings), or "eternity" (Moore), or "the fire and the rose" (Eliot), or, the final finale, "merely in living as and where we live" (Stevens, as we shall soon see, again).

Notes

1 See Lloyd Schwartz's performance suggestions in "Elliott Carter and American Poetry," CR and Tony Arnold's "Digging Deeper: Singing the Music of Elliott Carter" in the same issue.

2 Lawrence Kramer, who had written admiringly about *Syringa*, claimed that in the later songs "Carter often seems to take the mimetic-expressive model as an uncontested given." "Modern Madrigalisms," in CR.

3 Stevens' daughter Holly, born in 1923, could not be termed "parvula" at the time he wrote this poem. She was already married and divorced and the mother of Stevens' grandson, Peter.

4 For an extended reading of "Puella Parvula" see Bloom, *The Poems of our Climate*, 300–302.

5 I find Carter's compressed setting of the last two words, "Speak it," a bit awkward, requiring a stilted-sounding glottal stop to articulate the "k." As an easy fix, I would place a longish fermata on "speak," slightly extend the intervening rest, and then punch out "it" as a typically Carterian cadential click.

6 Richardson, vol. 2, 426, and Mariani, 395–6.

7 For the background of *Mad Regales* see CPLD, 340–343.

8 See Alex Houen's chapter "Anti-Semitism" in Nadel, and Stephen Sicaris' chapter "Pound after Pisa: 1945–1972."

9 See Ronald Bush's chapter "Pisa" in Nadel.

10 "Elliott Carter's Ezra Pound," CR.

11 Readers interested in the current state of Pound scholarship will find much of interest in two volumes: *Ezra Pound in Context*, edited by Ira Nadel (Cambridge University Press, 2010), and *A Poem Containing History*, edited by Lawrence S. Rainey (University of Michigan Press, 1997).

12 Liner notes to Bridge CD set. Music of Elliott Carter vol. 8.

13 I would strongly direct readers and performers to the detailed discussion of the cycle by poet Ray Ragosta, CR, 187–197.

14 Carter used the versions of the poems found in the collections edited by Grace Schulman in 1972 shortly after the poet's death. This edition restored poems and variants that Moore had deleted from previous collections.

15 Ackroyd, 262.

CHAPTER THIRTEEN

Farewell Symphonies

A T A CONCERT CELEBRATING HIS 103RD BIRTHDAY HELD AT NEW YORK'S
92nd Street Y on December 8, 2011, Carter heard the world
premieres of *A Sunbeam's Architecture, Mnemosyné, Rigmarole,* and *String
Trio,* along with American premieres of *Trije glasbeniki* and *Double Trio,* a
stunning display of post-centenary creative energy. Over the following
nine months, and despite increasingly debilitating symptoms of physical decline, Carter composed his last quasi-concerto, *Dialogues II,* which
premiered a month before his death, and three major works that would
not be performed until after his passing: *The American Sublime,* Five Poems
of Wallace Stevens for baritone and large ensemble, *Instances* for chamber
orchestra, and *Epigrams,* twelve short movements for violin, cello, and
piano. The score of *Epigrams* indicates that it was edited by others, mostly
a matter of slurs and dynamics that Carter had not yet added to the score.
For all three posthumously premiered works Carter did not live to make
the many fine adjustments, retouches, and *pentimenti* that normally arise in
the course of rehearsals for a first performance. All three valedictory scores
stand with one foot in this world, one in the next.

For his seventh and final large-scale song cycle Carter returned to
Wallace Stevens, elevating him to a unique place in his personal pan-
theon. In these five last songs the voices of the composer and the poet
became one. Where Carter had placed Pound on the witness stand, a
distancing strategy, he now used Stevens' words to sum up his own life

and oeuvre. Carter signaled his special relationship with the poet in both overt and coded forms. In placing "The American Sublime" first and using its title for the entire work, he triangulated the terms of convergence with Stevens. Of the six poets that he set in the late cycles, Pound and Eliot pursued international ambitions and renounced their national identity, while the other four affirmed it. Moore, Williams, and cummings wrote plain style poetry, while Eliot, Pound, and Stevens chose the grand style, though in different ways. Stevens alone pursued the grand style within an American framework. Carter, despite the considerable time he had spent in Europe, shared that goal. The title of his final poetic settings thus identified the location and rhetorical style of his oeuvre with Stevens' poetic project. Carter reaffirmed this alliance at the very end of the cycle. *The American Sublime* concludes with the very words from Stevens' "Esthéthique du Mal" that appeared at the top of Wilfrid Meller's chapter on Carter in *Music in a New Found Land*:

And out of what one sees and hears and out
Of what of what one feels, who could have thought to make
So many selves, so many sensuous worlds,

As if the air, the midday air, was swarming
With the metaphysical changes that occur
Merely in living as and where we live.

The singer intones Stevens' "thesis," which is also Carter's, unaccompanied, disarmed, unmasked, as if the composer were saying, one final time: "Here I stand."

In its scoring *The American Sublime* resembles the wind ensemble of *Three Explorations*, with four flutes, four double reeds, and two brass, but the addition of piano and percussion instantly evokes a different locale. We have left Venice and Europe and Missouri behind. With instruments such as the guiro and lion's roar, Carter summoned up the spirit of his Greenwich Village neighbor Edgard Varèse, bringing the music back to the United States, back along the Hudson, back to the 1920s, when Varèse's *Hyperprism, Intégrales*, and *Arcana* inspired Carter's compositional calling. Stevens figured in the backstory to that initial spark. A decade earlier Varèse and Stevens, along with Marcel Duchamp, Francis Picabia, Man Ray, and William Carlos Williams, had often gathered at Walter and Louise Arensberg's West 67th Street apartment to debate the future course of American modernism.

The five-movement arch form of the cycle weaves together two themes, one aesthetic, the other chthonic. The odd-numbered movements expound Stevens' artistic credo in two complete poems and a twelve-line excerpt from a third, "Esthétique du Mal," Stevens' extended meditation on the relation of poetry to human suffering. The even-numbered movements picture the erotic foundation of that credo in two contrasting poems from Stevens' very late and very early phases. The dates of the poems Carter set are as significant as their content.

Stevens wrote "The American Sublime" in 1935 in response to the Great Depression and as a companion to "Mozart in 1935." That year Carter returned to the United States from his studies in Paris. In the face of the economic crisis, many of his friends, including Marc Blitzstein and Aaron Copland, questioned the relevance of elitist, difficult art. Stevens' poem, the beginning of his own wrestling with that question, is not at all the Whitmanesque landscape its title might suggest. In 1935 Stevens did not hear America singing, but rather descending precipitously into cynicism, seeking momentary solace at the movies. The poem mirrors the national crisis with gnarly, at times opaque, language, expressing rage and frustration rather than an aesthetic program. It concludes with questions rather than answers: "What wine does one drink? / What bread does one eat?"

Stevens, a successful corporate lawyer with no leftist sympathies, lampooned the young radicals of 1935 as "mickey mockers," unable to rise above the vernacular triviality of mass culture or the food-on-the-table ("plated pairs") priorities of Marxism, unable to engage with the sublime, which "comes down / To the spirit itself." Carter responded to the Depression similarly—if less vehemently—with a choral work, *To Music*, that praised the spiritual power of music, rather than imitating the politically-engaged agitprop of Blitzstein's *The Cradle Will Rock* or Copland's *Second Hurricane*. We can hear the fierce, declamatory chords that punctuate Carter's setting of "The American Sublime" with mounting vehemence as a fanfare for the uncommon imagination, a retrospective response to the populist pretensions of Copland's enduringly popular tribute to the common man.

By presenting the two erotic poems in reverse order, Carter problematized chronology in order to frame a central movement whose subject is time. "Life is Motion," the fourth song, is (relatively) early Stevens, written in 1919. "The Woman in Sunshine," written in 1948, is part of a group of poems that ushered in Stevens' distinctive late style. 1948, we will recall, also marked a decisive turn in Carter's music from his final neo-classical work, the Woodwind Quintet, to the first composition that revealed his unique voice, the Cello Sonata.

"The Woman in Sunshine" is a mysterious poem. Its female subject may be a disembodied version of the *Ewig weibliche*, a poetic muse, or even the imagination itself, yet at the same time she possesses "warmth and movement" and bears "the odors of the summer fields." In his setting Carter signaled this ambiguity with the odd tempo indication "*Quasi tenero*," tender-ish, but the song, a love duet for voice and oboe with a few punctuations for the vibraphone and piano, emphasizes physical warmth over abstract thought. This sensuous, intimate reading agrees with that of literary scholars who interpret the poem as Stevens' way of recovering an emotion that he had once felt for his wife, a feeling snuffed out by their disastrously mismatched marriage. In Stevens' poetry the sun often symbolizes the first cause, instigator of the imagination. In "The Woman in Sunshine" he re-assigned that primal role to "the only love."[1]

In many of the poems collected in *Harmonium*, Stevens, who grew up in a Puritan household, mocked religion and celebrated sex. At times Stevens strutted his hedonism like a vaudevillian, replacing words with nonsense syllables, "tum–ti–tum" or "ki–ki–ri–ki" or "rou–cou–cou," or, as in "Life is Motion," a Valkyrie-like "ohoyaho, Ohoo," whooped in Oklahoma to celebrate "the marriage of flesh and air." Carter's laconic setting of "Life is Motion" for voice and sparse percussion seems, at first hearing, oddly lacking in both life and motion, strikingly so if we recall its equivalent in *What Are Years*, the scuttling "To An Intra-mural Rat." Here, too, the tempo indication is counterintuitive: "*Misurato*." The brevity and apparent lack of affect in this song make sense, however, if we hear it as an elderly composer's faint recollection, barely a glimmer, of youthful desire. The contrasting temporal perspectives of the two erotic poems, one describing a growth in intensity over time, the other a loss, anticipate and echo the argument about the nature of time at the cycle's core.

"This Solitude of Cataracts," the keystone of Carter's cycle, also dates from 1948. Its subject is time, here figured in the Heraclitean image of the river.[2] Carter had earlier explored similar themes and images in *Syringa*, *Tempo e Tempi*, and *Three Explorations*, but, as we have seen, the question of time stands at the "azury centre" of all his music, just as it does in this cycle. The poem opposes change—the river that "kept flowing and never the same way twice"—to the desire to "feel the same way over and over" and to "know how it would be / Just to know how it would feel released from destruction." Stevens figured the interplay of temporal reality and the ideal of "permanent realization," outside of time, in the reflected image of Mount Monadnock, a New Hampshire landmark celebrated by Emerson and Thoreau.

As we might expect, Carter's realization of this poem deploys his *scorrevole* style, with smoothly flowing lines moving throughout the large woodwind section. The trumpet counters that flow with staccato notes spread out widely in time, sometimes in regular pulses, sometimes not, like an erratically ticking clock. The apparent literalism in the way the music mirrors poetic images masks a larger, encompassing reflection of Carter's oeuvre. The ticking trumpet, for instance, recalls one of the most dramatic moments in the *Variations for Orchestra*. The watery wind figures revisit the last of the *8 Etudes*. Many of the musical events that at first seem like facile responses to images in the poem return later in the music free of the initial connection and suggesting different motives and connections in the poem. The flowing lines, for instance, seem obviously river-like until they suddenly evoke a flock of birds rising out of the lake and then, having taken flight, appear once more to contradict the words "There seemed to be an apostrophe that was not spoken," brashly, like gaggling geese. Gradually though, Stevens' image of "the bronze man . . . Breathing his bronzen breath" emerges from the flow as an organ-like chord in the winds and a properly ticking trumpet illuminate the word "time."

The attenuated, one-page setting of "Life is Motion" marks a downward turn from this celestial, "azury" apogee to the valedictory gesture of the final song, an envoi to the cycle and (a bit prematurely) to an entire life's work. Stevens began work on his long poem "Esthéthique du Mal" in June 1944, just after D-Day, in response to a letter from an American soldier that Stevens had read in the *Kenyon Review*. The letter concerned "the relation between poetry and pain."[3] A few months later Carter would respond to that question with his mistitled, misunderstood

Holiday Overture. Stevens' poem, written when he was sixty-five, is a summation of ideas he had explored extensively in "The Comedian as the Letter C," "The Man with the Blue Guitar," and "Notes Toward a Supreme Fiction." Carter's overture, by contrast, was just the beginning of his mature oeuvre, not yet in his own distinctive voice. We hear that voice emerge from its surroundings at the very end of this final song.

Setting only the last stanza of Stevens' fifteen-part meditation, Carter shaped the final song, "This is the thesis . . .," in two contrasting parts. It opens with rich declamatory chords for the winds, recalling the sounds that opened the first movement and closed the third, a musical correlative to the words "the reverberating psalm, the right chorale." The trumpet launches an arching line that twice extends the singer's voice upward *in excelsis*. Then, at the words "but the dark italics, it could not pronounce," the imaginary cathedral seems to vanish. The quartet of double reeds, piano, and percussion drops out. The remaining flutes, clarinets, and whispa-muted brass sustain long notes barely audibly—ghostly echoes. Following the words "metaphysical changes," all the instruments fall silent and the singer chants the final words, "that occur / Merely in living as and where we live" without accompaniment. This extraordinary gesture recalls two precedents, Haydn's "Farewell" Symphony (no. 45) and the concluding song, "*Der Abschied*," of Mahler's *Das Lied von der Erde*, two grandly staged farewells—Mahler's turning towards eternity, Haydn's just a plea for time off. Both of these farewells, like Carter's, would be followed by more music.

Carter completed *Instances*, his last orchestral composition, on April 8, 2012. Commissioned by the Tanglewood Music Center and the Seattle Symphony, and dedicated to that orchestra's conductor, Ludovic Morlot, this haunting eight-minute work calls for a large chamber orchestra of eight woodwinds, four brass, two percussion, piano, and at least twenty-two strings. The special character of the score, full of both humor and pathos, and a lifetime's wisdom, might be heightened if it were performed in tandem with two other final orchestral thoughts: Copland's *Inscape* and Stravinsky's *Huxley Variations*.

Instances begins like a kaleidoscope of Carterisms, with short bursts of phrases that echo his whirling, declamatory, lyrical, pointillist, joking, and tranquil manners. While the unpredictable play of fragments continues for most of the piece, the tranquil slow movement, initiated by the brass in the second measure, gradually envelopes the whole with a Boulanger-style "*grande ligne*" that also has an Ivesian aspect. *The Unanswered Question* seems to hover over the music, though it is never quoted. At the very end Carter's two contending musical parents continue to debate their differences into eternity. The strings, with help from flutes and clarinets, spin out an ultimate elegy. Against their expressive song, the piano, as if in a different, Ivesian, sphere, plays staccato notes at a barely-breathing pulse, just a notch faster than seven beats per minute. This coda, a second "*Abschied*," contracts the essential dialectic of Carter's music into a mysterious emblem. We can hear it as the end of a journey that began with the clash of sonorities and time worlds in the first movement of the Cello Sonata, or as a wordless reprise of the "enchantered space" of Enchanted Preludes, with the piano now portraying time, "the hooded enemy, the inimical music", while the strings, undeterred, sound the full diapason of felicity.

> What is an Epigram? A dwarfish whole,
> Its body brevity, and wit its soul.
>
> —Samuel Taylor Coleridge

Carter composed his final work(s), twelve *Epigrams* for violin, cello, and piano in the spring and summer of 2012. He made his last revisions on September 23, 2012, composing a replacement for an earlier version of the first movement, and so, one last time, heeding his own advice to write the beginning of a piece last. Rolf Schulte, Fred Sherry, and Ursula Oppens gave the first performance of *Epigrams* as part of a private memorial tribute at the Juilliard School on May 22, 2013. The official premiere took place a month later at the Aldeburgh Festival with Diego Toso, Valerie Aimard, and Pierre-Laurent Aimard. Carter dedicated the work to M. Aimard.

The published score states that Carter had not been able to make a thorough review of the final page proofs. Allen Edwards, Carter's long time copyist, John Link, and David Nadal therefore prepared a "performer's edition," which contains a list of all their editorial decisions. Despite the brevity of individual epigrams, their complete sequence produces a substantial work, nearly twice as long as *Instances*. Performers may be tempted to play individual movements or a selection from the twelve. I would not say that partial performances violate the spirit of the work, and the score does not rule them out.

The conclusion of the twelfth Epigram may not be the only possible ending, but it probably is the most effective and most Carterian button. I have found, however, that listening to the twelve movements one after another without a break feels constricting. I want time to savor and think about each movement. Perhaps they could be scattered across a concert, three or four at a time.

With his background as a classical scholar, Carter would have known the epigrams of ancient Greece and Rome that were engraved, often impiously, on tombstones. The more modern literary epigram is usually defined as a short, witty statement often containing a surprising twist. W.H. Auden, in the introduction to his anthology of aphorisms, said that an epigram needed only to be clever while an aphorism must express a universal truth, but it is hard to apply this distinction to instrumental music. Unlike John Cage and Milton Babbitt, two masters of the zinger, Carter rarely expressed himself, whether in words or music, in a snappy, quotable manner, but he had already tried out the aphoristic genre in several of his song cycles, particularly in "Una Colomba" from *Tempo e Tempi*, many of the Zukofsky poems, and also with Moore's "To an Intra-mural Rat" and Stevens' "Life is Motion."

While some of Carter's Epigrams include a sudden change in texture, suggesting the unexpected twists of the literary form, none of them feels like a fragment or even a haiku. They loom larger than their temporal dimensions might suggest. I hear them as a set of crystals, each a complete statement that reflects, through sonorities, gestures, and juxtaposition of ideas, some part of Carter's musical world. Having said goodbye so eloquently in *The American Sublime* and *Instances*, Carter completed his oeuvre with a lagniappe, more than we expected or deserved, twelve perfectly fashioned encores.

Notes

1 Richardson, vol. 2, 330.
2 For a superb detailed reading of the poem see J.H. Lesher, "Heraclitean Ideas in Stevens' 'This Solitude of Cataracts.'" *The Wallace Stevens Journal* 38, no. 1 (Spring 2014).
3 Richardson, vol. 2, 230.

CHAPTER FOURTEEN

Epilogue

"EVERY NOTE HAS LIFE IN IT."

ON YOUTUBE YOU CAN EASILY FIND A SEVEN-MINUTE VIDEO TITLED "Elliott Carter—The Last Interview." Actually it is less an interview than a coaching session, with cellist Alisa Weilerstein, filmed at the 12th Street apartment in July 2012, just before she recorded Carter's Cello Concerto. At the beginning, Weilerstein asks Carter where he was when he composed the piece, and he recalls a trip he and Helen took to Japan. In Kyoto they visited the Moss Garden. There Carter noticed little bamboo tubes in the watering system that would fill up and then suddenly flip, creating a snapping sound. In the concerto he evoked that sound with the snap pizzicato (aka "Bartók pizz.") for the cello, first heard in m. 5. Carter tells Weilerstein that this pizzicato is part of a "story" that runs through the entire work. She then uncases her cello and begins to play the opening solo of the concerto, but he quickly interrupts with precise, even microscopic, suggestions. He asks her not to rush through the brief silences that punctuate the solo because "they are the only silences in the piece." He describes with apparent glee the way the orchestra responds to the cello's plaintive line with slammed chords: "Wham! Wham!" He asks her to bring out a staccato B flat sixteenth note in the fourteenth bar, a seemingly trivial suggestion that changes the character of the phrase. He sings his wide-spanning, chromatic melodies to her exactly on pitch. After several tries Weilerstein finally gets his approval.

The one-hundred-and-three-year-old Elliott Carter in this video strikes me as the very same person I first met some forty years earlier. I hear the same voice, and I recognize the same sharp mind, and perfectly attuned ear and most of all the animated concern for the tiniest musical detail, a concern that I now see was at the very core of his musical aesthetic. In 1973, at my very first composition lesson, Carter briefly flipped through my score, then seized on a detail on its first page. Beneath a sustained open G on all the violins I had written a snare drum roll and marked it with the dynamic *mf* (*mezzo forte*, loud-ish). Carter pointed to the *mf* and said, "You can't do that." In itself this was not a surprising reaction. Composers learn early on that no two players will agree on what *mf* means unless it follows or anticipates a *p* or an *f*. Schoenberg forbade his students from using the *mf* indication in their scores for this pragmatic reason, but many composition teachers, myself included, routinely discourage beginners from using it to counteract their tendency to hedge musical bets somewhere safely between loud and soft. Carter may have questioned my *mf* quite legitimately for either reason, but his critique quickly leapt beyond questions of pragmatics or cowardice. Pointing to my non-committal snare drum notation he said, matter-of-factly and without any oracular inflections, "Every note has a shape. Every note has life in it." A snare drum roll, he continued, might crescendo or diminuendo. It might start with a sudden accent followed by a sharp drop, *sfzpp*, or it might simmer and then explode, *pp subito sforzando*. These were not, for him, just notational niceties. He was asking me to imagine each note I put on the page in precise detail, from the attack to the fade, and, beyond that, to think of each note virtually as a living thing. Each sound in a piece contained its own "story," and the vibrancy of each individual sound, its unique profile and way of unfolding, would be essential to the life of the piece as a whole.

As with many of the suggestions that Carter would make in future lessons, I think that he was speaking critically about his own music as well as mine. For him, endowing sounds with life, or unlocking the life within sounds, was a constant struggle, usually achieved through an arduous process of sketching and rewriting. Whatever the abstract schemes of a piece might be, Carter felt impelled to shape them into a "story" or "scenario" whose essence was not extra-musical, but inherent in the sounds themselves. In this foundational tenet of his musical aesthetics, Carter parted company early on with the neo-classical ideal of objectivity (Stravinsky famously said that his Octet was an object, like his nose), even as he wrote music that seemed to belong to the neo-classical camp. Later on he distanced himself from the de-personalizing strategies of total serialism and chance composition, once again while writing music that in many ways resembled the products of those procedures. To critics throughout his career, Carter's apparent misalliances marked him as an odd duck. In retrospect, though, I would say that his lifelong impulse to shape musical stories out of the life in each note is the key to his music both for performers and listeners, a key that unlocks some of its complexities and gives access to its pleasures.

But what did Carter actually mean by the "life" within a sound, or by "story"? Any of his works might suggest answers to these questions, but since this is an epilogue let's turn to three short works from 2011: *String Trio, Trije glasbeniki* (for flute, bass clarinet, and harp), and *Double Trio* (for violin, percussion, trombone and trumpet, piano, and cello.) All three pieces were performed at the concert honoring Carter's 103rd birthday, which took place at the 92nd Street Y on December 8, 2011. The concert was recorded and videoed. The next day, *The New York Times* reported that "Mr. Carter, with assistance, walked a short distance to the foot of the stage, where he basked in an ovation and listened as the musicians played and sang 'Happy Birthday,' with some interpolated bursts of Carterian instrumental complexity. Though Mr. Carter is physically frail, his eyes sparkled."

For Carter, the "life" within a note sprang from the fact that the sounds in his music were produced by living performers, not through any kind of mechanical or electronic synthesis. The beginnings of each of these three late works calls attention to the players' essential presence and to the unique attributes of their instruments. *String Trio* opens with an *espressivo* bowed G played on the C string of the viola, a sound whose intense vibrato, produced by tiny movements of the player's finger, would not be possible on the violin (where the same note can only be played on an open G string) and would not sound nearly as intense on the D string of the cello. Carter also marked the opening *molto sostenuto sempre*, calling attention to the controlled pressure of the player's bow arm. *Trije glasbeniki* opens with *staccatissimo* notes on the harp marked *sons etouffés*, or choked sounds. The harpist plucks the notes (snapping one of them) with one hand and then immediately stops the sound with the other. The unusual, unresonant sound draws our attention to the mechanics of the harp and the precise control of the sound by the player. The opening of *Double Trio* vaunts the abilities (or exposes the disabilities) of three of its six performers. The violin sounds a note in its highest register, the trombone in its lowest, and both already perilous notes must be played softly. Even more softly and perilously, the muted snare drum enters with a roll marked *ppp* (a much more provocative indication than my old *mf*).

In all three pieces Carter initiates a "story" with a stark juxtaposition of sounds. In *String Trio*, the violin and cello respond to the viola's expressive *sostenuto* with *spiccato* and *pizzicato*, respectively. We might hear these short dry notes—half music, half noise—as comical or dismissive. The flute and bass clarinet in *Trije glasbeniki* counter the harp's isolated, dry tones, with rapid legato, swirls with swelling dynamics. The trumpet, cello, and piano "trio" in *Double Trio* brashly intrude upon the tranquil, undemonstrative exposition of the opposing violin, percussion, and trombone, with fast, *marcato* notes that seem as unrelated to the other trio's sounds as possible. In each case the opening dramatic contrasts set the "story" in motion as efficiently as Bernardo's "Who's there?" in *Hamlet*. Much as the action of *Hamlet* amplifies both the "who" and the "there," Carter's "stories" pursue implications of their oppositional openings to unexpected outcomes.

The course of the String Trio is easiest to describe. It's all about the viola, the musical middleman. As its events unfold, the viola shrugs off the slings and arrows of its two surrounding companions, and even their apparent attempts to mimic its soulful line. At the conclusion it reasserts its uniqueness with a triumphant-sounding solo phrase, *ff* and *martellato*, ending emphatically on its open C string. In this final gesture we might hear a self-celebration, perhaps tongue in cheek, of the composer's own *via media*, his oft-derided insistence that an "emancipated" idiom could still retain the expressive function of earlier music. The six pitches of this last phrase state the all-triad hexachord, a Carter equivalent, we might imagine, to the FAF signature: "*Frei aber froh*," free, but happy, often attributed to Brahms.[1]

Within its two-minute duration, *Trije glasbeniki* ("Three Musicians") travels very far from its opening. In its first half the harp gradually appropriates the sounds of the two wind instruments, first by playing two slow lines, above and below their ranges, surrounding their quietly expressive notes with a ghostly halo. Without warning, though, it suddenly refashions the swirling figures that the winds played at the opening into a brilliant perpetual motion. By the end, the three instruments become one. Carter summarizes this compressed journey at the close by having the harp recall its opening choked (and snapped) expostulation and then striking a resonant eighteen-note double arpeggio that fills in the void between the winds' *tremolandi*.

Double Trio tells the most unexpected story of all. The title of this eight-minute composition inverts that of its lengthier predecessor, *Triple Duo*. In that piece Carter had divided the music three ways by pairing related instruments: two winds (flute, clarinet), two strings (violin and cello), and two percussion (a large assortment of pitched and unpitched percussion and the piano). The instrumentation of *Double Trio* is similar in total, with two brass instruments, trumpet and trombone, taking the place of the two winds, but here Carter builds each trio out of unrelated instruments. This counterintuitive arrangement sparks two different story lines. At the beginning, each oddly assorted threesome asserts a distinctive identity, very much as the three pairs of instruments do in *Triple Duo*, but in m. 46 the percussionist seems to change the rules. Moving from unpitched snare drum to marimba, the percussion imitates rapid legato figures played by the trumpet in the other trio just a few bars before. At first the violin and trombone seem to ignore the marimba's violation of boundaries, but the marimba returns with its idea in m. 74, and this time its departure from the work's proprieties has consequences. Soon the piano takes up the marimba's idea, and then it breaks out in the violin and cello, as if the natural affinities of the instruments have overcome their artificial divisions. A sense of an even higher unity, however, emerges from an unlikely source. At m. 127 the trombone, in its operatic tenor register, begins to sing out a warmly expressive melody, finally releasing the lyricism hinted at in its muted opening phrase. Its noble tones seem to charm all the other instruments out of their belligerence. Most unexpectedly of all, the piece closes with a fortissimo fanfare sounded at first by the reconnected familial pairings of piano and percussion, violin and cello, trumpet and trombone, and finally converging on a six-note (yes, *those* six notes) chord, sustained in a soft dynamic—one final surprise turn—to suggest the sweetness of musical communion. Elevating the music to this utopian *telos*, Carter celebrated his multi-storied art and his many-selved life.

Note

1 While the association of "FAF" with Brahms appears in program notes all the time, musicologists have found that the motto was invented by the music critic Max Kalbeck after the composer's death. See Michael Musgrave, "*Frei aber Froh*: A Reconsideration" in *19th-Century Music* 3, no. 3 (March 1980), 251–258.

Carter's Musical Signatures

Seikilos Song   All-interval tetrachords   All-triad hexachord

          (0.1.4.6)   (0,1,3,7)   (0,1,2,4,7,8)

Calendars

1. Chronology of Carter's Life

December 11, 1908   Born in New York City.

1914–1926   Student at Horace Mann School.

1926–1930   Undergraduate at Harvard; private study at Longy School.

1930–1932   Masters student at Harvard.

1932–1935   Studies with Nadia Boulanger at the Ecole Normale de Musique and privately.

1937–1939   Writes for *Modern Music*; musical director, Ballet Caravan.

1939   Married to Helen Frost-Jones (July 6).

1940–1944   Instructor in music, Greek and mathematics at St. John's College.

1943   Birth of David Carter (January 4).

1943–1945   Music consultant to Office of War Information.

1945   Awarded Guggenheim Fellowship to compose Piano Sonata.

1946–1948   Professor of Composition, Peabody Conservatory.

1948–1950   Teaches at Columbia University.

1950   Second Guggenheim Fellowship for String Quartet no. 1.

1953–1954   Fellow of the American Academy in Rome.

1954   Death of Charles Ives.

1955   Death of Elliott Carter, Sr.

1955–1956   Teaches at Queens College, New York.

1956   Elected to National Institute of Arts and Letters.

1958   Instructor at the Salzburg seminars.

1960   Pulitzer Prize in Music for Quartet no. 2

1960–1962   Teaches at Yale.

1961   Wins New York Critics' Circle Award for *Double Concerto*

1963   In residence at American Academy in Rome.

1964   Composer-in-residence, Berlin. Begins to teach at Juilliard.

1967–1968   Professor-at-large at Cornell.

1970   Death of Florence Chambers Carter.

1971   Gold Medal for Eminence in Music from National Institute of Arts and Letters. Publication of *Flawed Words and Stubborn Sounds: A Conversation with Elliott Carter*.

1973   Pulitzer Prize in Music for Quartet no. 3. Exhibit of sketches and scores at the Library and Museum of the Performing Arts of the New York Public Library at Lincoln Center.

1978   Awarded Handel Medallion by City of New York.

1981   Boosey and Hawkes becomes his publisher.

1984   Resigns from Juilliard.

1985   Ernst von Siemens Prize and National Medal of the Arts.

1988 80th birthday tributes at Tanglewood, and the Bath Festival. Sale of sketches and papers to Paul Sacher Stiftung.

1990   Sale of Waccabuc.

2003   Death of Helen Carter (May 17).

2008   Tributes on 100th birthday at Carnegie Hall, Tanglewood and IRCAM.

2011   103rd birthday concert at 92nd Street Y.

2012   Dies on November 5.

2. Chronological List of Published Compositions

(A detailed catalogue of Carter's works can be found at www.elliottcarter.com.)

1936   *Tarantella* for men's chorus (TTBB) and piano, four-hands.

1937   *Let's Be Gay* for women's chorus (SSAA) and two pianos; *Harvest Home* for chorus (SATB) a cappella; *To Music* for mixed chorus (SSAATTBB) a cappella.

1938   *Tell Me Where is Fancy Bred* for alto voice and guitar; *Heart Not so Heavy as Mine* for chorus (SATB) a cappella.

1939   *Pocahontas*, Ballet Legend in one act for orchestra; Canonic Suite for quartet of alto saxophones.

1940   *Pastoral* for viola or English horn or clarinet and piano.

1941   *The Defense of Corinth* for speaker, men's chorus and piano four-hands; Suite from *Pocahontas* for orchestra.

1942   *Three Poems of Robert Frost* (Dust of Snow, The Rose Family, The Line Gang) for voice and piano; Symphony no. 1 for orchestra.

1943   *Warble for Lilac Time* for soprano or tenor and piano; *Voyage* for medium voice and piano; *Elegy* for cello and piano.

1944   *Holiday Overture* for orchestra; *The Harmony of Morning* for women's chorus (SSAA) and chamber orchestra.

1945   *Musicians Wrestle Everywhere* for chorus (SSATB) with optional string accompaniment.

1946   Piano Sonata; *Elegy* (arranged for string quartet).

1947   *The Minotaur* ballet in one act and two scenes for orchestra; *Emblems* for men's chorus (TTBB) and piano.

1948   Woodwind Quintet; Sonata for Violoncello and Piano.

1950   Eight Etudes and a Fantasy for flute, oboe, clarinet, and bassoon; Six pieces for Kettledrums.

1951   String Quartet no. 1.

1952   Sonata for Flute, Oboe, Cello and Harpsichord; *Elegy* (arranged for string orchestra).

1955   Variations for Orchestra.

1956   Suite from the ballet *The Minotaur* for orchestra; Canonic Suite (arranged for four clarinets).

1959   String Quartet no. 2

1961   *Double Concerto* for Harpsichord and Piano with two chamber orchestras; *Elegy* (arranged for viola and piano).

1965   Piano Concerto.

1966   Adagio and Canto for timpani.

1969   Concerto for Orchestra.

1971   String Quartet no. 3; *Canon for 3: In Memoriam Igor Stravinsky*.

1974   Duo for Violin and Piano; Brass Quintet; A Fantasy about Purcell's "Fantasia upon One Note" for brass quintet.

1975   *Voyage* (orchestrated); *A Mirror on Which to Dwell*, six poems of Elizabeth Bishop for soprano and chamber orchestra.

1976   *A Symphony of Three Orchestras.*

1978   *Birthday Fanfare* for Sir William Glock's 70th for three trumpets, vibraphone, and glockenspiel; *Syringa* for mezzo-soprano, baritone, and chamber orchestra.

1980   *Night Fantasies* for piano; *Three Poems of Robert Frost* (orchestrated).

1981   *In Sleep, In Thunder*, six poems of Robert Lowell for tenor and chamber orchestra.

1983   *Triple Duo* for flute, clarinet, violin, cello, piano, and percussion; *Changes* for guitar.

1984   *Canon for 4—Homage to William* for flute, clarinet, violin, and cello; *Riconoscenza per Goffredo Petrassi* for solo violin; *Esprit rude/esprit doux* for flute and clarinet.

1985   *Penthode* for five instrumental quintets

1986   String Quartet no. 4; *A Celebration of some 100 x 150 notes* for orchestra.

1987   Oboe Concerto; *Pastoral* (orchestrated).

1988   *Enchanted Preludes; Remembrance; Birthday Flourish*

1989   *Anniversary; Three Occasions*

1990   Violin Concerto; *Con leggerezza pensosa* for clarinet, violin, and cello.

1991   *Scrivo in vento* for solo flute; Quintet for Piano and Winds.

1992   *Trilogy* for oboe and harp.

1993   *Gra* for solo clarinet; *Partita* for orchestra.

1994   *90 +* for piano; *Adagio tenebroso* for orchestra; *Figment 1* for solo cello; *Fragment no. 1* for string quartet; *Of Challenge and of Love*, poems of John Hollander for soprano and piano.

1995   *Esprit rude/Esprit doux II* for flute, clarinet, and marimba; String Quartet no. 5.

1996   Clarinet Concerto.

1997   *Allegro scorrevole* for orchestra; *Symphonia: sum fluxae pretium spei; A 6 Letter Letter* for English horn; Quintet for Piano and Strings; *Shard* for guitar; *Luimen* for trumpet, trombone, harp, vibraphone, mandolin, and guitar.

1998   *What Next?* Opera in one act to a libretto by Paul Griffiths.

1999   *Two Diversions* for piano; *Fragment no. 2* for string quartet; *Tempo e tempi* for soprano and ensemble; *Statement—Remembering Aaron* for solo violin; *Fantasy—Remembering Roger* for solo violin.

2000   *ASKO Concerto* for ensemble; *Retrouvailles* for piano; Cello Concerto; *Rhapsodic Musings* (for Robert Mann) for solo voiin; *Four Lauds* (*Statement, Riconoscenza, Rhapsodic Musings, Fantasy*).

2001   *Figment II: Remembering Mr. Ives*, for cello; Oboe Quartet; *Hiyoku* for two clarinets; *Steep Steps* for bass clarinet.

2002   *Au Quai* for bassoon and viola; *Retracing* for bassoon; *Boston Concerto* for orcheatra; *Of Rewaking*, three poems of William Carlos Williams for mezzo-soprano and orchestra; *Micomicón* for orchestra.

2003   *Dialogues* for piano and orchestra; *Call* for two trumpets and horn.

2004   *Réflexions* for ensemble; *Mosaic* for ensemble; *More's Utopia* for orchestra; *Fons juventatis* for orchestra; *Three Illusions (Micomicón, More's Utopia, Fons juventatis).*

2005   *Soundings* for piano and orchestra; *Intermittences* for piano.

2006   *In the Distances of Sleep* for mezzo-soprano and ensemble; Horn Concerto; *Caténaires; Two Thoughts for the piano* (*Intermittences* and *Caténaires*).

2007   *Interventions* for piano and orchestra; *Mad Regales* on poems of John Ashbery for six solo voices; *HBHH* for oboe; *Sound Fields* for string orchestra; *Matribute* for piano; *Figment III* for contrabass; *Figment IV* for viola; *La Musique* for soprano; Clarinet Quintet; *Elegy* (arr. Cello and piano).

2008   Flute Concerto; *Tintinnabulation; Duettino* for violin and cello; *Fratribute* for piano; *Sistribute* for piano; *Wind Rose* for wind ensemble; *On Conversing with Paradise* for baritone and ensemble; *Poems of Louis Zukofsky* for clarinet and soprano.

2009   *Tre Duetti* for violin and cello; *Figment V* for marimba; *Retracing II* for horn; *Retracing III* for trumpet; *What are Years,* five poems of Marianne Moore for soprano and chamber ensemble; Concertino for Bass Clarinet; *Nine by Five* for woodwind quintet.

2010   *A Sunbeam's Architecture*, six poems of e.e. cummings for tenor and chamber orchestra; *Conversations* for piano, percussion, and chamber orchestra or full orchestra; *Dialogues II* for piano and orchestra.

2011   *Three Explorations* drawn from T.S. Eliot's *Four Quartets* for voice and ensemble; *Trije glasbeniki* for flute, bass clarinet, and harp; *Double Trio* for violin, percussion, trombone/trumpet, cello, piano; String Trio; *The American Sublime* five poems of Wallace Stevens for baritone and large ensemble; *Two Controversies and a Conversation* for piano, percussion, and chamber orchestra or full orchestra; *Rigmarole* for cello and bass clarinet; *Mnemosyne* for solo violin; *Figment VI* for oboe; *Retracing IV* for tuba; *Retracing V* for trombone.

2012   *Instances* for chamber orchestra; *Epigrams* for violin, cello, and piano.

3. Chronology of American Composers

Scott Joplin (1867–1917)
Charles Ives (1874–1954)
Arnold Schoenberg (1874–1951)
John Alden Carpenter (1876–1951)
Carl Ruggles (1876–1971)
Ernest Bloch (1880–1959)
Bela Bartók (1881–1945)
Igor Stravinsky (1882–1971)
Edgard Varèse (1883–1965)
Charles Tomlinson Griffes (1884–1920)
Jerome Kern (1885–1945)
Charles Seeger (1886–1979)
Ernst Toch (1887–1964)
Darius Milhaud (1892–1974)
Douglas Moore (1893–1969)
Walter Piston (1894–1976)
James P. Johnson (1894–1955)
Paul Hindemith (1895–1963)
Dane Rudhyar (1895–1985)
William Grant Still (1895–1978)
Howard Hanson (1896–1981)

Roger Sessions (1896–1985)
Virgil Thomson (1896–1989)
Henry Cowell (1897–1965)
Erich Korngold (1897–1957)
George Gershwin (1898–1937)
Roy Harris (1898–1979)
Duke Ellington (1899–1974)
Randall Thompson (1899–1984)
George Antheil (1900–1959)
Aaron Copland (1900–1990)
Kurt Weill (1900–1950)
Ruth Crawford Seeger (1901–1953)
Harry Partch (1901–1974)
Stefan Wolpe (1902–1972)
Marc Blitzstein (1905–1964)
Leroy Anderson (1908–1975)
ELLIOTT CARTER (1908–2012)
Samuel Barber (1910–1981)
Paul Bowles (1910–1999)
William Schuman (1910–1992)
Frank Loesser (1910–1969)
Bernard Herrmann (1911–2007)
Gian Carlo Menotti (1911–2007)
Arthur Berger (1912–2003)
John Cage (1912–1992)
Conlon Nancarrow (1912–1997)
Hugo Weisgall (1912–1997)
Henry Brant (1913–2008)
Morton Gould (1913–1996)
Irving Fine (1914–1963)
David Diamond (1915–2005)
George Perle (1915–2009)
Vincent Persichetti (1915–1987)
Milton Babbitt (1916–2011)
Lou Harrison (1917–2003)
Leonard Bernstein (1918–1990)
George Rochberg (1918–2005)
Leon Kirchner (1919–2009)
Harold Shapero (1920–2013)
Ralph Shapey (1921–2002)
Lukas Foss (1922–2009)
Peter Mennin (1923–1983)
Ned Rorem (b. 1923)
Gunther Schuller (1925–2015)
Earle Brown (1926–2002)
Morton Feldman (1926–1987)
Jacob Druckman (1928–1996)

George Crumb (b. 1929)
Yehudi Wyner (b. 1929)
Donald Martino (1931–2005)
John Williams (b. 1932)
Morton Subotnick (b. 1933)
Mario Davidovsky (b. 1934)
Terry Riley (b. 1935)
Steve Reich (b. 1936)
David Del Tredici (b. 1937)
Philip Glass (b. 1937)
William Bolcom (b. 1938)
John Corigliano (b. 1938)
Alvin Curran (b. 1938)
Frederic Rzewski (b. 1938)
Harvey Sollberger (b. 1938)
Joan Tower (b. 1938)
Charles Wuorinen (b. 1938)
Ellen Taaffe Zwilich (b. 1939)
Meredith Monk (b. 1942)
John Adams (b. 1947)
John Luther Adams (b. 1953)
David Lang (b. 1957)
Wynton Marsalis (b. 1961)

4. American Classical Music: Chronology (Far from Complete) of Notable Premieres during Carter's Lifetime

1914   Carpenter: *Adventures in a Perambulator*
1915   Griffes: *The White Peacock*
1917   Cowell: *The Tides of Manaunaun*
1918   Griffes: Piano Sonata
1920   Ives self-publishes the *Concord Sonata*
1921   Varese: *Amériques*; Carpenter: *Krazy Kat*
1922   Rudhyar: Luciferian Stanza and Ravissement; Ives self-publishes *114 Songs*
1923   Varese: *Hyperprism*, New York premiere of *Pierrot Lunaire*
1924   Ruggles: *Men and Mountains*; Gershwin: *Rhapsody in Blue*; Varese: *Octandre*;
        Friml: *Rose-Marie*; Carpenter: *Skyscrapers*, New York premiere of *Le Sacre du printemps*
1925   Copland: *Music for the Theatre*; Piston: Three Pieces; Gershwin: Concerto in F;
        Varèse: *Intégrales*; Cowell: *The Banshee*
1926   Antheil: *Ballet mécanique*
1927   Antheil: Jazz Symphony; Varese: *Arcana*; Sessions: Symphony no. 1;
        Kern: *Show Boat*
1928   Rudhyar: Three Paeans; Gershwin: *An American in Paris*; Johnson: *Yamekraw*
1930   Copland: Piano Variations; Crawford: Piano Study in Mixed Accents
1931   Ruggles: *Sun Treader*; Crawford: String Quartet; Varese: *Ionization*;
        Still: Symphony no.1 "Afro-American"; American premiere of *Wozzeck*
1930   Hanson: Symphony no. 2

1933   Barber: Overture to *The School for Scandal*
1934   Thomson: *Four Saints in Three Acs;* Cowell: Ostinato Pianissimo
1935   Sessions: Violin Concerto; Gershwin: *Porgy and Bess*
1936   Barber: Symphony no. 1; Schoenberg: String Quartet no. 4;Varese: *Density 21.5*;
       Thomson: *The Plow that Broke the Plains*
1937   Copland *The Second Hurricane, El Salon Mexico*; Blitzstein: *The Cradle Will Rock*
1938   Barber: Adagio for Strings; Piston: *The Incredible Flutist*
1939   Ives: *Concord Sonata*; Copland: *Billy the Kid*; Cage: *First Construction in Metal*;
       Harris: Symphony no. 3
1940   Schoenberg: Violin Concerto, Chamber Symphony no. 2
1941   Barber: Violin Concerto; 1941 Schuman: Symphony no. 3
1942   Copland: *Rodeo;* Barber: *Second Essay*
1943   Hindemith: *Ludus Tonalis*; Piston: Symphony no. 2: Ellington: *Black, Brown
       and Beige*
1944   Copland: *Appalachian Spring*; Bernstein: Symphony no. 1, *Fancy Free*;
       Schoenberg: Piano Concerto; Bartók: Concerto for Orchestra; Hindemith: *The Four
       Temperaments*
1945   Schuman: *Undertow*
1946   Diamond: *Rounds*; Menotti: *The Medium*; Stravinsky: Symphony in
       Three Movements; Bartók: Piano Concerto no. 3; Schoenberg: String Trio;
       Copland: Symphony no. 3; Kurt Weill: *Street Scene*
1947   Thomson: *The Mother of Us All*; Barber: *Medea*; Piston: Symphony no. 3;
       Wolpe: *Battle Piece*
1948   Cage: *Sonatas and Interludes*; Stravinsky: *Orpheus*; Schoenberg: *A Survivor
       from Warsaw*; Barber: *Knoxville: Summer of 1915*; Copland: *The Heiress*;
       Thomson: *Louisiana Story*
1949   Blitzstein: *Regina*; Babbitt: *Composition for Four Instruments*; Barber: Piano Sonata;
       Schuman: Symphony no. 6
1950   Copland: Dickinson Songs; Menotti: *The Consul*; Cage: *String Quartet in Four
       Parts*; Piston: Symphony no. 4.
1951   Menotti: *Amahl and the Night Visitors*; Cage: *Music of Changes*; Stravinsky: *The
       Rake's Progress*; Ives: Symphony no. 2; Nancarrow: Study no. 1 for Player Piano
1952   Bernstein: *Trouble in Tahiti*
1953   Cage: *Williams Mix*; Partch: *U.S. Highball* (radio premiere)
1954   Bernstein: *On the Waterfront*; Menotti: *The Saint of Bleecker Street*; Sessions: Idyll
       of Theocritus;Varèse: *Déserts*
1955   Hovhaness: Symphony no. 2 "Mysterious Mountain";Toch: Symphony no. 3
1956   Moore: *The Ballad of Baby Doe*; Loesser: *The Most Happy Fella*
1957   Copland: Piano Fantasy; Bernstein: *West Side Story*; Stravinsky: *Agon*
1958   Barber: *Vanessa*;Varèse: *Poème electronique*; La Monte Young: String Trio
1959   Schuller: *Seven Studies on Themes of Paul Klee*
1960   Lukas Foss: *Time Cycle*; Bernard Herrmann: *Psycho*
1961   Davidovsky: *Synchronisms no. 1*
1962   Copland: *Connotations*
1963   Sessions: Piano Sonata no. 3
1964   Babbitt: *Philomel*;Terry Riley: *In C*;Wolpe: Chamber Piece no. 1;
       Sessions: *Montezuma*

1965   Ives: Symphony no. 4; Crumb: *Eleven Echoes of Autumn*

1966   Reich: *Come Out*; Barber: *Anthony and Cleopatra*

1966   Stravinsky: *Requiem Canticles*

1967   Subotnick: *Silver Apples of the Moon*

1969   Cage: *HPSCHD*; Wolpe String Quartet; Wuorinen: *Time's Encomium*

1970   Glass: *Music with Changing Parts*; Crumb: *Ancient Voices of Children, Black Angels*

1971   Bernstein: *Mass*; Reich: *Drumming*; Sessions: *When Lilacs Last in the Dooryard bloom'd*

1972   Rochberg: String Quartet no. 3; Reich: *Clapping Music*; Joplin: *Treemonisha* (first performance)

1974   Glass: *Music in Twelve Parts*

1975   Rzewski: *The People United Will Never Be Defeated*

1976   Reich: *Music for Eighteen Musicians*; Cage: *Renga*; Glass: *Einstein on the Beach*; Del Tredici: *Final Alice*

1977   Meredith Monk: *Quarry*; John Williams: *Star Wars*

1978   Adams: *Shaker Loops*

1979   Sondheim: *Sweeney Todd*

1981   Tower: *Sequoia*

1982   Zwilich: Symphony no. 1

1983   Bernstein: *A Quiet Place*; Glass: *Akhnaten*

1987   Adams: *Harmonium, Nixon in China*; Glass: Violin Concerto

1988   Reich: *Different Trains*; Nancarrow: Two Canons for Ursula

1990   Corigliano: Symphony no. 1

1991   Adams: *The Death of Klinghoffer*; Corigliano: *The Ghosts of Versailles*

1994   Marsalis: *Blood on the Field*

1999   Adams: *Naïve and Sentimental Music*

2005   Adams: *Doctor Atomic*

2008   Lang: *The Little Match Girl Passion*

Personalia

A short list of family, close friends and fellow musicians, not including well-known names such as Bernstein, Boulez, Copland, Ives, etc.

Babbitt, Milton (1916–2011). Composer, music theorist, and mathematician. He studied composition with Marion Bauer at New York University and with Roger Sessions at Princeton, and taught mathematics and music at Princeton and, after 1973, composition at the Juilliard School. Although he started out composing popular songs and wrote a musical based on Homer's *Odyssey*, he is best known for his extensions, as theorist and composer, of Schoenberg's twelve-tone method—parallel to but distinct from those pursued by European composers like Boulez and Stockhausen—and for his role in developing computer music at the Columbia-Princeton Electronic Music Center. His students included David Lewin, Paul Lansky, Donald Martino, and Stephen Sondheim.

Blackwell, Virgil (1942–). Clarinetist and bass clarinetist. In 1971 he co-founded Speculum Musicae along with other musicians, including Fred Sherry, Rolf Schulte, and Ursula Oppens who had played in the Juilliard Ensemble, formed by Luciano Berio in 1967. From 1976 to 1986 he also was a member of the Steve Reich Ensemble. In 1988 he became Elliott Carter's personal manager. He has served as executive vice president of the Amphion Foundation, and also as producer of recordings and videos of Carter's music.

Blitzstein, Marc (1905–1964). Composer, lyricist, and librettist. Originally trained as a pianist, he studied composition at the Curtis Institute, with Arnold Schoenberg, and with Nadia Boulanger. He achieved fame in 1937 with the agit-prop theater work *The Cradle Will Rock*, for which he composed the Kurt Weill-inspired music and the Brecht-inspired lyrics and book. His other theatrical works, including *No for an Answer* (1941) and the opera *Regina* (1949), based on Lillian Hellman's play *The Little Foxes*, were important influences on the musical theater works of his close friend Leonard Bernstein. His English translation of the Brecht/Weill *The Threepenny Opera* played a total of 2,707 performances at the Off-Broadway Theater de Lys from 1954 onward.

Carter, David Chambers (1943–). Due to his parents' frequent travels, he was largely brought up by his paternal grandmother until he was placed in the Brooks School in 1956, after his grandfather's death. Educated at Yale, University of Chicago, the Sorbonne, and Indiana University, he left academia to become a farmer and bookstore owner. After a crippling accident he became an advocate for people with disabilities. Elliott Carter composed Figment V for marimba in 2009 for David's son Alexander.

Carter, Helen Frost-Jones (1907–2003). Born in Jersey City, New Jersey, she studied with Alexander Archipenko at the Art Students League in New York. Worked as a sculptor and as a director of the Works Progress Administration art program in New York. She met Elliott Carter in 1936, and they were married on July 6, 1939. Her bust of Marcel Duchamp is in the collection of the Wadsworth Atheneum, Hartford, Connecticut, and one of her husband is on display at the New York Public Library. After their marriage she abandoned her work as a sculptor and dedicated herself to supporting his musical career.

Cowell, Henry (1897–1965). Composer, born in Menlo Park, California. Studied with Charles Seeger at University of California at Berkeley. Seeger helped him prepare his book *New Musical Resources*, begun in 1919 but published in 1930. His music encompassed innovative piano works that introduced the tone-cluster and performing on the strings rather than the keyboard, music for percussion ensemble that absorbed non-Western influences, and works based on American folk music. Throughout his life, Cowell helped organize and promote new music, especially by fellow ultra-modernists Ives, Ruggles, Rudhyar, Varèse, Ornstein, and Crawford. He organized the New Music Society and the Pan-American Association of Composers, founded the periodical New Music in 1927, and established New Music Recordings in 1934. His influence was particularly important on the music of John Cage and Lou Harrison.

Crawford Seeger, Ruth (1901–1953). Composer and folk music scholar. At the American Conservatory of Music in Chicago she studied piano with Heniot Levy and Louis Robyn, and composition and theory with Adolf Weidig. She continued her studies with Djane Lavoie Herz who introduced her to Dane Rudhyar and Henry Cowell. In 1929 she began studies with Charles Seeger, and was greatly influenced (as were Cowell and Ruggles) by his ideas about dissonant counterpoint. In 1930 she became the first woman to receive a Guggenheim Fellowship and composed her String Quartet while living in Berlin and Paris. She married Seeger in 1932. From 1936 onward she devoted herself to American folk music, transcribing recordings for John and Alan Lomax, and for her own collection *Our Singing Country* (1941). She returned to classical composition only in the last year of her life.

Fromm, Paul (1906–1987). Bavarian-born Chicago wine importer and patron of contemporary music. He became interested in new music early in his life, attending festivals at Donaueschingen between 1921 and 1926, but entered his family's wine-making business. He emigrated to the United States in 1938 and established a foundation to support new music in 1952. In its early years the foundation commissioned music by Carter and Babbitt, though later on it broadened its stylistic range. The Fromm Foundation is now based at Harvard.

Furness, Clifton Joseph (1898–1946). Literary scholar and pianist. He studied at Northwestern University. In 1922, after an exchange of letters about the *Concord Sonata*, Ives helped him secure a teaching position (English and music) at the Horace Mann School for Boys where Carter was a student. He worked at Harvard from 1929 to 1934 and also taught a variety of musical and nonmusical subjects at the New England Conservatory. He was regarded as an authority on Walt Whitman, with *Walt Whitman's Workshop* (Harvard University Press, 1928) and *Walt Whitman's Estimate of Shakespeare* (1932).

Glock, Sir William (1908–2000). One of the most important figures in British musical culture in the second half of the twentieth century, he was born in London, he studied at Cambridge, where he was organ scholar at Gonville and Caius College, and had piano lessons from Arthur Schnabel in Berlin from 1930 to 1933. Back in London, he worked as a journalist and, in 1939, became the chief music critic for the *Observer*. After serving in the RAF during the war, he established a summer school of music, first at Bryanston, Dorset, and, in 1953, at Dartington Hall, Devon. Here he introduced the younger generation of British composers, including Peter Maxwell Davies and Alexander Goehr, to major figures including Nadia Boulanger, Enescu, Hindemith, and Stravinsky, and younger modernists including Carter, Wolpe, Boulez, and Stockhausen. In 1949 he founded the periodical *The Score*, and in 1959 was named Controller of Music at the BBC. In this position he transformed the Henry Wood Promenade Concerts (aka "The Proms") and made advanced contemporary music a central part of the repertory of the BBC Symphony.

Goldman, Richard Franko (1910–1980). Conductor, educator, scholar, and music critic. His father was the trumpet-player, conductor, and band leader Edwin Franko Goldman. He studied at Columbia University, and with Nadia Boulanger and Wallingford Riegger. He shared the conducting post at the Goldman Band with his father from 1937 until his father's death in 1956, when he took over as director. He taught at the Juilliard School, where he helped develop the Literature and Materials curriculum with William Schuman, and also at Princeton, and was director of the Peabody Conservatory of Music in Baltimore. He was New York critic for *The Musical Quarterly* and editor of *The Juilliard Review*, and he wrote the libretto for Hugo Weisgall's opera *Athalia*. He also wrote three books about band music and a harmony textbook.

Hanson, Howard (1896–1981). Nebraska-born composer, conductor, and educator, educated at the Institute of Musical Art and Northwestern University. From 1921–1924 he was a Fellow at the American Academy in Rome. In 1924, after the New York premiere of his Symphony no. 1 ("Nordic") he was named director of the Eastman School of Music in Rochester, New York, a position he held for forty years. Here he created the Eastman-Rochester Orchestra and many festivals of American music. His reputation as a composer was affirmed with the premieres of his Symphony no. 2 ("Romantic") by Koussevitsky and the Boston Symphony Orchestra in 1930 and of his opera *Merry Mount* at the Metropolitan Opera in 1934. As a conductor, his performances (including the premiere of Carter's Symphony no. 1) and recordings were vastly influential in shaping a sense of the canon and tradition of American music.

Harris, Roy (1898–1979). Oklahoma-born composer. After lessons with Arthur Bliss and Arthur Farwell he studied with Nadia Boulanger from 1926 to 1929. As early as 1936, Aaron Copland wrote that Harris' name was "analogous with 'Americanism' in music." His Symphony no. 3, premiered by Koussevitsky and the Boston Symphony Orchestra in 1939, made him famous and became the model for many later American symphonies, especially those by his student William Schuman. Its "pioneer" style fused American folk songs and hymns with Soviet-style populism and Sibelius-inspired organicism. Although he composed much music after that, including ten more symphonies, and remained active and productive his reputation declined rapidly after the Second World War.

Harrison, Lou (1917–2003). Portland, Oregon-born composer. Studied with Henry Cowell and Arnold Schoenberg. Like Cowell and Cage, he composed music for percussion ensemble strongly influenced by East Asian traditions. In the 1940s he worked as a music critic for *The New York Herald Tribune*, and became good friends with Charles Ives, working with Cowell to prepare the score and part of Ives' Symphony no. 3 for its Pulitzer Prize-winning premiere, and with Carter, on the scores for *Three Places in New England* and *Central Park in the Dark*. His many compositions, including symphonies and operas, are a unique and compelling fusion of Eastern and Western musical ideas.

Heyman, Katherine Ruth (1874–1944). California-born pianist, composer, and disciple of Alexander Scriabin. Author of *The Relation of Ultramodern to Archaic Music* (1921). Founded the Scriabin Circle in 1934. She was a close friend of Ezra Pound (who called her his "Beatrice") and H.D. (Hilda Doolittle), his previous muse.

Jacobs, Paul (1930–1983). New York-born pianist. After studying at the Juilliard School he performed with Robert Craft's Chambers Arts Society. He moved to Paris in 1951 and performed in Pierre Boulez's Domaine musical concerts. In 1957 he gave the world premiere of Karlheinz Stockhausen's aleatory *Klavierstück XI*. He returned to New York in 1961 to become the pianist of the New York Philharmonic. He soon became one of Elliott Carter's closest friends, and Carter composed the piano part of *A Symphony of Three Orchestras* to showcase his pianism. Jacobs was also a sophisticated cook and a delightful raconteur, and his musical tastes were eclectic, ranging from the sonatas of Boulez to the ragtimes of William Bolcom—both composers were his good friends. He was one of the first known victims of the AIDS epidemic. Near the end of his life, when he could no longer see, he nevertheless attended the launch party at the Lincoln Center for MEC83, with his partner Paul Levenglick.

Kennedy, Edith Forbes (1890–1942). A Bostonian "muse" (not related to the prominent Forbes family), she was married, in 1908, to Albert Joseph Kennedy, a pioneer of the settlement house movement. They had three sons, and divorced in 1929. After that she spent two years in Paris, then returned to Boston, where she held salons at her small house on Shepard Street. The poet and novelist May Sarton described her as "an island of light, fun, wisdom" who "listened to music passionately and critically all her life" and "who could hold her own with, and stimulate, friends as various as Ernest Simmons, Edwin Cohn, George Sarton, Nancy Hale and Elliott Carter" (*A World of Light*, 90–91).

Kirkpatrick, John (1905–1991). New York-born pianist, educated at Princeton. Studied piano in Paris with Nadia Boulanger and Isidor Philipp. On returning to New York in 1931, he became a proponent of the piano music of Copland, Ives, and Ruggles. On January 20, 1939 he gave the first complete public performance of the *Concord Sonata* at Town Hall. Four years later he gave the premiere of Copland's Piano Sonata. In later years he was curator of the Charles Ives archives at Yale, and in 1972 he edited and annotated an edition of Ives' *Memos*.

Kirkpatrick, Ralph (1911–1984). Massachusetts-born harpsichordist and musicologist. He began his study of the harpsichord as an undergraduate at Harvard (B.A. 1931), and then went to Paris to study with Wanda Landowska. He also worked with Nadia

Boulanger and Arnold Dolmetsch. With the support of a Guggenheim Fellowship, he began his musicological research on seventeenth- and eighteenth-century performance practice in 1937. He was particularly noted for his critical edition and performances of Domenico Scarlatti, and for his biography of that composer (1953). He taught at Yale from 1940 to 1976. With Charles Rosen, he gave the world premiere of Elliott Carter's *Double Concerto*.

Kirstein, Lincoln (1907–1996). One of the most important figures in twentieth-century American culture, Kirstein was born in Rochester, New York, where his maternal grandparents had a clothing business (Stein-Bloch & Co.) that became successful producing uniforms for the Union Army during the Civil War. He grew up in Boston, where, in 1911, his father, Louis Kirstein became a partner (with Lincoln and Edward Filene) in Filene's, the largest department store in the city. While an undergraduate at Harvard he co-founded (with Varian Fry) the literary quarterly *Hound & Horn*. After seeing a performance of the ballet *Apollo* by the Ballets Russes he decided to bring the choreographer George Balanchine to America. In 1933, with several wealthy friends, he founded the School of American Ballet. Here Balanchine created his first American work, *Serenade*. Kirstein also founded the American Ballet, Ballet Caravan, Ballet Society and, in 1948, the New York City Ballet, which he led until 1989. He commissioned his Harvard classmate, Elliott Carter, to write the scores for *Pocahontas* and *The Minotaur*, and planned to have Anthony Tudor create a ballet to the *Double Concerto*, although this never happened. Kirstein commissioned and helped to fund the design for the New York State Theater at Lincoln Center by his friend, the architect Philip Johnson. As a connoisseur of the visual arts he was particularly devoted to the work of Pavel Tchelitchew, Elie Nadelman, and his brother-in-law Paul Cadmus. His many writings include the classic *Movement and Metaphor: Four Centuries of Ballet* (1970).

Lederman Daniel, Minna (1896–1995). Founder and (from 1924 to 1946) editor of *Modern Music*. Born in New York City, she graduated from Barnard College in 1917 after spending one year at Vassar, and studied piano and theory at the Institute of Musical Art (which became the Juilliard School). With her friends Claire Reis, Louis Gruenberg, Frederick Jacobi, and Alma Wertheim helped found the League of Composers in 1923. At the helm of *Modern Music*, originally titled *The League of Composers Review*, Lederman cultivated a group of composer-critics that would include Aaron Copland, Virgil Thomson, Marc Blitzstein, John Cage, Paul Bowles, Leonard Bernstein, and Elliott Carter. In 1947 she edited the anthology *Stravinsky in the Theater*, and, in 1974, *The Life and Death of a Small Magazine*. She was married to the painter Mell Daniel.

Longy-Miquelle, Renée (1898–1979). Paris-born music theoretician and teacher. At age four she won the Pleyel Grand Piano prize, and studied eurhythmics with Jean d'Undine. When her father, Georges Longy became first oboist of the Boston Symphony in 1914, she moved to the United States and the following year she and her father founded the Longy School of Music. She also taught at the New England Conservatory, and, beginning in 1926, at the Curtis Institute. There, in 1940 and 1941, she taught solfège and score-reading to Leonard Bernstein, and they became close friends. She taught these subjects at the Juilliard School from 1963 to her death. Once each year her advanced students at Juilliard would give a recital where they would sight-read complex music with many different clefs and transposition following her methods or rhythmic and intervallic analysis.

Moore, Douglas (1893–1969). New York-born composer and educator, best known for his operas *The Devil and Daniel Webster* (1938) and *The Ballad of Baby Doe* (1956). He studied at Yale, and after service in the Navy, went to Paris to study with Nadia Boulanger, Vincent D'Indy, and Ernest Bloch. From 1926 to 1962 he taught at Columbia University, where he hired—and fired—Elliott Carter. Moore encouraged Carter to accept a teaching position at Princeton but Carter did not pursue that post, or any other full-time academic position.

Nabokov, Nicolas (1903–1978). Russian-born composer, writer, and cultural agent, first cousin of the novelist Vladimir Nabokov. After the Russian Revolution his family moved to Paris where he studied at the Sorbonne and became close friends with Stravinsky and Prokofiev. The Ballets Russes gave the premiere of his *Ode* in 1928. In 1933 he moved to the United States, and in 1934 the Ballets Russes de Monte Carlo presented *Union Pacific*, a highly successful ballet on which Nabokov collaborated with the poet Archibald Macleish. None of his later works would enjoy a comparable success. His largest later compositions are the opera *Rasputin's End* (libretto by Stephen Spender, 1958) and the ballet *Don Quixote* (choreographed by George Balanchine, 1966). Nabokov taught at Wells College in upstate New York from 1936 to 1941, then at St. John's College, Annapolis, Maryland, and the Peabody Conservatory in Baltimore. During the Second World War, Nabokov offered his services to the State Department, initially as a translator. He soon met Isaiah Berlin and other diplomats who were posted to the Soviet Union during the war. His friends now included Charles Bohlen, George Kennan, the poet-diplomat Alexis Leger, author, under the nom de plume St.-John Perse, of *Vents*, and W. H. Auden. In 1949 Nabokov's role in cultural politics became public at the Conference for World Peace, held at New York's Waldorf-Astoria Hotel. According to Vincent Giroux's account, Nabokov publicly demanded that Shostakovich make clear if he agreed with a recent *Pravda* article that labeled Hindemith, Schoenberg, and Stravinsky as "obscurantists," "decadent bourgeois formalists," and "lackeys of imperialism." Shostakovich, seated next to a KGB "nurse," agreed, and Nabokov was greeted with unanimous booing. In 1950 Nabokov was appointed to the secretariat of the newly-founded Congress for Cultural Freedom. While the Congress was covertly funded by the CIA, Nabokov always claimed (Giroux, 240) that he was not aware of the funding source. The CIA's involvement became a public scandal when it was first revealed in *Ramparts* in February 1967. Nabokov's globe-spanning work with the CCF included supporting cultural magazines, like *Encounter*, organizing international music festivals, and involvement with the American Academy in Rome. On the side he also acted as agent for Stravinsky, arranging the commissions for *Threni, Movements* for Piano and Orchestra, and *The Flood*, even though he lamented Stravinsky's "conversion" to serialism. Nabokov's important role in Carter's life and career began soon after Carter returned to New York from Paris in 1935. Chez Carter Nabokov was known for his talents as mimic and raconteur (the latter gift amply displayed in his two autobiographical books) and for his five wives.

Nancarrow, Conlon (1912–1997). Arkansas-born composer. Originally a jazz trumpeter, he studied at the Cincinnati College-Conservatory of Music from 1929–1932 and then privately in Boston with Nicolas Slonimsky, Walter Piston, and Roger Sessions. In 1936 he went to Spain to fight in the Abraham Lincoln Brigade. Returning to New York he became active as a composer and a critic for *Modern Music*. In 1940 the State Department refused to renew his passport because of his leftist political views, and he moved to Mexico City. There he purchased two Ampico player pianos and began to compose directly on piano rolls. Except for one brief visit he did not return to the USA until 1981. Late in his life Nancarrow's music was praised by György Ligeti and in 1982 he was awarded a MacArthur "genius" award. Elliott Carter met Nancarrow in 1939. As editor of *New Music*, he published the score of Study No. 1 for Player Piano in October 1951, and he quoted bits of that work in his String Quartet no. 1, a work for which Nancarrow expressed great admiration (CPLD, 138–139). Carter's letters to Aaron Copland and Minna Lederman in the PSS reveal, however, that Carter's connection to Nancarrow was complicated, and Carter often rejected the idea that he had been influenced by Nancarrow's music, but they remained friends for many years (CPLD, 200–201).

Oppens, Ursula (1944–**).** New York-born pianist. She studied first with her mother, Edith Oppens, then with Leonard Shure, and earned degrees from Radcliffe (1965) and Juilliard (1967). At Juilliard she studied with Rosina Lhevinne and Felix Galimir. She served as a founding member of Speculum Musicae from 1971 to 1982, and has taught at Northwestern University, the Tanglewood Music Center, and the Conservatory of Music at Brooklyn College. She commissioned and recorded works by a wide-range of composers including Anthony Braxton, Anthony Davis, Julius Hemphill, Conlon Nancarrow, Tobias Picker, Frederic Rzewski, Charles Wuorinen, and many more. She honored Elliott Carter's one hundredth birthday with a recording of his complete piano works.

Petrassi, Goffredo (1904–2003**).** Composer, conductor, and teacher, born in Palestrina, Italy, east of Rome. A late bloomer like Carter, he began musical studies at the Rome Conservatory when he was twenty-four, but he achieved fame in 1933 with the Amsterdam premiere of his Partita for Orchestra. He directed the Teatro La Fenice in Venice from 1937 to 1940 and taught composition at the Academia di Santa Cecilia from 1959 to 1974. He is best known for his series of Concertos for Orchestra and for his choral music. His students included Peter Maxwell Davies, Franco Donatoni, and Ennio Morricone.

Piston, Walter (1894–1976**).** Composer and teacher born in Maine of Italian descent. After playing saxophone in the Navy band during the First World War, he enrolled at Harvard (B.A. summa cum laude, 1924) where he studied with Archibald Davison and Edward Burlingame Hill. He was awarded a John Knowles Paine Traveling Fellowship and studied with Nadia Boulanger, Paul Dukas, and George Enescu in Paris between 1924 and 1926. He taught at Harvard from 1926 until 1960. His students included Leroy Anderson, Leonard Bernstein, Elliott Carter, Irving Fine, and many more (see Pollock, *Harvard Composers*). His textbooks *Harmony, Counterpoint*, and *Orchestration* became fixtures of American musical education. Aside from the entertaining score for *The Incredible Flutist* (1938), Piston was mainly known, and honored, for his eight Symphonies. His Symphony no. 3 (1948) and Symphony no. 7 (1961) earned Pulitzer Prizes.

Reis, Claire Raphael (1888–1978). Texas-born music promoter and writer, "the single most indispensable woman to modernist musicians in New York" (Oja, 214), whose family moved to New York in 1898. She took an early interest in childhood education, particularly in the Montessori method, and in 1911 she founded the People's Music League, which presented concerts for newly arrived immigrants. In 1916, after meeting Leo Ornstein through her friends Waldo Frank and Paul Rosenfeld, she launched her role as a proponent of new music with four recitals of his music at her home on Madison Avenue, while at the same time continuing to work in charitable and educational fields. In 1922 she became executive director of the International Composers' Guild, and the following year founded the League of Composers. In 1930 she published *American Composers of Today*, the first catalog of music by living American composers, which she updated and expanded in 1938 with *Composers in America*.

Rosen, Charles (1927–2012). New York-born pianist and writer. He studied with Moritz Rosenthal at the Juilliard School, and studied French literature at Princeton. He became known for his recordings of contemporary music, including Carter's Piano Sonata and *Double Concerto*, Stravinsky's Movements for Piano and Orchestra and the three sonatas of Boulez, and also recorded music of Scarlatti, Bach, Beethoven, and Schumann. His first book, *The Classical Style*, was published in 1971, followed by *Sonata Forms* (1980) and *The Romantic Generation* (1995). His reviews appeared frequently in *The New York Review of Books*. Three of his writings about Elliott Carter, including his vivid account of the premiere of the *Double Concerto*, were published by the Library of Congress in 1984 as *The Musical Languages of Elliott Carter*. He was one of the Carters' closest friends, and he kindly let me work on the first draft of MEC83 in his West Side Manhattan apartment (across the street from the Museum of Natural History) while he was in Paris for the summer. I discovered, there, that he had a little-known interest in comic literature. He owned complete sets of P.G. Wodehouse's novels and stories, and Walt Kelly's *Pogo* comics.

Saminsky, Lazare (1882–1959). Ukraine-born composer, conductor, and critic, educated at the Odessa conservatory and the Imperial conservatory in St. Petersburg where his teachers included Rimski-Korsakov, Anatoli Liadov, and Nicolai Tcherepnin. He was a founder of the Society for Jewish Folk Music. He left the Soviet Union in 1918 and came to America in 1920, soon joining the International Composers Guild and helping to found its rival group, the League of Composers. From 1924 to his death he was music director at Temple Emanu-El, New York's largest and most socially prominent Reform Jewish congregation. Here he strove to develop a musical liturgy distinct from the nineteenth-century German idiom then in place, but also far from the popular and Hassidic influences heard in Orthodox synagogues. To this end he encouraged younger Jewish composers like Frederick Jacobi and David Diamond, and, in 1936, established an annual Three Choir Festival that premiered works, both sacred and secular, by George Rochberg, Miriam Gideon, Hugo Weisgall, and Elliott Carter.

Schuman, William (1910–1992). New York-born composer, educator, and administrator. He started out playing violin, banjo, and bass in dance bands, and, after meeting Frank Loesser, began to write popular songs. He only became interested in classical music when he first heard Toscanini conduct the New York Philharmonic in 1930. He dropped out of NYU where he was preparing for a business degree, studied at the Malkin Conservatory in Boston and, from 1933 to 1938, privately with Roy Harris. He also earned a degree in music education at Teachers College, Columbia University. In 1942 his *Cantata no. 2 A Free Song* earned him the first Pulitzer Prize in Music. From 1935 to 1945 he taught at Sarah Lawrence College, and in 1945 became president of the Juilliard School, where he introduced the Literature and Materials curriculum that integrated the studies of music theory and history, and also founded the Juilliard String Quartet. In 1961 he became president of Lincoln Center. As a composer he is best known for his ten numbered symphonies (he withdrew the first two) and other orchestral works including *Credendum* and *In Praise of Shawn*, and for his orchestration of Charles Ives' *Variations on "America."* In 1951 Aaron Copland praised the "experimental attitude" of Schuman's String Quartet no. 4, its instrumental writing, and, in particular, its rhythms, "so skittish and personal, so utterly free and inventive."

Seeger, Charles (1886–1979). Composer, theorist, and musicologist, born in Mexico City where his father had business interests. He graduated from Harvard in 1908. As a theorist he is associated with "dissonant counterpoint," an idea he expounded in *Modern Music* 7, no. 4 (June–July 1930), and which was particularly influential on the music of Henry Cowell, Carl Ruggles, and Ruth Crawford, who became Seeger's second wife. Seeger played an even more influential role in the development of ethnomusicology. Three of his children, Pete (by his first wife Constance Edson), Peggy, and Mike (by Crawford) became famous folklorists and performers.

Sessions, Roger (1896–1985). Brooklyn-born composer and teacher. He graduated from Harvard at age eighteen, then studied composition at Yale with Horatio Parker and Ernest Bloch. Although he spent much of the 1920s in Europe, he helped establish the Copland-Sessions concerts in New York in 1928, as a showcase for the "younger generation of American composers." Writing in 1926, Copland described Sessions "on the basis of hearsay" as a "revolutionary," but by 1936 he came to realize that Sessions was "the classicist par excellence," composer of "a musician's music" not aimed at a large audience, a judgement confirmed by Sessions' later career. Sessions taught at Princeton from 1936 to 1945 and at the University of California at Berkeley from 1945 to 1953, and after that back at Princeton and at the Juilliard School. His students included Milton Babbitt, Edward T. Cone, David Diamond, Miriam Gideon, Robert Helps, Andrew Imbrie, Leon Kirchner, Donald Martino, Leonard Rosenman, and Ellen Taaffe Zwilich (among many others). He is best known for the *Black Maskers Suite* (1928), Violin Concerto (1935), *From My Diary* (1940), Symphony no. 2 (1946), *Idyll of Theocritus* (1954), and three Piano Sonatas (1930, 1946, 1965). His musical style evolved from the neo-classicism of his Symphony no. 1 (1927) to a chromatic expressionism—heard as early as *From My Diary*—close to Schoenberg, although he did not employ the twelve-tone method until the Solo Violin Sonata of 1953.

Sherry, Fred (1948–). New York-born cellist. At Juilliard he studied with Leonard Rose and played with the Juilliard Ensemble. In 1971 he co-founded Speculum Musicae, and in 1973 he co-founded Tashi, along with violinist Ida Kavafian, clarinetist Richard Stoltzman, and pianist Peter Serkin. From 1989 to 1993 he served as Artistic Director of the Chamber Music Society of Lincoln Center. He has taught at the Juilliard

School, the Manhattan School of Music and the Mannes College of Music. His extensive discography includes recordings of music with Chick Corea and John Zorn, as well as music of prominent "uptown" composers such as Milton Babbitt, Charles Wuorinen, Mario Davidovsky, and Elliott Carter, and also Bach and Schoenberg.

Wolpe, Stefan (1902–1972). Composer. Born in Berlin, Wolpe studied with Schreker and Busoni, and, after fleeing—as both a Jew and a Communist—from the Nazis, with Anton Webern in Vienna, before moving to Palestine in 1934. In 1938 he emigrated to the United States. In 1950 he began to attend meetings of the Eighth Street Artists' Club, along with painters Franz Kline, Mark Rothko, Willem and Elaine De Kooning, and Jack Tworkov. From 1952 to 1956 he taught at Black Mountain College, and after 1956, at C.W. Post College, but he also taught composers, performers, jazz musicians, and painters privately at his Greenwich Village apartment. In 1956 he lectured at Darmstadt on contemporary American music, including that of Milton Babbitt, Earle Brown, John Cage, Elliott Carter, and Christian Wolff. His music combined elements of Schoenberg's methods with engaged leftist political sympathies and often displayed an agitated surface recalling the painterly side of Abstract Expressionism.

Woodworth, G. Wallace (1902–1969). Boston-born choral director. Known as "Woody," he graduated from Harvard in 1924 and served on the Harvard faculty for forty-four years. He taught Music I, an introductory course that usually attracted three hundred students, conducted the Harvard Glee Club and the Radcliffe Choral Society, and served as University organist and choirmaster. On the occasion of the Harvard Glee Club's one-hundredth anniversary he conducted the Harvard-Radcliffe chorus and the Boston Symphony in Bach's B Minor Mass.

Bibliography

Reference abbreviations

CEL Carter, Elliott. *Collected Essays and Letters 1937–1995*
CIR Perlis, Vivian, ed. *Charles Ives Remembered: An Oral History*
CPLD Meyer, Felix and Anne C. Shreffler. *Elliott Carter: A Centennial Portrait in Letters and Documents*
CR *Elliott Carter: Settings. Chicago Review* 58, no. 3/4 (Summer 2014)
CS Boland, Marguerite and John Link. *Elliott Carter Studies*
FW Edwards, Allen. *Flawed Words and Stubborn Sounds: A Conversation with Elliott Carter*
MEC83 Schiff, David. *The Music of Elliott Carter*
MEC98 Schiff, David. *The Music of Elliott Carter*. Second, revised edition
WEC Stone, Kurt and Elsa, eds. *The Writings of Elliott Carter*

Periodical abbreviations

MM *Modern Music*
MQ *The Musical Quarterly*
NYHT *New York Herald Tribune*
NYT *The New York Times*
PNM *Perspectives of New Music*
Ackroyd, Peter. *T.S. Eliot: A Life*. New York: Simon and Schuster, 1984.
Adams, Hazard, ed. *Critical Theory Since Plato*. New York: Harcourt, Brace, and Jovanovich, 1971.
Adorno, Theodor W. *Philosophy of Modern Music*. Anne G. Mitchell and Wesley V. Blomster, trans. New York: Continuum, 1985.
Arnold, Tony. "Digging Deeper: Singing the Music of Elliott Carter," CR: 161–170.
Apel, Willi. *French Secular Music of the Late Fourteenth Century*. Cambridge: Medieval Society of America, 1950.
Ashbery, John. *As We Know*. Harmondsworth: Penguin Books, 1979.
Ashbery, John. *A Wave: Poems*. New York: Penguin Books, 1985.
Ashbery, John. *Houseboat Days*. Harmondsworth: Penguin Books, 1977.
Auden, W.H. and Louis Kronenberger. *The Viking Book of Aphorisms*. New York: Viking, 1966.
Babbitt, Irving. *Rousseau and Romanticism*. Cleveland: Meridian, 1955.
Bernard, Jonathan. "Elliott Carter and the Modern Meaning of Time." *Musical Quarterly* 79 (1995): 644–82.
Bernard, Jonathan. "The Evolution of Elliott Carter's Rhythmic Practice." *Perspectives of New Music* 26, no. 2 (1988): 164–203.
Bernard, Jonathan. "An Interview with Elliott Carter." *Perspectives of New Music* 28, no. 2 (Summer 1990): 180–214.
Bernard, Jonathan. "The true significance of Carter's early music," in CS: 3–32.

Bishop, Elizabeth. *The Complete Poems 1927-1979*. New York: Farrar, Straus, and Giroux, 1980.

Bishop, Elizabeth. *One Art: Letters Selected and Edited by Robert Giroux*. New York: Farrar, Straus, and Giroux, 1994.

Bloom, Harold. *Agon: Towards a Theory of Revisionism*. Oxford: Oxford University Press, 1982.

Bloom, Harold. *The Anxiety of Influence: A Theory of Poetry*. Second edition. New York and Oxford: Oxford University Press, 1997.

Bloom, Harold. *Wallace Stevens: The Poems of Our Climate*. Ithaca and London: Cornell University Press, 1977.

Boland, Marguerite. "Ritornello form in Carter's *Boston* and *ASKO* concertos," in CS: 80–109.

Boland, Marguerite and John Link. *Elliott Carter Studies*. Cambridge: Cambridge University Press, 2012.

Boulez, Pierre. *Stocktakings from an Apprenticeship*. Stephen Walsh, trans. Oxford: Clarendon Press, 1991.

Broyles, Michael. *Mavericks and Other Traditions in American Music*. New Haven and London: Yale University Press, 2004.

Budiansky, Stephen. *Mad Music: Charles Ives the Nostalgic Rebel*. Lebanon, NH: ForeEdge, 2014.

Bürger, Peter. *Theory of the Avant-garde*. Michael Shaw, trans. Minneapolis: University of Minnesota Press, 1984.

Burkholder, J. Peter. *All Made of Tunes: Charles Ives and the Uses of Musical Borrowing*. New Haven: Yale University Press, 1995.

Burkholder, J. Peter. *Charles Ives: The Ideas Behind the Music*. New Haven: Yale University Press, 1985.

Burkholder, J. Peter, ed. *Charles Ives and His World*. Princeton: Princeton University Press, 1996.

Bush, Ronald. "Quiet, Not Scornful?" The Composition of the Pisan Cantos, in Rainey, ed.: 169–212.

Bush, Ronald. "Pisa," in Nadel, ed.: 261–273.

Butterworth, Neil. *The American Symphony*. Aldershot: Ashgate, 1998.

Cage, John. *Silence: Lectures and Writings*. Middletown: Wesleyan University Press, 1961.

Capuzzo, Guy. *Elliott Carter's What Next? Communication, Cooperation, and Separation*. Rochester: University of Rochester Press, 2012.

Caro, Robert A. *The Power Broker: Robert Moses and the Fall of New York*. New York: Vintage, 1975.

Carter, Elliott. *Collected Essays and Letters 1937–1995*. Jonathan W. Bernard, ed. Rochester: University of Rochester Press, 1997.

Carter, Elliot. *Harmony Book*. Nicholas Hopkins and John F. Link, eds. New York: Carl Fischer, 2002.

Carter, Elliot. *The Writings of Elliott Carter*. Else Stone and Kurt Stone, eds. Bloomington and London: Indiana University Press, 1977.

Carter, Elliott and John Ashbery. "The Origins of *Syringa*." CR: 114–123.

Clark, T. J. *The Painting of Modern Life: Paris in the Art of Manet and his Followers*. Princeton: Princeton University Press, 1984.

Copland, Aaron. *Copland on Music*. Garden City: Doubleday, 1960.

Copland, Aaron. *The New Music 1900–1960*. Revised and enlarged edition. New York: Norton, 1968.

Copland, Aaron and Vivian Perlis. *Copland 1900 through 1942*. New York. St. Martin's, 1984.

Cowell, Henry. *New Musical Resources*. New York: Something Else Press, 1969.

Cowell, Henry and Sidney. *Charles Ives and His Music*. London: Oxford University Press, 1955.

Craft, Robert. *Down a Path of Wonder: Memoirs of Stravinsky, Schoenberg and other cultural figures.* Naxos Books, 2006.

Crane, Hart. *The Complete Poems of Hart Crane.* New York: Liveright, 1933.

cummings, e.e. *50 Poems.* New York: Grosset and Dunlap, 1940.

Dickinson, Emily. *The Complete Poems of Emily Dickinson.* Thomas H. Johnson, ed. Boston: Little, Brown, 1960.

Dickinson, Emily. *Final Harvest: Emily Dickinson's Poems.* Thomas H. Johnson, ed. Boston: Little, Brown, 1961.

Doering, William T. *Elliott Carter: A Bio-Bibliography.* Westport: Greenwood, 1993.

Duplessis, Rachel Blau. "Elliott Carter's Ezra Pound," CR: 173–186.

Edwards, Allen. *Flawed Words and Stubborn Sounds: A Conversation with Elliott Carter.* New York: Norton, 1971.

Eliot, T.S. *The Complete Poems and Plays 1909-1950.* New York: Harcourt, Brace, and World, 1962.

Eliot, T.S. *The Sacred Wood and Major Early Essays.* Mineola: Dover, 1998.

Emmery, Laura. "Rhythmic Process in Elliott Carter's Fourth String Quartet," *Mitteilungen der Paul Sacher Stiftung,* no. 26, April 2013.

Fauser, Annegret. *Sounds of War: Music in the United States during World War II.* Oxford: Oxford University Press, 2013.

Feder, Stuart. *Charles Ives: "My Father's Song." A Psychoanalytic Biography.* New Haven: Yale University Press, 1992.

Giroud, Vincent. *Nicolas Nabokov: A Life in Freedom and Music.* Oxford: Oxford University Press, 2015.

Glass, Philip. *Words Without Music: A Memoir.* New York: Liveright, 2015.

Glock, William. *Notes in Advance: An Autobiography in Music.* Oxford: Oxford University Press, 1991.

Goldman, Richard Franko. *Selected Essays and Reviews 1948–1968.* Dorothy Klotzman, ed. Brooklyn: Institute for Studies in American Music, 1980.

Gordon, Eric A. *Mark the Music: The life and work of Marc Blitzstein.* New York: St. Martin's Press, 1909.

Greenberg, Clement. *Art and Culture: Critical Essays.* Boston: Beacon Press, 1961.

Griffiths, Paul. *Modern Music: A Concise History.* Revised edition. London: Thames and Hudson, 1994.

Griffiths, Paul. *Modern Music and after: Directions Since 1945.* Oxford: Clarendon, 1995.

Guberman, Daniel. "Composing Freedom: Elliott Carter's 'Self-Reinvention' and the Early Cold War," PhD diss., University of North Carolina at Chapel Hill, 2012.

Guberman, Daniel, "Elliott Carter as (Anti-)Serial Composer." *American Music* 33, no. 1, Spring 2015.

Hamilton, Ian. *Robert Lowell: A Biography.* New York: Random House, 1982.

Hodeir, Andre. *Since Debussy: A View of Contemporary Music.* Noel Burch, trans. New York: Grove Press, 1961.

Houen, Alex. "Anti-Semitism," in Nadel, ed.: 391–401.

Ives, Charles. *Essays Before a Sonata, The Majority and Other Writings.* Howard Boatwright, ed. New York, Norton, 1970.

Ives, Charles. *Selected Correspondence.* Tom C. Owens, ed. Berkeley: University of California Press, 2007.

Jacobs, Jane. *The Death and Life of Great American Cities.* New York: Vintage, 1992.

Kalstone, David. *Becoming a Poet: Elizabeth Bishop with Marianne Moore and Robert Lowell.* New York: Farrar, Straus, and Giroux, 1989.

Kalstone, David. *Five Temperaments. Elizabeth Bishop, Robert Lowell, James Merrill, Adrienne Rich, John Ashbery.* New York: Oxford University Press, 1977.

Kern, Stephen. *The Culture of Time and Space 1880–1918.* Cambridge, Harvard University Press, 1983.

Kirstein, Lincoln. *By With To & From: A Lincoln Kirstein Reader.* Nicholas Jenkins, ed. New York: Farrar, Straus, and Giroux, 1991.

Kirstein, Lincoln. *Mosaic: Memoirs.* New York: Farrar, Straus, and Giroux, 1994.

Kleeblatt, Norman L., ed. *Action Abstraction: Pollock, De Kooning and American art 1940–1976.* New Haven and London: Yale University Press, 2008.

Kolisch, Rudolph. "Tempo and Character in Beethoven's Music," *Musical Quarterly* 29, no. 2 (1943): 16–87 and 29, no. 3 (1943): 291–312.

Kramer, Lawrence. *Music and Poetry: The Nineteenth Century and After.* Berkeley: University of California Press, 1984.

Kramer, Lawrence. "Modern Madrigalisms: Elliott Carter and the Aesthetics of Art Song." CR: 124–133.

Krutch, Joseph Wood. *The Desert Year.* London: Penguin, 1977.

Lang, Paul Henry, ed. *Problems of Modern Music: The Princeton Seminar in Advanced Musical Studies.* New York: Norton, 1960.

Lederman, Minna. *The Life and Death of a Small Magazine.* Brooklyn: Institute for Studies in American Music, 1983.

Lesher, J.H. "Heraclitean Ideas in Stevens' 'This Solitude of Cataracts.'" *The Wallace Stevens Journal* 38, no. 1, Spring 2014.

Link, John. *Elliott Carter: A Guide to Research.* New York and London: Garland Publications, 2000.

Link, John. "Elliott Carter's late music," in CS: 33–54.

Lowell, Robert. *The Dolphin.* New York: Farrar, Straus, and Giroux, 1973.

Lowell, Robert. *History.* New York: Farrar, Straus, and Giroux, 1973.

Lowell, Robert. *For Lizzie and Harriet.* New York: Farrar, Straus, and Giroux, 1973.

Lowell, Robert. *For the Union Dead.* New York: Noonday, 1967.

Lowell, Robert. *Notebook 1967–68.* New York: Farrar, Straus, and Giroux, 1969.

Lowell, Robert. *Selected Poems.* New York: Farrar, Straus, and Giroux, 1976.

Lucretius. *The Way Things Are: The De Rerum Natura of Titus Lucretius Carus.* Rolfe Humphies, trans. London: Indiana University Press, 1969.

Machlis, Joseph. *Introduction to Contemporary Music.* New York: Norton, 1961.

Magee, Gayle Sherwood. *Charles Ives Reconsidered.* Urbana: University of Illinois Press, 2008.

Mann, Thomas. *The Magic Mountain.* H.T. Lowe-Porter, trans. New York: Alfred A. Knopf, 1961.

Mariani, Paul. *The Broken Tower: The Life of Hart Crane.* New York: Norton, 1999.

Mariani, Paul. *The Whole Harmonium: The Life of Wallace Stevens.* New York: Simon and Schuster, 2016.

McConville, Brendan P. "Refinement through revision of compositional methods: "The recent music of Elliott Carter as a paradigm for composers in the 21st century," *iSCI: The Composer's Perspective* 1, no. 1.

Mead, Andrew. "Review of *The Music of Elliott Carter,*" *Notes* 40, no. 3 (March 1984).

Mellers, Wilfrid. *Music in a New Found Land: Themes and Developments in the History of American Music.* New York: Hillstone, 1964.

Merrill, James. *From the First Nine: Poems 1946–1976.* New York: Atheneum, 1984.

Meyer, Felix. "Left by the wayside: Elliott Carter's unfinished Sonatina for Oboe and Harpsichord," in CS: 217–235.

Meyer, Felix and Anne C. Shreffler. *Elliott Carter: A Centennial Portrait in Letters and Documents*. Woodbridge: The Boydell Press, 2008.

Meyer, Felix and Heidy Zimmermann, eds. *Edgard Varèse: Composer, Sound Sculptor, Visionary*. Woodbridge: Boydell, 2006.

Millier, C. Brett. *Elizabeth Bishop: Life and the Memory of It*. Berkeley: University of California Press, 1993.

Moe, Orrin. "The Music of Elliott Carter." *College Music Symposium* 22, no. 1 (1982): 7–13.

Moore, Marianne. *Complete Poems*. New York: Penguin, 1994.

Moore, Marianne. *Observations: Poems*. Lenda Leavell, ed. New York: Farrar, Straus, and Giroux, 2016.

Moore, Marianne. *The Poems of Marianne Moore*. Grace Schulman, ed. New York: Penguin, 2005.

Nabokov, Nicolas. *Bagázh: Memoirs of a Russian Cosmopolitan*. New York: Athenium, 1975.

Nabokov, Nicolas. *Old Friends and New Music*. Boston: Little, Brown, 1951.

Nadel, Ira, ed. *Ezra Pound in Context*. Cambridge: Cambridge University Press, 2010.

Noubel, Max. *Elliott Carter ou le temps fertile*. Geneva: Éditions Contrechamps. 2000.

Noubel, Max. "*Three Illusions* . . . and maybe a fourth: a hermeneutic approach to Carter's recent music," in CS: 253–270.

Noubel, Max, ed. *Hommage à Elliott Carter: textes réunis, traduits et introduits par Max Noubel*. Le Vallier: éditions Delatour France, 2013.

Oja, Carol. *Making Music Modern: New York in the 1920s*. New York: Oxford University Press, 2000.

Oja, Carol and Judith Tick, eds. *Aaron Copland and his World*. Princeton: Princeton University Press, 2005.

Owens, Tom C., ed. *Selected Correspondence of Charles Ives*. Berkeley and Los Angeles: University of California Press, 2007.

Paul, David C. *Charles Ives in the Mirror: American Histories of an Iconic Composer*. Urbana: University of Illinois Press, 2013.

Perlis, Vivian, ed. *Charles Ives Remembered: An Oral History*. New Haven: Yale University Press, 1974.

Perse, St.-John. *Vents suivi de Chronique*. Paris: Gallimard, 1960.

Pescatello, Ann M. *Charles Seeger: A Life in American Music*. Pittsburgh, University of Pittsburgh Press, 1992.

Poggioli, Renato. *The Theory of the Avant-garde*. Gerald Fitzgerald, trans. Cambridge: Belknap Press, 1968.

Pollack, Howard. *Aaron Copland: The Life and Work of an Uncommon Man*. New York: Henry Holt, 1999.

Pollack, Howard. *Harvard Composers: Walter Piston and His Students, from Elliott Carter to Frederic Rzewski*. Metuchen: Scarecrow Press, 1992.

Pollack, Howard. *Marc Blitzstein: His Life, His Work, His World*. Oxford: Oxford University Press, 2012.

Pope, Alexander. *Selected Poetry and Prose*. William K. Wimsatt, Jr., ed. New York: Holt, Rinehart and Winston, 1951.

Porter, Andrew. *Music of Three Seasons 1977–1980*. New York: Alfred A. Knopf, 1981.

Pound, Ezra. *The Cantos of Ezra Pound*. New York: New Directions, 1996.

Proust, Marcel. *Swann's Way*. C.K. Scott Moncrieff, trans. New York: Modern Library, 1956.

Ragosta, Ray. "Textures and Contrasts: Elliott Carter's Poems of Louis Zukofsky" CR: 187–197.

Rainey, Lawrence S. "'All I Want to Do Is to Follow Orders': History, Faith, and Fascism in the Early Cantos," in Rainey, ed., 63–116.

Rainey, Lawrence S., ed. *A Poem Containing History: Textual Studies in The Cantos.* Ann Arbor: University of Michigan Press, 1997.

Restagno, Enzo. *Elliott Carter in Conversation with Enzo Restagno for Settembre Musica 1989.* Brooklyn: Institute for Studies in American Music, 1991.

Richardson, Joan. *Wallace Stevens: A Biography: The Early Years 1879–1923.* New York: William Morrow, 1986.

Richardson, Joan. *Wallace Steven: A Biography: The Later Years 1923–1955.* New York: William Morrow, 1988.

Rockwell, John. *All American Music: Composition in the Late Twentieth Century.* New York: Vintage, 1984.

Rohwer, Jörn Jacob. "Und Was Jetzt?," *Das Magazin,* 11 November 2008.

Rorem, Ned. *Critical Affairs: A Composer's Journal.* New York: Braziller, 1970.

Rosen, Charles. *The Musical Languages of Elliott Carter.* Washington, DC: Library of Congress, 1984.

Rosenberg, Harold. *The Tradition of the New.* New York: McGraw-Hill, 1965.

Rosenfeld, Paul. *An Hour with American Music.* Philadelphia: Lippincott, 1929.

Ross, Alex. *The Rest is Noise: Listening to the Twentieth Century.* New York, Farrar, Straus and Giroux, 2007.

Salzedo, Carlos. *Modern Study of the Harp.* New York: G. Schirmer, 1921.

Sarton, May. *A World of Light: Portraits and Celebrations.* New York: Norton, 1976.

Saunders, Francis Stonor. *The Cultural Cold War.* New York: The New Press, 1999.

Schiff, David. *The Music of Elliott Carter.* London: Eulenburg Books, 1983.

Schiff, David. *The Music of Elliott Carter.* Second, revised edition. Ithaca, Cornell University Press, 1998.

Schiff, David. "A Mirror on Which to Dwell," *New York Arts Journal,* April 1977.

Schiff, David. "Carter in the Seventies," *Tempo* 130 (September 1979): 2–10.

Schiff, David. "Carter for Winds," *Winds Quarterly* (Fall 1980): 2–6.

Schiff, David. "In Sleep. In Thunder: Elliott Carter's Portrait of Robert Lowell," *Tempo* 142 (September 1982): 2–9.

Schiff, David. "Elliott Carter's Harvest Home," *Tempo* 167 (December 1988): 2–13.

Schiff, David. "Carter's New Classicism," *College Music Symposium* 29 (1989) 115–22.

Schiff, David. "First Performances: Carter's Violin Concerto," *Tempo* 174 (September 1990): 22–24.

Schiff, David. Review of "The Later Music of Elliott Carter," *notes* 47, no. 3, March 1991.

Schiff, David. "Carter as Symphonist," *The Musical Times,* December 1998.

Schiff, David. "Magna Carter," *The Nation,* 11 February 2013.

Schiff, David. "Interview." CR: 102–113.

Schoenberg, Arnold. *Style and Idea: Selected writings.* Leonard Stein, ed. Leo Black, trans. Berkeley and Los Angeles: University of California Press, 1975.

Schwartz, Lloyd. "Elliott Carter and American Poetry." CR: 46–60.

Scott, William B. and Peter M. Rutkoff. *New York Modern: The Arts and the City.* Baltimore: The Johns Hopkins University Press, 1999.

Seldes, Gilbert. *The Seven Lively Arts.* New York: Barnes, 1924.

Shreffler, Anne C. "Elliott Carter and his America," *Sonus* 14, no. 2 (Spring 1994): 38–66.

Shreffler, Anne C. "Instrumental Dramaturgy as Humane Comedy," *Musik Theater Heute: Internationales Symposion der Paul Sacher Stiftung*, Hermann Danuser and Mattias Kassel, eds., 147–171.

Sicari, Stephen. "Pound after Pisa: 1945–1972," in Nadel, ed.

Simeone, Nigel, ed. *The Leonard Bernstein Letters*. New Haven: Yale University Press, 2013.

Skulsky, Abraham. "Elliott Carter," *Bulletin of American Composers Alliance* 3, no. 2 (Summer 1953): 2–16.:

Soderberg, Stephen. "At the edge of creation: Elliott Carter's sketches in the Library of Congress," in CS 236–252.

Stevens, Wallace. *The Collected Poems*. New York: Vintage, 1982.

Stevens, Wallace. *Opus Posthumous: Poems/Plays/Prose*. Milton J. Bates, ed. New York: Alfred J. Knopf, 1989.

Stevens, Wallace. *The Palm at the End of the Mind: Selected Poems and a Play*. Holly Stevens, ed. New York: 1971.

Stone, Kurt and Elsa, eds. *The Writings of Elliott Carter*. Bloomington: Indiana University Press, 1977.

Stravinsky, Igor. *An Autobiography*. New York: Norton, 1962.

Stravinsky, Igor. *Poetics of Music in the Form of Six Lessons*. New York: Vintage, 1956.

Stravinsky, Igor and Robert Craft. *Dialogues and a Diary*. Garden City: Doubleday, 1963.

Stravinsky, Igor and Robert Craft. *Stravinsky in Conversation with Robert Craft*. Harmondsworth: Penguin, 1960.

Swafford, Jan. *Charles Ives: A Life with Music*. New York: Norton, 1996.

Taruskin, Richard. "Afterwards: Nicht blutbefleckt?" *The Journal of Musicology* 26, no. 2 (2009): 274–284.

Taruskin, Richard, review of Vincent Giroux, *Nicolas Nabokov: A Life in Freedom and Music*. *Times Literary Supplement*, August 5, 2016.

Taruskin, Richard, "Standoff (II): Music in History: Carter." In *The Oxford History of Western Music*. Oxford University Press, 2004, vol. 6, pp. 261–306.

Thomson, Virgil. *The Art of Judging Music: Music and Musical Life in America and Europe, 1944-1947, as Seen by the Wise and Witty Critic of the New York Herald Tribune*. New York: Alfred A. Knopf, 1948.

Thomson, Virgil. *Music Reviewed 1940–1954*. New York: Vintage, 1967.

Thompson, Virgil. *The Virgil Thomson Reader*. New York: Dutton, 1984.

Thurmaier, David. "'A Disturbing Lack of Musical and Stylistic Continuity'? Elliott Carter, Charles Ives, and Musical Borrowing," *Current Musicology*, 96 (Fall 2013).

Tick, Judith. *Ruth Crawford Seeger: A Composer's Search for American Music*. New York: Oxford University Press, 1997.

Tommasini, Anthony. *Virgil Thomson: Composer on the Aisle*. New York: Norton, 1997.

White, Edmund. "The Man Who Understood Balanchine," *New York Times*, November 8, 1998.

Whitehead, Alfred North. *Process and Reality: An Essay in Cosmology*. New York: The Humanities Press, 1929.

Whitman, Walt. *Complete Poetry and Selected Prose*. James E. Miller, Jr. ed. Boston: Riverside, 1959.

Whittall, Arnold. "The search for order: Carter's Symphonia and late-modern thematicism," in CS: 57–79.

Wierzbicki, James. *Elliott Carter*. Urbana, Chicago and Springfield: University of Illinois Press, 2011.

Williams, William Carlos. *The Collected Poems of William Carlos Williams. Volume I 1909–1939*. A. Walton Litz and Christopher MacGowan, eds. New York: New Directions, 1986.

Williams, Willam Carlos. *The Collected Poems of William Carlos Williams. Volume II 1939–1962.* Christopher MacGowan, ed. New York: New Directions, 1988.

Wilson, Edmund. *Axel's Castle: A Study in the Imaginative Literature of 1870 to 1930.* New York: Scribner, 1931.

Periodicals

Chicago Review 58, no. 3/4

Sonos 14, no. 2

Die Reihe

Index